Teaching for Deep Comprehension

Teaching for Deep Comprehension

A Reading Workshop Approach

Linda J. Dorn
Carla Soffos
Foreword by Carol A. Lyons

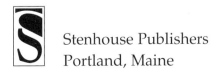

Stenhouse Publishers
Portland, Maine

Stenhouse Publishers
www.stenhouse.com

Copyright © 2005 by Linda J. Dorn and Carla Soffos

All rights reserved. No part of this publication may be reproduced or transmitted in any form or by any means, electronic or mechanical, including photocopy, or any information storage and retrieval system, without permission from the publisher.

Every effort has been made to contact copyright holders and students for permission to reproduce borrowed material. We regret any oversights that may have occurred and will be pleased to rectify them in subsequent reprints of the work.

Credits
Page 10: "Thank You, Stormy" copyright © 1994 by Nancy Springer. Reprinted from *Music of Their Hooves* by Nancy Springer. Reprinted by permission of Boyds Mills Press.

Page 20: From *Tiger, Tiger* by Beverley Randall in the PM Reader Series. Copyright © 1994 Thomson Learning Australia. Reprinted by permission.

Library of Congress Cataloging-in-Publication Data
Dorn, Linda J.
　Teaching for deep comprehension : a reading workshop approach / Linda J. Dorn, Carla Soffos.
　　p. cm.
　Includes bibliographical references and index.
　　ISBN 1-57110-403-8
　　1. Reading comprehension—Study and teaching (Elementary) I. Soffos, Carla. II. Title.
LB1573.7.D67 205
372.47—dc22　　　　2005049021

Cover and interior design by Martha Drury

Manufactured in the United States of America on acid-free paper
17 16 15 14 13　　14 13 12 11 10 9

To the literacy coaches and classroom teachers in our network, whose commitment to children and teachers is making a real difference in the literacy lives of all

Contents

Contents of the DVD Chapters	*ix*
Foreword by Carol A. Lyons	*xi*
Acknowledgments	*xv*
Introduction	*1*
1. **Understanding Comprehension**	**5**
2. **Reading for Deep Comprehension**	**13**
3. **Language for Literacy Learning**	**27**
4. **Teaching for Strategic Processing**	**37**
5. **Understanding Language for Comprehending Texts**	**51**
6. **A Workshop Approach to Literacy Learning**	**65**
7. **Creating Literature Discussion Groups**	**79**
8. **Designing Mini-Lessons for Deep Comprehension**	**95**
Appendix	
Section I: *Shared Reading Aids*	*109*
Section II: *Professional Development Activities*	*127*
Section III: *Glossary of Genres; Book Lists by Genre and Grade Level; Genre Descriptions, Questions, and Text Maps; Graphic Organizers*	*131*
Section IV: *Rubrics for Assessment*	*157*
Section V: *Correlation of DVD Chapters and Segments to Book Chapters*	*163*
References	*169*
Index	*175*

Contents of the DVD Chapters

1. **Shared Reading**
   Segment 1: *The Little Red Hen*
   Segment 2: *Who's in the Shed?*
   Segment 3: *Caterpillar Diary*
   Segment 4: Share Time and Self-Reflection

2. **Author Study**
   Segment 1: Listening for Powerful Language
   Segment 2: Share Time
   Segment 3: Mini-Lesson (Learning from Author)
   Segment 4: Small-Group Mini-Lesson
   Segment 5: One-to-One Conferences

3. **Teacher Discussion**
   Segment 1: *Black-Eyed Susie*
   Segment 2: *Beachmont Letters*

4. **Character Analyses**
   Segment 1: Mini-Lesson (*An Angel for Solomon Singer*)

5. **Literature Discussion Groups**
   Segment 1: *The Summer My Father Was Ten*
   Segment 2: *Honeysuckle House*

Foreword

Ensuring that all children comprehend what they read is critical to their subsequent success in school and throughout their lives. Increasing the effectiveness of teaching practice in this critical area is therefore a priority. In this book, Linda Dorn and Carla Soffos present a complex view of comprehension by asking—and answering—profound questions: What does it mean to comprehend? How do we teach *for* comprehension?

This well-written book is unique for several reasons. First, it engages the reader immediately. As I read the first few pages, I felt myself entering into a kind of social relationship with the author. Writing in the first person, Linda shares how specific language in books such as Laura Hillenbrand's *Seabiscuit: An American Legend* and Toni Morrison's *Beloved* stimulated her thoughts, feelings, and imagination, activated memories, and promoted deeper understanding, which she refers to as deep comprehension.

I was captivated by her response to James Patterson's poignant novel *Suzanne's Diary for Nicholas*. Linda's emotional reaction to descriptions of how people balance five balls throughout their lives—family, friends, faith, integrity, and work—had a marked effect on her thinking. Although I had a different response to the book, we both encountered new ideas and ways of confronting ourselves and our views of life that changed our thinking and behavior in remarkable ways.

Second, the book describes, in clearly written language, the complexity of the comprehension process. In discussing her personal response to John Steinbeck's classic novel *The Grapes of Wrath*, Linda shows us that comprehension is a constructive process regulated by perceptual, emotional, cognitive, and social experiences that cannot occur without thought. She provides a theoretical explanation and explicit examples to demonstrate how readers use prior knowledge or nonvisual information stored in the brain to make sense of visual information in the text and a range of strategies that helps them monitor and sustain meaning as they interpret and synthesize ideas.

Third, the book includes professional development activities within a reading workshop format that mirrors students' experiences. Teachers experience for themselves the struggle that is an essential part of the learning process. Being involved as a learner provides teachers opportunities to discuss, think about, and experience deep comprehension, and subsequently create rationales and understand how to teach for deep comprehension. Teacher learning is personal and solitary and also shared and collegial.

Participation in the workshop activities gives teachers firsthand experience of the constructivist notion of teaching and learning that is central to the development of a conceptual understanding of the comprehending and learning process, higher-order thinking, and problem solving. Teachers who have participated in these workshops report that the intellectual and emotional stimulation gave them the courage to try out new ideas, refine their lessons, and engage students differently in the classroom. They become involved in an exciting and powerful learning cycle: the more they learn, the more they open up to new possibilities, and the more they become part of a trusted professional community of learners.

This book is about comprehension, learning, teaching, and professional development. Both explicitly and implicitly, it suggests that learning, like comprehension, is a constructive process that is modified by what we already know from interacting with the people and the world around us. There are several key principles about learning and teaching supported by the student and teacher activities presented and discussed in the book.

On learning:

- Learning (comprehension) occurs not by retelling information but by interpreting it.
- Adults and children learn to the degree in which they are actively involved in the construction of knowledge through shared activities. In other words, we learn only as we actively participate in the learning process.
- People of all ages learn with more depth and understanding when they are able to share ideas with others, think together, consider alternative points of view, and broaden their own perspectives.

On teaching:

- Organize classroom and professional development activities to engage individuals in social interactions that involve active inquiry, problem solving, and personal reflection.
- Provide students and teachers many opportunities to engage directly in the struggles of learning, risk taking, and the thrill of generating new ideas.
- Realize that the role of the teacher is not to indoctrinate children and adults into a certain perspective or way to think, but instead to provide opportunities for individuals to analyze and think for themselves and develop the skills and capacities they need to take charge of their own thinking and their own lives.

For more then a decade, Linda Dorn and Carla Soffos have worked closely with many classroom teachers—and their interactions with both these teachers and the children in their classrooms have enabled them to write this book. Insights they have gained through these experiences have informed the way they make sense of the comprehension process and explain what it means to comprehend. Personal reflection and powerful examples from real classrooms provide a much-needed look at the complexities of comprehension and how to effectively teach for deep comprehension.

Linda Dorn and Carla Soffos practice what they preach. Their model for professional development is the same kind of learning teachers are being asked to provide for their students. The authors also have a commitment to the learning process and a tremendous respect for learners of all ages. They have written a book that provides ways for students and teachers to nurture their capacities as learners and enable them to be independent thinkers. *Teaching for Deep Comprehension: A Reading Workshop Approach* will simultaneously challenge and delight its readers.

Carol A. Lyons

Acknowledgments

In *Apprenticeship in Literacy* (Dorn, French, and Jones 1998), my coauthors and I concluded our book with this statement: "Systemic change lies in our understanding how our children learn and in our ability to problem-solve with colleagues who work with our children, who share our common experiences, and who speak our language of literacy" (p. 160). This quote represents a vision of teachers working together toward a common goal, but it also captures the need for a common language and shared experiences that foster constructive problem solving within the group. For the past twelve years, Carla and I have worked alongside teachers to discover best literacy practices. Our work in schools is a kind of apprenticeship situation, one that builds on a constructivist theory of literacy learning in social contexts. Our social contexts have been classrooms, where literacy coaches and classroom teachers are living their literacy lives alongside their young students.

Our book would not be complete without the contributions of a special group of educators who collaborated with us on the DVD that accompanies our book. At Sallie Cone Elementary in the Conway School District, we thank Vicki Altland, first-grade teacher, for her willingness to share her classroom with us. At Gibbs International Magnet School in the Little Rock School District, we thank Felicia Hobbs, principal; Teresa Richardson, literacy coach; Melanie Miller, second-grade teacher; and Jill Johnson and Priscella Leibig, fourth-grade teachers. Special thanks to our state leaders, who allowed us to videotape their book discussion: Debbie Coffman, Reading Program Director at the Arkansas Department of Education; Pam East, K–12 Literacy Specialist in the Conway School District; and Laurie Harrison and Patsy Conner, Reading Recovery Teacher Leaders at the University of Arkansas at Little Rock.

Thanks to Carol Lyons, who wrote the foreword to this book. Carol has always been one of our most influential mentors: her dedication to struggling readers and her belief that all children can become literate have set a standard for our own work. I use Carol's book, *Teaching Struggling Readers: How to Use Brain-Based Research to Maximize Learning* (2003) with my graduate students, and I am always amazed by her ability to describe complex theory in practical terms. Also, thanks to P. David Pearson and Linda Hoyt for their endorsement of our book: Carla and I are humbled by their words of support. I first read David's work on comprehension when I was a graduate student over twenty years ago. His text, *Teaching Reading Comprehension* (1972), coauthored with Dale Johnson, has become a classic, one of the most influential books on reading comprehension. More recently, I discovered Linda Hoyt. I'm impressed with Linda's work because of her strong collaboration with teachers, using an apprenticeship approach as she works alongside teachers in their classrooms. In her latest text, *Spotlight on Comprehension: Building a Literacy of Thoughtfulness* (2005), Linda presents a diverse collection of articles on comprehension written by leading experts, authors, and classroom teachers. We also acknowledge our colleagues, Barbara Schubert and Karen Scott, for their support. Their endorsements mean a great deal to Carla and me, because Barbara and Karen have worked closely with us in providing training to literacy coaches. We appreciate all of these distinguished leaders for taking the time to read our manuscript and endorse our work in reading comprehension.

Carla and I also thank the teachers and literacy coaches who contributed the illustrations for the book: Susan Gerke, literacy coach, and Regina Logan, second-grade literacy lab teacher, at Skyline Elementary in Sedalia, Missouri; Vicki Altland, first-grade teacher, and Rebecca Keith, Reading Recovery and intervention specialist, at Sallie Cone Elementary in Conway, Arkansas; Donnie Skinner, literacy coach at Boone Park Elementary in North Little Rock, Arkansas; and Laurie Harrison, Reading Recovery teacher leader at the University of Arkansas at Little Rock.

We would also like to acknowledge the literacy coaches and Reading Recovery teacher leaders at our university (UALR). Special thanks to Janet Behrend, Ruth Keogh, Vicki Wallace, Laurie Harrison, Patsy Conner, and Karen James for their dedication to a comprehensive literacy model in our schools. Without these committed educators, our work in schools would be incomplete. We would also like to express our appreciation to Pauline Moley, who has assumed a leadership role in expanding the K–5 comprehensive literacy model to middle school teachers. We are indebted to Angela Sewall, Dean of the College of Education at UALR, who demonstrates her advocacy to literacy in her actions as well as her words. She supports our literacy endeavors through her work with the Arkansas State Legislature, her service on the board of directors for the Reading Recovery Council of North America, and her presentations at literacy conferences. We are also grateful for the literacy leaders at the Arkansas Department of Education. We offer special thanks to our friend and colleague, Debbie Coffman, the Reading Program Director, for her support of our work in Reading Recovery and Comprehensive Literacy programs. Former director Krista Underwood, now with the Little Rock School District, continues to support the Comprehensive Literacy model, including fully implemented Reading Recovery programs and literacy coaches in all schools. Thanks also to Connie Choate, Reading First Director, for her support of Reading Recovery and Comprehensive

Literacy programs in Reading First schools. These individuals have been our partners in literacy, and we appreciate their commitment to the teachers and children of our state.

Carla and I would also like to acknowledge all the literacy coaches in our network. Currently there are over one hundred coaches, including twenty-six new elementary and midlevel coaches participating in the 2004–2005 training year. These individuals are effecting changes in curriculum and student achievement; we are indebted to them for their hard work and their commitment to literacy. Special thanks to Donnie Skinner, literacy coach at Boone Park Elementary, North Little Rock School District, and Teresa Richardson, literacy coach at Gibbs Magnet School, Little Rock School District. These two coaches have gained a national reputation with visitors coming from across the United States to observe in their schools. Their exemplary literacy programs are led by two of the most effective school principals we have ever known: Mavis Cherry at Boone Park and Felicia Hobbs at Gibbs Magnet. You can observe these amazing administrators on the "Leadership for Literacy" segment of our video series, *Results That Last: A Model for School Change*.

Over the past seven years, our work in comprehensive literacy programs has expanded beyond Arkansas to schools in Missouri, Wisconsin, California, North Carolina, Illinois, Michigan, and other states. Our acknowledgments would not be complete without recognizing the special contributions of the literacy coaches in these schools. First, we would like to thank Karen Scott, district literacy coach in Springfield, Missouri, and her dynamic team of coaches across the district—Kristie Hallam at Bissett, Glenda Dow at Bowerman, Becky Southard at Boyd, Susan Conover at Campbell, Ginder Wittkorn at Fairbanks, Denise Slagle at Fremont, Cheryl Roy at Pittman, Janet Gore at Portland, Barbara Head at Robberson, Shelly Shaver at Shady Dell, Denise Kelly at Watkins, Kerri Bruce at Weaver, Robin Pettijohn at Weller, Lois Anderson at Westport, and Debbie Lambeth at York. You can hear their voices on the message board of our Web site (www.arliteracymodel.org) as they discuss teaching and learning issues and celebrate the work of their teachers and students. These coaches are serving as mentors for other teachers, always ready to respond with advice and constructive feedback to any teacher seeking assistance from a literacy coach. From the bottom of our hearts, we thank the Springfield coaches for all they are doing to support literacy.

Thanks also to our dear friend and colleague, Barbara Schubert of Saint Mary's College in Morago, California. Our collaborative relationship has resulted in a new state we call *Arcofonia!* Barbara's endless energy, humor, and passion for teaching and learning constantly amaze both Carla and me. Barbara has been in Arkansas so often this year that we consider her an Arkansas resident. In fact, she has shown me Arkansas restaurants and sights I never knew existed! Thank you, Barbara, for collaborating with us on the Comprehensive Literacy model.

As always, Carla and I acknowledge the help of the Stenhouse team. Heartfelt thanks to Philippa Stratton and Brenda Power, our editors. To the entire staff at Stenhouse, thank you for your support of our work. Special thanks to Tom Seavey, our marketing director, who has worked diligently to spread our theories and practices to teachers across the country.

In closing, Carla and I acknowledge the experts from whom we have learned. The most influential has been Marie Clay, whose theories of literacy processing have shaped our definitions of comprehension. Her most recent work, *Change Over Time in Children's Literacy Development* (2001), presents a neurological perspective on reading acquisition, including Harry Singer's theory of working systems for solving reading problems. We believe that comprehension is perceptual, emotional, cognitive, and social; and a variety of experts have helped to shape our beliefs: P. David Pearson (comprehension); David Wood (contingent scaffolding), Lev Vygotsky (thought and language), Barbara Rogoff (apprenticeship), Don Holdaway (self-regulation), Mel Levine (cognitive processing), and Carol Lyons (emotion). These experts have been our mentors: we have read their words and filtered their teachings through our own perceptions and experiences. In the process, Carla and I have created our own theory of comprehension.

Linda J. Dorn

Introduction

Recently during a conference presentation, I asked teachers three questions: (1) Can comprehension be taught? (2) When does a model become a barrier to comprehension? (3) When does the tool become the reason for reading? These questions stimulated an interesting discussion, and the issues raised by these questions are important and relate to the themes of the present book. Thus, it is appropriate to begin this book with a brief response to the three questions.

Can comprehension be taught? Generally, teachers will answer yes, comprehension can be taught. They then explain how they teach comprehension strategies and skills. In Chapters 1 and 2, I attempt to explain the cognitive and social sides of comprehension. It would have been easier to discuss comprehension from a skills perspective. Yet because comprehension is a cognitive process we must move beyond teaching discrete skills to creating problem-solving conditions that will prompt learners to process information at deeper levels. Comprehension is also a constructive process, personalized by the ideas and thoughts of the individual reader. So we might ask: Can ideas and thoughts be taught, or are they developed through personal connections? Certainly we can read a common text and come away with a standard version of what the author meant. Yet this standard version is most likely a literal-level interpretation, a brief experience with a text that will likely be forgotten in a short amount of time. Deeper comprehension requires a reader to go beyond the author's message, assimilating the text experience into his or her own background and in the process creating a new message. To move deeper into the text implies that readers are moving deeper into their own minds. At the same time, such thoughtful analysis of the author's message could actually lead one to a different interpretation. That's the problem with teaching comprehension—the task is very complex at the level of the mind. So, to return to our opening question: Can comprehension be taught? I doubt that we can teach meaning, because meaning exists only in the mind of the reader. A text can stimulate meaning, but it cannot create meaning. Comprehension and meaning are one and the same—an inner reflection of the reader's mind. What can teachers do to *promote* comprehension? We can create a set of literate conditions that activate students' thinking processes, but that is probably all we can do. What tools may we use for accomplishing this complex task? The most important tool is the language teachers use to engage students in talking about books. Our classrooms must be alive with literate talk—rich conversations about books that apprentice students into deeper comprehension.

When does a model become a barrier to comprehension? To respond to the question of when a model may become a barrier to comprehension, we must first define what a model is. Simply put, a model is a good example of constructive thinking with generalizable value. Models are not scripted or standard; rather, they are specific examples of how to deal with comprehension problems. When students observe good models, they file these examples into a mental toolbox of effective strategies and practices. Models are beneficial only if the reader knows when to activate the appropriate one to solve a particular problem. Readers must not perceive the model as the goal; if they do, the model becomes only a behavior to copy, an imitation of someone else's thinking. Without guided practice, a model can become a barrier to learning. How much time should pass before the learner moves from observation of the model to practice? A connection between model and practice must happen immediately. In short, the purpose of a model is to demonstrate to learners constructive ways of thinking while providing them with opportunities for flexible practice over time and across different contexts.

When does the tool become the reason for reading? Too often, students perceive the goal of reading as using sticky notes or writing in response logs. These tools are important, but they are *not* the reason we read. When students view reading as "visualizing" or "making text-to-life connections," for example, this narrow perspective can impair deep comprehension. A good reader will automatically visualize and make connections, but never in isolation from other comprehension strategies. The process of comprehension requires that readers assemble flexible strategies to solve problems. From this point of view, the orchestration of strategies—not single strategies—is a condition of deep comprehension.

Overview of the Chapters

Chapter 1 provides the framework for subsequent chapters in the book. In this chapter I describe comprehension as a strategic process having some of the same features as everyday problem-solving. The driving force behind all strategic actions is the need to make meaning from the particular event, whether it is the child learning to button a shirt or a teacher modeling a visualization strategy. In each case, the learner must orchestrate a range of strategic actions aimed toward a meaning-making goal.

Chapter 2 outlines the differences between comprehension as an outcome and comprehending as an active, ongoing process. The complexity of comprehension is again featured, specifically how comprehension fits into a processing puzzle that includes four types of interrelated knowledge. In this chapter, I explain the challenge of teaching for self-reflection, the deepest level of comprehension, and focus on the role of character analysis in comprehension, including some practical ideas for the classroom.

Chapter 3 connects language to literacy. Here I explain how the oral language system is the foundation for the written language system, and how shared reading can provide a supportive context for bridging oral and written language. This chapter provides an apprenticeship framework for implementing shared reading.

Chapters 4 and 5 describe ten strategic behaviors for both reading and language, with practical examples for the classroom. Chapter 6 explains how the readers' workshop meets the goals of differentiated instruction—that is, a framework of whole-group, small-group, and individual instruction. Chapter 7 shows how literature discussion groups can provide a social context for talking about books. This chapter emphasizes the distinction between automatic and literate language. Chapter 8 presents detailed mini-lessons for the ten strategic reading behaviors described in Chapter 4. The Appendix provides resources that supplement the chapters.

The DVD presents examples of comprehension strategies during shared reading, author studies, mini-lessons, one-to-one conferences, literature discussion groups, and teacher book clubs. Together, the book and DVD provide a valuable resource for teachers in teaching for deep comprehension.

Who We Are

Carla and I have been friends and colleagues for twelve years. I trained Carla as a Reading Recovery teacher leader in 1993, and we bonded immediately. Our colleagues say that we perfectly balance each other, although they add that we are identical in our obsession with literacy. I have spent the past fifteen years at the University of Arkansas at Little Rock. My experience is diverse: I've taught in the primary and intermediate grades, I'm trained in Reading Recovery, and, most recently, I've trained literacy coaches. I am grateful that my university job keeps me in close contact with teachers and children. Carla has taught in the primary grades and is trained in Reading Recovery and literacy coaching. She is strongly connected to the classroom, where she spends time each day working with literacy coaches and model classroom teachers. A talented teacher, Carla can accelerate the learning rate of any child. My earlier book, *Apprenticeship in Literacy: Transitions Across Reading and Writing* (Dorn, French, and Jones 1998), uses transcripts of videotapes from Carla's classroom for many of its examples. Carla also appears in the videotape *Organizing for Literacy*, coaching first-grade teacher Teresa Treat as she attempts to establish a balanced literacy classroom. Since then, Carla and I have written two books together and coauthored several video series. In this, our latest book, we decided that I would write the text in the first person, and Carla would provide feedback and examples. In this way, I can present theories and discuss personal reading experiences naturally, while Carla has been a valuable writing partner, providing classroom examples from her work in the field. The two of us have worked closely together to implement literacy changes in our state. We share a literacy partnership that I hope is captured in the pages of this, our new book on comprehension.

Understanding Comprehension

The women sat among the doomed things, turning them over and looking past them and back. This book. My father had it. He liked a book. Pilgrim's Progress. *Used to read it. Got his name in it. And his pipe—still smells rank. And this picture—an angel. I looked at that before the fust three come—didn't seem to do much good. Think we could get this china dog in? Aunt Sadie brought it from the St. Louis Fair. See? Wrote right on it. No, I guess not. Here's a letter my brother wrote the day before he died. Here's an old-time hat. These feathers—never got to use them. No, there isn't room.*

How can we live without our lives? How will we know it's us without our past? No. Leave it. Burn it.

They sat and looked at it and burned it into their memories. How'll it be not to know what land's outside the door? How if you wake up in the night and know—and know the willow tree's not there? Can you live without the willow tree? Well, no, you can't. The willow tree is you. The pain on that mattress there—that dreadful pain—that's you.

And the children—if Sam takes an Injun bow an' his long roun' stick, I get to take two things. I choose the fully pilla. That's mine.

Suddenly, they were nervous. Got to get out quick now. Can't wait. We can't wait. And they piled up the goods in the yards and set fire to them. They stood and watched them burning, and then frantically they loaded up the cars and drove away, drove in the dust. The dust hung in the air for a long time after the loaded cars had passed.

John Steinbeck, *The Grapes of Wrath*

This past summer, I reread *The Grapes of Wrath* by John Steinbeck. I first read it nearly thirty years ago. Since then, I have acquired new experiences and memories that have shaped and reshaped my perceptions of life. Now when I read Steinbeck's book, I read it differently. My mind has been shaped by my experiences of the world, and my memories redefine the meaning of this and every book I read. I ponder Steinbeck's words "How can we live without our lives? How will we know it's us without our past?" These are powerful words that don't go away when the page is turned. "Can you live without the willow tree?" "The pain on that mattress there—that dreadful pain—that's you." I try to imagine how the Joad family must have felt, knowing they were leaving everything behind for a new life. I remember how I felt twenty years ago, a mother with two children, all alone, moving from Tennessee to Arkansas. Steinbeck's words stimulate these memories, retrieving the fears I once felt when leaving my past behind to start a new life in a strange place. I am building an emotional rapport with the characters in the book, a text-to-life bond that will influence how I interpret their thoughts and their actions. It is integral to my comprehending the book.

A few weeks later, I was reading a picture book, *What You Know First* (1995) by Patricia MacLachlan. In this story, a little girl must leave her cherished home on the prairie. Just like the Joad family in *The Grapes of Wrath*, she struggles with leaving her past behind. MacLachlan uses language to portray fear and uncertainty, as the young girl tries to convince the family to take the baby and leave her behind: "He [the baby] doesn't know about the slough where the pipits feed. When the geese sky-talk in the spring. That baby hasn't even seen winter with snow drifting hard against the fences, and the horses breathing puffs like clouds in the air, ice on their noses, the cold so sharp it cuts you." How can the child say good-bye to all the things she loves—the endless sky, the ocean of grass, her cottonwood tree? These memories represent the very core of a person, and the fear of leaving them behind is symbolized in forgetfulness. MacLachlan captures this emotion in her words: "What you know first stays with you, my Papa says. But just in case I forget, I will take a twig of the cottonwood tree." As I reflect on MacLachlan's words, my comprehension is enriched by my previous experiences with Steinbeck's writing. The visual images of the two texts become blurred, and a new experience is created from my reading.

Our perceptions and our emotions become embedded into the fabric of every book we read, and our understanding is shaped by the memories and experiences we bring to the author's message. Without these personal experiences, our comprehension is limited to the author's words. As a result, we are denied the opportunity to expand the experience, and by so doing, lift our understanding to new heights.

A Complex Process

Reading is a complex process involving a network of cognitive actions that work together to construct meaning (Baker and Brown 2002; Block and Pressley 2002; Pearson 2002; Farstrup and Samuels 2002; Ruddell, Ruddell, and Singer 1994). A reader's comprehension is influenced by a range of internal factors, including perceptions, beliefs, motivation, and problem-solving strategies. The line between perception and cognition is blurred (Lyons 2003; Ratey 2001). Both form the basis of comprehension. In other words, we perceive what our brain tells us to notice. If we do not have the background experience to relate to the reading event, the message can be meaningless. Comprehension results from the mind's ability to make links and ask questions regarding the particular reading event.

If the mind cannot formulate questions about the reading, true comprehension is impossible. When teaching for comprehension, our challenge is twofold: (1) to understand the complexity of the comprehending process, and (2) to apply this knowledge to our work with students. These goals guide the discussion throughout this book.

Consider the distinction between *comprehension* (a noun) as an outcome of our thinking, and *comprehending* (a verb) as the active process of our thinking. Although both words mean *understanding,* these distinctions are important because they can influence our teaching and assessment practices. From an *outcome* point of view, when the reading act has terminated, our understanding is represented in the knowledge we have gleaned from the reading experience. From a *process* point of view, however, the meaning-making is still under construction after the act of reading, and comprehension depends on the problem-solving strategies that the reader uses to interpret what has been read. In other words, comprehending is an ongoing process that continues as long as the reader is thinking about the message. For instance, after my recent reading of *The Grapes of Wrath,* I found myself thinking about particular passages and discussing them with my friends. This motivation, internally driven, was based on my need to understand Steinbeck's words and images and to fit his ideas into my own set of experiences. The comprehending process required me to use a flexible range of strategies, including constant monitoring, searching, connecting, and inferring—all with the goal of deepening my understanding of the author's message (see Figure 1.1). As teachers, when we realize that *comprehending* is the instructional goal of reading, we will teach differently. Our emphasis will be on problem-solving strategies, and we will seek out opportunities for our students to deepen their understanding through reflective thinking.

Figure 1.1 Thought Processes for Learning and Remembering

> Some of the same processes in the human brain that allow us to mature in our general thinking are used in the specific tasks of learning and remembering. These include:
>
> Perceiving objects in the environment
> Classifying information into related categories of knowledge
> Monitoring and evaluating responses
> Searching for new information
> Forming new hypotheses
> Making new attempts
> Choosing alternative routes
> Making links and discoveries
> Self-correcting

The Problem-Solving Process

From a cognitive point of view, whatever influences our general thinking (or our problem solving) also influences our reading comprehension (Clay 2001; Duke and Pearson 2002; Levine 2002; Smith 1976). This is a powerful statement, for it suggests that the strategies we use for comprehending life in general are comparable to those we use when we seek to comprehend a written message. What is the common ground between these two types of activity? The answer is simple: our background experience is the foundation for our problem solving (comprehending). This suggests that context plays a critical role in our using appropriate strategies to solve a particular task. Consider the following three situation-specific events, all of which require the learner to apply certain strategies for constructing meaning.

Problem-Solving Strategies for General Thinking

By an early age, children acquire an extensive repertoire of problem-solving strategies for dealing with real-life situations (Rogoff 1990; Vygotsky 1978; Wood 1998). They learn how to monitor their behaviors and initiate new searching actions toward achieving personal goals. These experiences provide them with a cognitive base (schema) for making discoveries and expanding their knowledge. Simultaneously, they are developing systematic problem-solving strategies that can be transferred to other learning tasks. Consider a young girl who is learning how to button her shirt (Figure 1.2). What are some problem-solving strategies she applies as she carries out this task? First, she must be aware of the relationship between the buttons on her shirt and the shirt itself. This is a basic cognitive requirement for initiating any shirt-buttoning plan. The child must also have a model in her head that represents how a correctly buttoned shirt looks; this will enable her to predict and monitor her actions as she begins to execute the necessary steps. Now suppose that she buttons the shirt incorrectly; she looks in the mirror and notices that one side is hanging lower than the other side. Here, the child is applying important cognitive strategies: she activates her background experience (her schema for a correctly buttoned shirt) and she compares this image with her own model. Without this comparison, she would not be able to monitor her performance. In other words, the youngster would not know that an error had taken place in her buttoning attempt. At this point, the child begins to think of the steps she will need to correct herself. She may decide to unbutton the top button and move it down to the second hole, but when she looks in the mirror after doing that, the problem still exists. Her self-monitoring will prompt her to make a second attempt. These self-monitoring strategies provide the child with feedback and help sustain her momentum for problem solving. Through subsequent attempts, one of three outcomes can occur: (1) the child solves the problem, (2) the child abandons the

Figure 1.2 This youngster is applying general strategies to the task of buttoning her shirt, including self-monitoring as she strives to complete her goal. She will use the same cognitive strategies when she learns how to problem-solve while reading.

problem, or (3) the child receives outside help in solving the problem. Here I should point out that *the problem-solving process is more important than the outcome.* The child is learning how to use meaning-making strategies, including such processes as activating background knowledge, predicting, comparing, discriminating, confirming, rejecting, monitoring, and searching, all of which can be used for other tasks. In time, with practice and guidance, the shirt-buttoning task will become automatic—a subroutine (unthinking) process in the brain. Until it does, the greatest benefit for the child lies in her learning strategies for determining the steps needed to accomplish an important goal. These same strategies are used during the reading process.

Visual Imagery for Increasing Understanding

Visual imagery is an important strategy used in general problem solving, particularly as it relates to organizing and monitoring information in unfamiliar or new situations (Gambrell and Koskinen 2002; Kaufmann 1979). For example, suppose a friend is giving you directions to the airport. She describes specific landmarks that are familiar to you: "On your right, you'll see an elementary school." As your friend talks, you construct mental pictures of the landmarks she mentions, using your background knowledge as the foundation for interpreting the new information. On your way, you will continue to use this strategy to organize your thoughts and monitor your comprehension. Or imagine that your husband calls you to describe the car he has just purchased. As he talks, you turn his words into a visual representation of the car. Here's another example: on your way home from work, you are listening to music on your radio. The song reminds you of a particular day you spent with your friend, and once again you use a visualization strategy to create images in your mind. This strategy for comprehension is a natural reaction of our brain, provided that the background schema is appropriate for stimulating the mental images.

Visualization Strategies in Text Reading

As in the examples just described, if a reader has sufficient background knowledge, he or she will automatically create visual pictures in an attempt to clarify and deepen understanding. Good writers create texts that activate visual images in the minds of their readers. For instance, in the book *Out of the Dust,* Karen Hesse (1997a) uses symbolic and figurative language that requires the reader to think beyond the text—in other words, to use visual imagery to enhance comprehension. The book to me symbolizes a journey of hope that is illustrated in two ways: through the story of a young girl who suffers emotional and physical hardships, yet by the end of the story has managed to find her way; and through the story of the Oklahoma dust storm. Hesse uses vivid language that stimulates the senses, breathing life into her words and placing the reader right in the middle of the dust storm: "a red dust like a prairie fire, hot and peppery, searing the inside of my nose, the whites of my eyes. Roaring dust, turning the day from sunlight to midnight." As I turn the pages of the book, the images of fire and hardship continue to build. The kerosene left on the stove, the mother burning to death, the baby dying, the blame and the storm suffocating the living. Then, at the moment when despair seems overpowering, hope appears in the form of snow and rain. Hesse uses verbs that create living images as she describes how the snow "soothed the parched lips of the land." Her words breathe life into death, as the rain nourishes the dry and barren land. "Soft and then a little heavier, helping along what had already fallen into the hard-pan earth until it rained, steady as a good friend who walks beside you, not getting into your way, staying with you through a hard time. And because the rain came so patient and slow at first, and built up strength as the earth remembered how to yield, instead of washing off, the water slid in, into the dying ground and softened its stubborn pride, and eased it back toward life." At the end of the book, hope is represented in forgiveness. Like the persistent rain on the dying ground, it was only when the daughter was able to forgive her father that she was able to forgive herself as well. "As we walk together, side by side, in the swell of the dust, I am forgiving him, step by step, for the pail of kerosene. As we walk together, side by side, in the sole-deep dust, I am forgiving myself for all the rest." The reader's ability to construct pictorial images from the writer's words is essential for deepening the reader's comprehension. In fact, deep comprehension is greatly impaired—if not impossible—if the reader is unable to construct mental bridges between the author's message and the reader's experiences.

Teaching Visualization Strategies

The question is: Can comprehension strategies be taught to students? I believe that teaching for comprehension is grounded in the same theoretical principles that apply to problem-solving strategies in life. (Notice that I use the phrase "teaching *for* comprehension," as I think it highly unlikely that one can teach comprehension). In addition, teachers can model think-aloud processes that demonstrate how good readers use flexible strategies to comprehend the author's message (Hoyt 2004; Pinnell and Scharer 2003). For example, third-grade teacher Donnie Skinner verbalizes her thought processes for using imagery while reading a passage aloud to her students (see Figure 1.3). During a reading mini-lesson, she models how good readers apply various strategies as they read, thus increasing their comprehension of the message. She understands that a familiar text—one that her students have already read and enjoyed—can provide a meaningful context for demonstrating the strategy of visualization. Today, Donnie has selected the poem "Thank You, Stormy" from Nancy Springer's book *Music of Their Hooves* (1994). The poem is about a young girl, Lisa, who writes a letter to her horse, Stormy, thanking him for taking her up the mountain. The students are familiar with the author's writing style, and they have enjoyed many of her poems, including this one.

Donnie begins the lesson by introducing the new strategy: "Today we are going to talk about a new strategy called visualizing. All good readers visualize when they read. A good writer like Nancy Springer will use words that help us visualize what her poem is all about. Her words are like paint on a paintbrush, and we can use them to draw pictures in our minds. These mind pictures help us to think more deeply about her message." Then, Donnie reads the first four lines of the poem:

Figure 1.3 Donnie Skinner models how to use a visualization strategy to create mental pictures in her mind as she reads.

My horse I'm writing you
To thank you for taking me
Up the wildflower trail
Where the air smelled like angels

She pauses for a moment. "Yes," Donnie says, thinking aloud, "I see a young girl sitting at her desk, remembering the afternoon climb. The lingering scent of wildflowers on her clothes, a special reminder of the day she shared with her horse as they climbed the mountain trail." She continues to read.

And getting me around the fallen tree
And being calm when the grapevine
Grabbed you under the belly
And backing up when I asked you to
Even though you don't like to do it

As Donnie reads the words, she hesitates at the right places to let the language soak into the minds of her students and create the visual images. Again she thinks aloud: "I see the horse carefully watching his steps, trusting the girl to guide his movements with a soft voice. Backing up at her command, even though he doesn't like to. A sense of teamwork, a type of dance, girl and horse working together to reach the top of the mountain."

She continues:

Thank you for bringing me home
When I got kind of lost
Up there on the mountain
And thank you for standing still
As a tree trunk when we met up with
The skunk

Again, Donnie stops and ponders on the author's words, saying, "I feel the bond between the girl and horse—a loving horse whose goal is to protect the girl and bring her home safely. The horse, still as a tree trunk. A black and white skunk brushing against them, totally unaware of their existence. Close your eyes and imagine this scene. What pictures are you visualizing in your mind?" The children shut their eyes, and Donnie reads again, slowly and deliberately.

I promise I will bring you
Wild pears like the deer eat
And shampoo your mane and tail
And never let your water go dry
Again

"What are you visualizing? What are you thinking?" Donnie asks the students. One student says, "I can see her sitting at her desk, trying to explain on paper how much she loves her horse. She feels grateful to him, in a way that she has never felt before. It's like their time together on the mountain has changed her inside." Another student remarks, "It's almost like she feels guilty. The horse took such care of her on the mountain, and now she wants to repay him, bringing him special treats, shampooing his mane and tail." Another child says, "I think they took care of each other on the mountain, and this experience has made her more aware of her love for the horse."

Donnie finishes the poem:

I'm not a perfect human
You are not a perfect horse
But today we were a team
Thank you Stormy
I love you
Forever,
Lisa

Donnie then says to her students, "You are using visualization strategies to deepen your understanding of Nancy Springer's message. Now turn to your partner and talk about what this poem really means to you." In this example, the teacher has encouraged her students to reflect more deeply about a particular text and, more important, she has demonstrated the power of using imagery, or visualization, as a strategy that can be used in comprehending text.

Comprehension as a Process of Orchestration

The reciprocity of comprehension to learning (and vice versa) is complex, simply because of the intricate nature of problem solving. Comprehending strategies are motor reactions of the brain—*and they cannot exist in isolation*. The mind constructs meaning through a flexible range of comprehending strategies that work together (perhaps unconsciously) to maintain the highest possible order of understanding. Research on reading comprehension clearly illustrates how proficient readers orchestrate a range of flexible strategies toward the goal of meaning-making. This implies that being strategic is much more than knowing individual strategies (Clay 1998; Pinnell 2001; Routman 2003); rather, it means knowing how to select and coordinate the best strategies for solving the problem at hand and constructing the deepest understanding. To illustrate, let's revisit previous examples. During my readings of *The Grapes of Wrath* and *What We*

Know First, my brain was making connections (text to text, text to life), but I also was simultaneously applying other mental strategies, such as inferring, predicting, monitoring, searching, analyzing, and synthesizing. In a similar way, the child who was learning to button her shirt used a range of strategies aimed toward her goal. Finally, Donnie, who demonstrated a visualization strategy, could just as easily have discussed her use of other strategies—for example, analyzing, inferring, predicting, or reflecting. In summary, our understanding depends on our mind's ability to think through relational strategies. From this perspective, we can make two important assumptions regarding comprehension:

1. The human mind is a well-organized network of knowledge, skills, and strategies, and it is unreasonable to expect these systems to work in isolation.
2. Teachers can spotlight a particular strategy in isolation, but the goal is that students incorporate the strategy into a larger network of related actions that work together to comprehend messages.

Closing Thoughts

In this chapter, I have tried to explain a difficult concept, the process of comprehending. Because of the perceptual and cognitive sides of meaning, we can only make tentative assumptions about how the comprehending process occurs. More important, our assumptions must be guided by our observations of students as they strive to construct meaning from literate experiences. Here are some important concepts regarding reading comprehension.

The mind is structured to construct meaning—to resolve conflict and restore order. The same cognitive strategies that a learner uses to solve general problems can be utilized to solve reading problems—*if* the teacher values processing strategies as inquiry tools for constructing knowledge.

The goal of all reading is to develop deep (reflective) comprehension. Deep comprehension requires the reader to make inferences, ask questions, and build connections between related sources of knowledge. It is important for teachers to prompt their students for depth and density of understanding, as this knowledge provides a cognitive base for new literate discoveries.

Reading for Deep Comprehension

I am an avid reader, and I select books to meet a particular purpose. Some of the books I read are quick reads. I call these my "airport" or "mindless" reads—paperback novels I can read between flights or short teaching breaks. I give most of these books away, simply because I'm not motivated to reread them. In contrast, my shelves are full of books that have affected me emotionally—books I find I must talk about with someone. For example, when reading *Suzanne's Diary for Nicholas* (2001), I was intrigued by James Patterson's ability to apply his mystery writing skills to a love story that caught me off guard at the ending. These surprising elements made me want to discuss the book with others. I responded even more strongly to the author's vivid descriptions of how people balance five balls throughout their lives: family, friends, faith, integrity, and work. What a profound thought! This simple message was especially relevant for me at the time because teachers were being asked to compromise their beliefs about reading instruction to accommodate political trends. I discussed this with my friends, and we contemplated the consequences of dropping our integrity ball. We asked questions: How do we define integrity in teaching? How can some educators compromise their beliefs so easily? What does integrity have to do with depth of understanding and commitment? We became so absorbed in this notion of the integrity ball that one friend proposed that we interview teachers to explore our ideas further. Now, when I think back on Patterson's book, I realize that the "integrity ball" was an insignificant—almost incidental—part of his story. Yet for me, the reader, it was memorable because of the effect it had on my thinking. When a writer creates a message that influences the thinking of the reader, making the reader's experience personal, comprehension moves beyond the surface level to the conceptual level. A similar experience happened to me when I read *Seabiscuit* by Laura Hillenbrand (2001), the story of a little racehorse and his racing team, which overcame numerous obstacles to win the biggest race of all time. Why was this story of a racehorse so memorable to me? The author told a story of passion and determination—a conviction that anything is possible if you believe in yourself. For me, the reader, the story of Seabiscuit made me think of the children we teach—those who are struggling in literacy—and their teams of passionate teachers who never give up on these kids. Recently at a reading conference, a teacher shared a similar reaction, saying, "The story reminds me of what we can accomplish if we work together to ensure that all children can learn to read." These examples illustrate how our perceptions directly influence the comprehending process. As readers, our comprehension is shaped by our ability to use our imagination and think beyond the author's literal message. When we are influenced by a writer's words, the experience of reading has a mental effect on us—changing the way we think and learn.

Levels of Comprehension

Comprehension is a complex process regulated by cognitive, emotional, perceptual, and social experiences. When individuals read, they apply a range of comprehending strategies to monitor and sustain their meaning. Comprehending involves interpreting and synthesizing ideas in ways that influence the reader's mind. What we call deep reading has the potential to change the way we think and learn. Consider my experiences with Patterson's text. This was not a difficult book to read; most readers would probably view it as a simple love story. I, however, interpreted it differently. A writer is never sure how his or her words will be taken in the reader's mind: the reader's experiences will determine the significance of the writer's ideas. The mind stores and processes information at two levels of comprehension: surface and deep. In any act of reading, these cognitive processes are controlled by our memory functions and our personal reading goals. Consider these two levels of thinking and how each can shape our comprehension:

- *Surface level.* The surface level of comprehension is a literal level of understanding represented by the ability to recall factual information from the text. This retrieval process involves short-term memory; thus, this level of understanding directly relates to the recency of the reading. The desire to think beyond the surface level requires motivation. A reader might possess the strategies to think deeper, yet lack the interest to do so. A steady diet of surface-level reading will inhibit the mind's potential for growth in knowledge.
- *Deep level.* The deep level of comprehension is a conceptual level of understanding that results from the reader's ability to think beyond the text, thus integrating the author's intentions with the reader's point of view. At this level, the author's message serves as a pivotal point in regulating the reader's deeper thinking. The text becomes reconstructed or tailored in the reader's mind to accommodate the reader's background experience and personal goals. Deep comprehension is the result of the mind's analyzing and synthesizing multiple sources of information, thus lifting a reader's comprehension to new levels of meaning. Discussing a book with others has a significant influence on one's depth of comprehension.

Obviously, teachers' theories of comprehension will influence the methods they use to assess their students' understanding of texts. For instance, if we believe that comprehension can be taught as a set of objective outcomes (that is, subskills of reading), we are likely to test accordingly. Such testing of standardized information is fairly simple to measure, and this is why schools are set up to assess discrete items of knowledge. But if we believe that comprehension is personalized—not standardized—our assessments will include opportunities for the reader to display deep-level comprehension. Because comprehension at this level is more subjective, since it represents a reflection of the reader's mind, it becomes difficult (if not impossible) to measure with simplistic assessments. The challenge for teachers is to understand the purpose, as well as the limitation, of comprehension measures at each level.

- *Surface level.* A story retelling immediately following the reading of a new book can provide a teacher with important information about a child's instructional reading level. The retelling simply assesses the reader's recall (i.e., short-term memory) of important facts based on an independent reading of a new story. Although assessment of the surface level of comprehension thus serves a purpose, teachers should recognize that its value in interpreting the reader's comprehending process is limited.
- *Deep level.* The deep level of comprehension is more difficult to assess, because the reader's interpretations are directly influenced by his or her background experiences. This means that an interpretation that is true and meaningful for one person might not mean anything to another. Deep comprehension is developed through reflective opportunities, such as engaging in literature discussion groups and writing in literature response logs (Figure 2.1). To assess deep thinking,

Figure 2.1 A student writes in her literature response log. Writing and reading work together to shape deeper comprehension.

teachers must observe and interact with students during these language-based experiences.

Processing Relationships

Good readers integrate four types of knowledge to sustain and expand their reading comprehension: generic, text, strategic, and reflective (adapted from Graesser and Clark 1985). Deep comprehension depends on the dynamic interplay between the four sources of knowledge. Figure 2.2 symbolizes this relationship as a puzzle, where each piece represents one knowledge source. Deep comprehension is represented by the complete puzzle; if one part is missing, comprehension is affected.

Generic knowledge is the reader's background information—his or her general theory of the world (schema). Generic knowledge is the nonvisual (cognitive) information that the reader activates to construct meaning for a text. Made up of the reader's beliefs and perceptions, generic knowledge influences the reader's interpretation

Figure 2.2 In this processing puzzle for deep comprehension, four types of knowledge come together to shape deeper comprehension. If one piece of the puzzle is missing, the depth of comprehension is adversely affected.

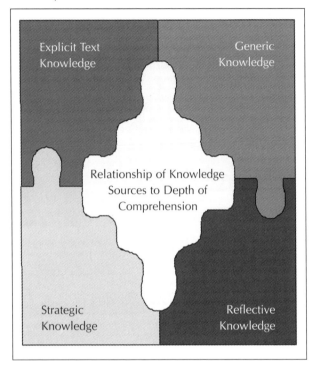

of the text. Without adequate background knowledge, a reader's comprehension will be limited to the surface level.

Text knowledge relates to the precise message of the text, including content knowledge, vocabulary meanings, and text structure (i.e., knowledge of how texts are organized). This is the information the reader uses when directly interacting with the text. Without sufficient text knowledge, comprehension will be scanty, resulting in a narrow interpretation of the author's message.

Strategic knowledge is the reader's knowledge of specific strategies for problem solving, including cognitive strategies for sustaining and expanding the meanings of a text. These strategies include the ability to monitor comprehension, search for meaningful solutions, integrate a range of knowledge sources, and make self-corrections—all of which reflect the process of making meaning. Without strategic knowledge, the reader may rely on ineffective or haphazard attempts to solve words, overemphasizing word accuracy instead of using flexible strategies for comprehending text.

Reflective knowledge is the mind's ability to think abstractly. It involves thinking beyond the text. Reflective knowledge requires the reader to process information at deep levels, including the ability to synthesize, analyze, and critique information. Self-reflection requires both a deep understanding of the content itself and the motivation to relate this information to personal goals. Such reflection represents a unique transaction between reader, writer, and text, resulting in a personalized recreation of the author's message. Reflective knowledge can restructure our perceptions, organize our ideas, expand our knowledge, and influence our minds in long-lasting ways. It is the ultimate goal of reading.

Teaching for Self-Reflection

The question for teachers is: Can we teach self-reflection? In the preceding section I have tried to demonstrate the connection between deep comprehension and self-reflection, though these concepts are difficult to explain because they have as much to with what is in the brain as what is on the page. The reader must orchestrate a range of textual and world experiences to achieve deep understanding. Self-reflection is metacognitive—that is, a conscious, deliberate examination of specific information. It calls for the reader to mentally gather the necessary information to interpret and extend the text knowledge. Thus, it involves much more than simply reacting, connecting, or summarizing information; furthermore, it requires the motivation to analyze thinking at a deeper level.

Chapter 2 Reading for Deep Comprehension

As a teacher of teachers, I have struggled with the notion of self-reflection for some time. I believe that the first step in understanding how to help children self-reflect is for teachers to understand the process within themselves. To help teachers understand the complexities of comprehending, I asked a group of them to examine their own self-reflections as they responded in journals to professional readings. They used highlighters and sticky notes to flag their thinking as they read professional materials and wrote reflections on their reading in response logs. As the teachers shared highlighted passages, we analyzed why some passages were marked and others were not. Kim identified meaningfulness and relevance as critical factors: "When I read this paragraph, it spoke directly to me." She continued to describe how the author's words stimulated memories from her classroom. "I could see the faces of my kids and I wondered how I could use this information to help them." Lee Ann flipped through several pages of the reading, which contained no highlighting, and commented, "I can't believe I actually read these pages! I didn't mark anything, and I just don't remember that much about them!" Leslie looked at the same pages and became very excited over her marked passages. As she read aloud what she had highlighted, she shared her reflections, and in the process took the group's understanding to a new level. We discussed what makes a passage worthy of remembering, and how important relevant and meaningful materials are for our students. As the teachers shared their reflections, they took the process a step further and began to analyze their depth of comprehension. Interestingly, they noticed that they were more apt to reflect at lower levels, with text-to-life connections being the most common. For instance, when reading a chapter on the reading and writing process, Jennifer wrote in her reflection log, "In our school, reading and writing are not taught together. In fact, writing is rarely taught. This is very frustrating for me." During our class discussion, we pondered whether this was self-reflection or simply a reaction to a life situation. Is there a defining feature that would help us understand the distinction? We decided that self-reflection displays a depth of comprehension that goes beyond the author's message. In other words, the act of self-reflection is a reconstructive process, wherein the reader is able to create new meanings through the integration of his or her text and world experiences.

If self-reflection is critical to deep comprehension, how does this translate to the classroom? The teachers had observed that many elementary students were reflecting at lower levels (in many cases, their reflections were simply reactions to previous mini-lessons or teaching prompts). We all agreed that a reaction is a lower level of thinking; it does not extend comprehension to a higher level. A reaction can be a type of self-reflection, but lower-level reflections alone may not lead to deeper comprehension. We considered what makes a passage worthy of remembering; and we discussed the importance of this information in teaching our students. We asked: Can teachers create a set of learning conditions for promoting self-reflective readers? In the end, we identified four essential conditions for enabling deeper comprehension:

1. The student must have adequate background knowledge to understand the content.
2. The material must be meaningful, relevant, and motivating, thus enabling the reader to sustain attention over time and for different purposes.
3. The student must have sufficient time to process the information, including time to reread, clarify, analyze, and research the content, as needed.
4. Talking with other interested persons about the content helps the reader notice relation-

ships among knowledge sources and thus to deepen comprehension.

A few days later, I was telling Carla about how the teachers were examining their own self-reflections to better understand how self-reflection might help their students. Carla recalled a third-grade classroom where she was coaching and mentioned that self-reflection was a concern in that class. She pulled out Megan's reading log and told me about the conference she had had with Megan about one of the entries. The students had read a beautiful Indian fairy tale entitled *The Rough Faced Girl* by Rafe Martin (1992). In this story, as in many fairy tales, good triumphs over evil, and the mistreated heroine (the rough faced girl) wins the affection of the hero (the Invisible One). In one scene, the rough faced girl walks into the lake, whereupon the waters heal her burns and she becomes beautiful again. After reading the story, the students were asked to reflect on it and record their thoughts in their reading logs. In the reading conference, Carla observed that Megan's response to the story was simply an off-task, low-level text-to-life connection that had nothing to do with the story: "This book reminds me of when I went camping and I walked down to the lake." Carla prompted Megan to reflect on her reading at a deeper level, "Is that what the story is really about? What did you learn from the author's message?" Megan then turned to a page where she had placed a sticky note and commented, "I learned that it doesn't matter what you look like. What matters is what you think of yourself." She looked up at Carla, thoughtfully, and added, "You know, that's what my mother always says to me." Carla asked, "Is that a meaningful connection to the story?" "Yes, I think so," Megan responded, as she picked up her pencil and recorded this text-to-life connection in her reflection log. Toward the end of the conference, Carla turned to page 16 in the book, where Megan had flagged another passage with a sticky note. Carla asked, "Was there some reason that you flagged this page?" "Yes," Megan replied. "I really like how the author used the words 'flip, flap, flapped like duck feet' to show the reader that the moccasins were too loose on her feet." "Yes," Carla responded, "Good writers will use words to create pictures in the minds of their readers. You might want to add this reflection in your log." Later, when Carla and I discussed this interaction, we agreed that too often children's reflections are simply low-level reactions to a text. However, talking with another person about a concept helps the reader build links between knowledge sources, thus promoting deeper comprehension.

Inferential Thinking

As stated earlier, comprehension is a cognitive process that depends on the mind's ability to see connections among multiple sources of knowledge. A written text can convey only a limited amount of information to a reader; the reader's mind must fill in the gaps with logical inferences. The ability to make inferences is a necessary function of the mind; it enables one to eliminate chaos and maintain order in general life. In reading, one makes inferences by going beyond the literal text and constructing mental bridges between one's general experiences and the author's intended message. Inferential thinking arises out of the questions the reader has about information not explicitly stated in the book.

According to Glaessar, Haberlandt, and Koizumi (1987), readers generate approximately four times as many inferences when they read narrative text as they do when they read expository text. Expository texts require more specialized knowledge sources, while narrative texts utilize many of the same structures from general life (e.g., problems and solutions, cause and effect). Sentences that prompt many inferences are processed faster than those that prompt fewer inferences. This is only logical, because the mind uses background information to anticipate the text information even before the eyes process the printed word. This is important information for teachers to know: text is processed faster when the reader can generate a greater number of inferences; and the number of inferences a reader can generate depends on the relationship between the reader's background knowledge and the author's intended message. This has critical implications for both fluency issues and comprehension.

Successful comprehension occurs when the reader has sufficient knowledge to fill in the blanks between the author's meaning and the surface features of the text. Therefore, if the reader is unable to make inferences while reading, comprehension will be severely limited. Proficient readers constantly make inferences as they read, using their background experiences to monitor and guide their comprehension. Here, two important questions come to mind: (1) Do beginning readers make inferences while they read? (2) Does the type of text influence the comprehension of the emergent reader?

To answer these questions, let's consider what happens in the mind of an emergent reader who is attempting to construct meaning from an easy patterned text. Even a simple story is full of complex relationships, and the reader's comprehension is dependent on the mind's ability to see these relationships. For instance, in *Tiger, Tiger* (Randall 1994) the author places three animals (Mother Monkey, Baby Monkey, and Tiger) in the same setting to create a dynamic interplay between the characters, the problem, the resulting action, and in the end a satisfying solution.

However, if the reader does not know that tigers pose a threat to monkeys, the whole point of the story will be missed. In addition, the reader must have the schema to infer how a particular character might act in one setting versus another, being able to ask such questions as: Why doesn't Mother Monkey go down the tree to rescue Baby Monkey? What will happen to Baby Monkey if Tiger comes along? Will Mother Monkey risk her own life to save Baby Monkey? Would Mother Monkey act differently if Tiger were not around? Here the text acts as a stimulus, activating the mind of the reader to question the author. If the reader is unable to ask questions and infer actions, comprehension is limited, if not impossible.

The following page shows an example of one young reader's interaction with the text of *Tiger, Tiger*.

Character Relationships

Stories revolve around characters, so deep comprehension depends on the reader's ability to analyze character relationships. A good writer will develop a strong character as the focal point of the plot and resulting action. If a reader doesn't understand the character, comprehension will be impaired. Take, for instance, the characters from *Seabiscuit*. Comprehension of this book requires an understanding of the characters' motives and how their interactions influenced particular outcomes. Deep comprehension is also shaped by the reader's ability to analyze the characters' relationship to various settings. The setting of *Seabiscuit*, for example, is during the Depression, when people were looking desperately for something to raise their hopes and lift their spirits. Would a change in setting influence the characters' actions and resulting events? Good readers are sensitive to questions such as this, and they use their awareness of

Author's Message (in the text)	Reader's Questions (in the mind)
Tiger is asleep.	What is a tiger?
Mother Monkey is asleep.	Does the tiger have anything to do with the monkeys?
Baby Monkey is asleep.	
Baby Monkey wakes up.	Where is the baby monkey going?
Here comes Baby Monkey.	Where is the tiger? Can tigers climb trees?
Baby Monkey is hungry.	Will Baby Monkey go find something to eat? Will Tiger wake up? Will Mother Monkey wake up? What will happen to Baby Monkey if Tiger comes along? Does Baby Monkey know that tigers are dangerous?
Tiger wakes up.	Uh, oh, what will happen? Will Tiger eat Baby Monkey? Will Mother Monkey wake up?
Tiger is hungry.	
Mother Monkey wakes up.	Why is Mother Monkey calling Baby Monkey? Why doesn't she just run down the tree to get him?
"Baby Monkey! Come up here! Come up here!"	
Here comes Tiger!	Does Tiger know that Baby Monkey is nearby? Will he chase Baby Monkey up the tree? Will he eat Baby Monkey?
Baby Monkey is up in the tree.	How does Baby Monkey feel? Did Tiger ever see Baby Monkey? Will Baby ever get anything to eat? Will he be able to go down the tree for food? What did Baby Monkey learn?
Baby Monkey is safe.	

such questions to think more deeply about the author's message.

Let's look at another example, this time from Richard Peck's book *A Year Down Yonder* (2000). This humorous story is about Mary Alice, a teenage girl who leaves her Chicago home to spend the summer in a small country town with her eccentric grandmother. From the first page, the reader is constructing knowledge of the characters, which in turn will enable the reader to anticipate and confirm subsequent actions as the story unfolds. Consider the following episode, which occurs about midway through the book. The scene opens with "bloody screams mingled with other screams and crashing and banging noises." Grandma runs down the stairs with a shotgun. The complexity of the story is further enhanced as two new characters (Arnold Green, the boarder, and Maxine Patch, the postmistress) are brought into the setting. To understand their relationship to this particular scene, it is important to recall that earlier in the story Grandma had invited Arnold to use the attic as his art studio, and that in previous chapters, the author has hinted that Maxine is romantically interested in Arnold. The words "mingled with other screams" allow the reader to predict that at least two people, probably Arnold and Maxine, are in the attic. The puzzling element of the passage has to do with all the noise. However, the scene with Grandma is perfectly logical, just the type of action we might expect from her tempestuous character. Grandma gallops into the front room, wearing an old bathrobe and Grandpa's house shoes, her spectacles hanging from one ear, and holding a twelve-gauge Winchester shotgun. As the story continues, the dynamic relationships between characters, actions, settings, and problems become more entwined. Maxine comes thundering down the stairs, with a large black snake "draped and coiled all over her sizable body, as though it had fallen from the ceiling on

Chapter 2 Reading for Deep Comprehension   21

Figure 2.3 A Character Map Analyzing the Role of the Central Character to Nine Secondary Characters from *Because of Winn-Dixie*.

Character	How the Character Influenced Opal	How Opal Influenced the Character
Winn-Dixie	He connected Opal to all the other characters.	Opal rescued and protected Winn-Dixie.
The Preacher	He gave Opal the truth about her mother.	Opal helped the preacher come out of his shell.
Miss Franny Block (librarian)	She was a friend to Opal who connected Opal to a friend her own age.	Opal was a friend to Miss Franny and connected her to friends her own age.
Old pinch faced Amanda Wilkinson (child)	She helped Opal realize that everyone had a loss.	Opal helped her realize that Amanda could still care for others.
Gertrude (parrot)	Gertrude helped Opal get a job.	Opal helped Gertrude get over her fear of dogs.
Sweetie Pie Thomas	She was Opal's first connection with a child and the town.	Opal let her play with and love Winn-Dixie.
Stevie & Dunlap Dewberry (neighbor boys)	The boys aroused Opal's curiosity in friendship.	Opal helped the boys learn to not judge people so quickly.
Gloria Dump (neighborhood lady)	She taught Opal that everyone has a past and how to deal with it.	Opal was Gloria's eyes and provided companionship.
Otis (pet store worker)	He opened Opal's eyes that people can be good even though they have a background.	Opal provided an opportunity for him to play his music for people.

her." As the reader visualizes this passage, it seems logical to assume that a snake of that size must have been living in the attic for a long time. (Earlier in the book, it was established that loud noises could be heard in the attic). Maxine's behavior is further complicated as the author describes that "the snake was all that Maxine wore!" This is a bit of humor, perhaps out of character for a spinster postmistress, yet not totally unexpected if the reader has been tuned in to Maxine's romantic interest in Arnold. A good reader will use text information to analyze characters, infer their actions, and make realistic assumptions about relationships between character and action. In this example, the idea that Grandma's spirited personality could be responsible for the snake in the attic and subsequent consequences is a natural attempt on the part of the reader to construct meaning on reading this humorous passage. My point is that deep comprehension is dependent on the reader's ability to think beyond isolated events and to construct greater understanding through the relationships of elements in a story.

As teachers, we ourselves should engage in activities that will deepen our knowledge of the process of comprehension. For instance, during literacy team meetings, teachers can conduct book discussions around a common text, then create a text map that focuses on character analysis. In Figure 2.3, for example, a team of coaches analyzed the central role of the main character, Opal, to nine secondary characters in the story *Because of Winn-Dixie* (DiCamillo 2000). In the example on the next page, from *Stone Fox* (Gardiner 1980), a group of coaches created a text map that focused on characteristics of strong characters, supported by evidence from the text.

Strong Characters	What Made the Character Strong	Evidence
Grandfather	Never gives up Taught Willie important life lessons Hardworking and caring	Got out of bed Don't accept help if you can't pay (p. 18) Took Willie in
Willie	Determined Compassionate Courageous	Kept the farm going Convinced he would win, took care of Grandpa Went to talk to Stone Fox
Stone Fox	Stoic Compassionate	Determined to buy back his people's land Made sure Willie won the race
Searchlight	Loyal Determined	Did everything she could to help Willie and Grandfather Worked so hard to win

In his book *On Writing* (2000), Stephen King explains how an author shows, rather than tells, the reader about the character. For example, in his description of Annie Wilkes, the psychotic nurse in *Misery*, King writes: "We see her go through dangerous mood-swings, but I tried never to come right out and say 'Annie was depressed and possibly suicidal that day' or 'Annie seemed particularly happy that day'" (p. 191). King explains how a writer uses language that shows the actions of the character, thus enabling the reader to infer particular traits and motives. "I can show you a silent, dirty-haired woman who compulsively gobbles cake and candy, then have you draw the conclusion that Annie is in the depressive part of a manic-depressive cycle" (p. 191). Thus, for deep comprehension, the reader's mind and thoughts must engage with the writer's words.

Given these facts, I propose that comprehending strategies used by fluent readers, as described in the last examples, are no different than the strategies used by emergent readers, such as the young person who was responding to *Tiger, Tiger*. Simply put, the difference is not in the process itself, but rather in the extent of the reader's content knowledge and problem-solving experience in activating and sustaining comprehending strategies. This is important for teachers to know, for it places comprehension instruction along a continuum that increases in depth and efficiency through meaningful and relevant reading experiences. Furthermore, it implies that the author is responsible for writing a comprehensible text to which readers can apply reliable strategies for constructing meaning. There is no greater barrier to reading comprehension than a poorly written text with illogical relationships; such a text denies the mind the opportunity to infer beyond the printed page.

From Theory to Practice

In summary, comprehension is grounded in a reader's ability to understand relationships, specifically how the parts come together to represent deeper meanings. A book's characters are at the center of multiple relationships; this suggests that deep comprehension is dependent on the reader's ability to infer and analyze characters. An important question for teachers is: How can we teach students how to analyze characters and thus promote deeper comprehension? Here are some questions teachers can use to prompt young readers to integrate multiple sources of information for inferring and analyzing character relationships:

- Who are the important characters in the story? How do you know this?
- What are the characteristics of one or more of the characters?
- How do the characters in the story feel about each other?
- How do you feel about the characters in the story? Do you like them? Would you like to have them for a friend?
- Is the time or place in the story important to the characters? Would it make a difference if the time and place were different? In what ways would it make a difference? How would the characters act differently if the time and place were changed?
- What are the problems faced by the characters, and how do they solve their problems?
- Why did the characters act the way they did? Was it right or wrong for the characters to act this way?
- Would you have solved the problems the characters faced in the same way as the characters did? What other solutions might there be to solving the problem? Would these solutions work better? Why do you think so?
- What lessons did you learn from the character's actions?
- Does the character remind you of anyone you know?

During reading workshop, teachers can use mini-lessons for teaching students about character analysis. They can show students how to use sticky notes for highlighting particular passages that illustrate how characters interact with other story elements. They can demonstrate how good readers reflect on characters as they read, recording their thoughts and impressions in a reading log. This process may be carried over to book discussions and reading conferences, where teachers prompt students to delve more deeply into character relationships. A unit of study can be developed to promote an in-depth analysis of characterization. During independent work, teachers can create comprehension task cards for scaffolding students as they develop strategies to understand and analyze characters. Explicit experiences such as these provide students with a temporary scaffold for thinking more analytically about character relationships. A comprehension task card might look something like this:

1. Choose a book to read.
2. Identify a character to be analyzed.
3. Write in your response log three or more words that best describe the character.
4. Record evidence in your text to support your analysis.
5. Explain why you think the character acts the way he or she does.

Understanding Text Structure

Another important relationship in reading comprehension is that of text structure (Fitzgerald 1984; Lattimer 2003; McGee 1982; Taylor 1992). Text conventions are sets of rules that outline how texts are typically organized. These conventions specify the main components of a text, the type of information that occurs at various locations, and the relationships among these text elements. As readers acquire more experience with texts, they build a knowledge base for understanding how authors write, including knowledge of text conventions, story structure, and organizational techniques. A good writer is always attentive to the reader's needs, ensuring that the text is well-written in order to promote the reader's comprehension. Therefore, knowledge of text structure and organizational conventions is just as important for the writer as it is for the reader.

Figure 2.4 Teacher and students have created an anchor chart that emphasizes the reading and writing connections. The charts are hung in the classroom and are used as a resource by the students.

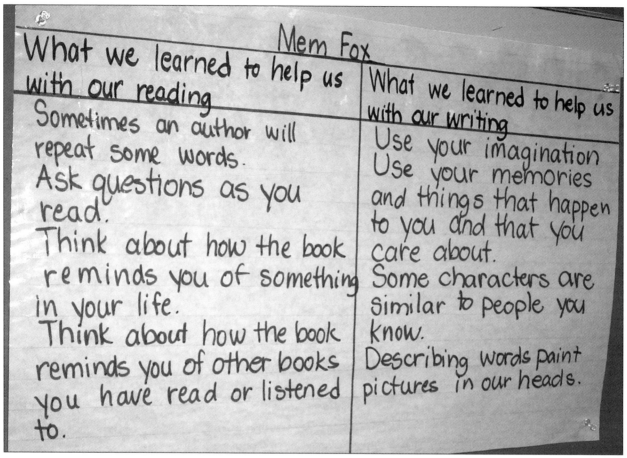

All texts have certain conventions that distinguish them as a particular genre. This becomes evident when we reflect on the different styles of writing to be found in newspapers, magazines, reports, novels, and so forth. Even in the specific category of books, there are many different types of texts, and each book is uniquely structured as part of a particular genre. For example, a tall tale generally contains heroes and heroines, unusual obstacles to overcome, and exaggerated events. Realistic fiction, by contrast, contains (as its name suggests) more realistic characters who encounter universal problems in a believable story line; and informational text is intended to communicate facts in a clear and concise format.

When young readers can recognize genre and text conventions, they can use this knowledge to guide their comprehension. Teaching the basic structure of texts can help students in both reading and writing.

In her book *How Writing Works,* Gloria Houston (2003) highlights the importance of readers understanding how a text is organized. As a writer of children's books, Houston uses examples from her own writing to illustrate the link between comprehending and composing. As readers read, they develop an internalized sense of the main elements and structures of text. This knowledge prompts readers to expect texts to be organized in particular ways, and this knowledge promotes comprehension even before the page is turned. If a text dishonors the conventions of good writing, the reader becomes frustrated and the comprehending process is disrupted. Section III of the Appendix contains several resources to help teachers develop author and genre studies, including descriptions of text types for teaching text conventions. These organizational frameworks can also be used for creating language charts within and across text structures. (See Figure 2.4.)

Closing Thoughts

Recently I presented a reading workshop to elementary teachers; several middle and high school teachers were also in attendance. My goal was to illustrate how a process approach to reading and writing is based on similar strategies regardless of whether you are teaching first graders or college-age students. The process is the same; only the content knowledge and depth of experience are different. To illustrate, I gave two examples: one of first graders who were learning how to write a fairy tale, and the other of graduate students who were learning how to write a research report. In both cases, the students had read numerous texts in each genre; they had examined these texts for common structures; they had utilized text organizers and rubrics to develop their compositions; and they had clarified and extended their knowledge through sharing their thoughts with others. Below are the similarities.

My point is that learners of all ages apply similar strategies to comprehend messages; and the teaching goal is to help students see the relationship among the common sources of information.

In summary, from first grade to high school, then on to college, readers acquire a wealth of literate experiences that enable them to think at deeper levels. As they accumulate knowledge, they can move beyond surface details and focus on deeper analysis. This is an important message for teachers—one that focuses on a seamless transition of knowledge, strategies, and skills that increase in power and flexibility over time and across grades.

First Graders Writing a Fairy Tale	**Grad Students Writing a Research Study**
Read lots of fairy tales.	Read lots of research studies.
Discuss organizational structure for fairy tales.	Discuss organizational structure for research genre.
Develop planning chart for composing fairy tales.	Develop planning chart for conducting research.
Share checklist or rubric with students.	Share checklist and rubric with students.
Read like a writer, analyzing fairy tale structures	Read like a writer, analyzing sections and conventions of research.
Write a draft of a fairy tale.	Write a draft of a research paper.
Use checklist or rubric to self-assess.	Use checklist or rubric to self-assess.
Revise, edit, and publish fairy tale.	Revise, edit, and publish research study.
Share fairy tale with others.	Share research study with others.

Language for Literacy Learning

I have just completed a workshop for a group of California teachers on the topic of language before literacy, and I rush to the airport for my return flight to Arkansas. As I settle into my seat, a young mother and her two daughters walk down the aisle, climbing into the three seats directly behind me. They are adorable little girls, about two and three years of age, chattering with excitement about what is apparently their first airplane flight. "It's going to be a long trip for these two," I think to myself. "Three hours of sitting still, strapped into their seats with nothing to do." While the mother buckles the children's seat belts, she directs their attention to the sign on the overhead panel and explains, "See the pictures of the seat belts? When the picture lights up, we'll need to have our seat belts buckled." The children comment about the large X that covers the picture. "I'm glad you noticed that," the mother responds. "It means that you do not unbuckle your seat belt. We'll be sure to watch this important sign while we are flying." Within twenty minutes of our flight, the mother takes out a bag of books. "Look, girls, I have a new book. We've never read this one before. It's all about a little girl who becomes a ballerina." "Read it to us first, Mommie," the older girl responds," then I can read it to you and Lindsey." The mother begins to read, occasionally stopping to elicit comments from the girls. "Tell me about this picture. What do you think is going to happen?" Lindsey, the younger child, responds, " She becomes a ballerina!" The mother asks, "What makes you think that?" Lindsey points to the picture and says, "She has on ballerina shoes!" At the end of the story, Sierra, the oldest child, exclaims, "Mommy, let me read it now. I can read it now!" "Yes, you certainly can," says her mother, and Sierra begins to read, using the same expression and intonation she has learned from her mother's voice. "It's like an apprenticeship into literacy," I think to myself. I glance at my watch and realize that we have been flying for over an hour and the children show no signs of boredom or discomfort. During the next hour of our flight, I continue to listen to story after story the three read together, interspersed with conversations about the clouds and frequent checks on the status of the lighted seat belt sign. The flight attendant drops by and offers the girls an activity book. As Sierra works in the book, I hear the mother ask her daughter problem-solving questions, such as "Why did you select that picture? Is that the right one? How do you know?" On her other side, Lindsay is coloring, and her mother prompts Lindsay to talk about her picture: "Tell me about your picture. What are you coloring?" Soon the plane begins to descend, and the clouds part to show the city beneath. The girls' discussions with their mother take a new direction, with new discoveries to talk about. The wheels on the plane make a large thumping noise as they are released, and Sierra comments that the plane is getting its wheels ready to land. "Yes," says the mother, "the wheels are going down." At the same time, Lindsey begins to sing softly, "The wheels on the bus go up and down, up and down, up and down." As the three-hour flight comes to an end, I smile as the mother and her two children look again at the seatbelt sign, unbuckle their belts, and walk down the aisle to new discoveries.

Becoming Literate Through Language

How do children become literate? In the previous example, the girls were acquiring knowledge of critical literacy concepts through conversations with their mother. Lev Vygotsky (1986) believed that language is the tool for shaping literate development. In other words, literacy is the outgrowth of language, a result of interactive discourse with a more knowledgeable person around reading and writing situations. In contrast, the theory that literacy precedes language implies that literacy can be taught as meaningless and isolated skills. As teachers, we need to examine our own beliefs about language and literacy, as our beliefs will influence how we teach for comprehension. If we view language as an instructional tool, we will create language-rich environments where children are mentored into literacy.

One of the most important literacy experiences we can give children is to read to them. Reading aloud introduces children to the special language of books. When children hear literary language, they deposit these structures in their minds, where they remain and are recalled as needed, to support reading, writing, and speaking. As they hear books read aloud, children acquire knowledge about print concepts, story structures, literary language, and specialized vocabulary and begin to anticipate that particular structures will occur within books. They discover recurring relationships between various texts and discourse patterns. This knowledge gives children a personal foundation for making meaningful predictions as they read stories on their own (Dorn, French, and Jones 1998, p. 30).

In the opening example, the preschoolers in the plane had already acquired a toolbox of literary and linguistic structures, which they will use to bring meaning to new experiences. For example, they had learned such essential reading concepts as predicting from pictures, making inferences, confirming information, using intonation to express meaning, and reading with fluency. One of the greatest benefits of reading aloud is its potential to build memory capacity, whereby children learn to listen for chains of language and remember these meaningful chunks over time. Having a network of background memories that can be easily mobilized to understand a particular event is needed for deep comprehension.

A few weeks ago, I received an e-mail message from a principal who was considering eliminating read-aloud time from the classroom literacy block. Her rationale was that this block of time would be more usefully spent in reading instruction. Yet research has clearly documented a significant link between reading aloud to children and early reading achievement. (Durkin 1966; Wells and Chang-Wells 1992). However, reading aloud is much more than simply sharing a great book with children: children should experience a variety of genres that expose them to a range of literary and linguistic patterns. Lester Laminack (2004) identified six types of texts that teachers should read aloud each day to students:

1. books that build community;
2. books that expose children to the beauty of language;
3. poetry books;
4. books that have been read before and so can now be used for reading and writing mini-lessons;
5. nonfiction books that support the content curriculum;
6. chapter books that are read over an extended period of time.

Recently Rosa Abernathy, a literacy coach from Conway, Arkansas, revised the elementary schedules in her school to incorporate these six types of daily read-alouds. At the beginning of the school day, the teacher gathers the children in a circle and reads a picture book that illustrates the importance of working and solving problems together, and respecting differences. Throughout the day, the teacher integrates four other text types into shared reading, interactive read-aloud, content mini-lessons, and the reading and writing workshops. At the end of the day, the teacher pulls the children together and reads a chapter or two from a favorite book. In this way children are mentored into the language of books, building a solid foundation for comprehending texts during independent reading.

Rhythmic Patterns in Literacy Learning

Recently I reread Don Holdaway's (1979) classic text, *Foundations of Literacy* and, as always, I was fascinated by his simple explanations of complex learning. He describes the rhythmic nature of all organic learning, and applies this notion to our everyday living experiences: our "heart beats and rests, we breathe in and out, we work and rest" (p. 96). According to Holdaway, "the secret to any learning is in the rhythm of challenge and relaxation, tension and reward. This rhythm, intrinsically controlled, sustains the mind in almost fatigueless activity" (p. 96). What a powerful concept! This simple notion of rhythmic patterns can be applied to any type of literacy learning; it suggests simply that literacy learning should be balanced to include spans of easy processing interspersed with a few challenges. The easy work helps the mind build momentum for solving problems with speed and efficiency. New learning becomes orchestrated with old learning, and comprehension is increased through integration of the two. To illustrate, let's revisit the opening example with the mother and daughters on the airplane. Although the three-hour flight was full of literacy experiences, the youngsters did not tire. Why? Most activities were easy for the them, so when challenges did occur, the children could meet them with motivation and energy. The interactions themselves were grounded in the children's existing knowledge, thus preventing frustration from occurring. The mother, as the more knowledgeable person, adjusted her support to ensure that the children were mentally engaged in the literacy process. The rhythms of easy and challenging work were naturally balanced to ensure that literacy learning was fun, motivating, and self-extending. These same rhythms should be evident in the interactions between teachers and students in the classroom.

Shared Reading

Shared reading is an excellent example of how easy and challenging experiences can be orchestrated to provide children with a "fatigueless" learning experience. The activity is grounded in language—specifically, shared reading is an interactive language experience between a more knowledgeable person (the teacher) and a group of novices (the students) around a literate event. The teacher uses an enlarged text to model, coach, and scaffold the children's learning about written language. During the process, the children experience the joy of reading, the richness of language, and the stimulation of sharing ideas and information with their peers. The teacher carefully observes the knowledge and skills the children display and prompts them to use existing information to learn something new. This kind of in-and-out support is similar to a carefully executed dance, with the teacher regulating assistance to create a smooth rhythm of easy and challenging moves on the part of the students (Dorn, French, and Jones 1998).

With the teacher's guidance, children acquire knowledge of the reading process, specifically how the elements of reading (phonemic awareness, phonics, comprehension, fluency, and vocabulary) are integrated to represent meaning. Shared reading is an excellent complement to guided reading, as it exposes children to critical concepts and comprehending strategies needed for independent reading. The charts in Section I of the Appendix illustrate how shared reading can be placed on a learning continuum from emergent to transitional readers, and how shared reading relates to guided reading. For example, during shared reading with emergent readers, one teaching goal is to learn about print conventions. To promote this knowledge, the teacher models and invites the students to locate early concepts of print, such as directionality, one-to-one matching, first and last, and concepts of letter, word, and punctuation. During guided reading, the children's knowledge is further developed and practiced, but this time with less assistance from the teacher. During shared reading with transitional readers, the teacher no longer needs to focus on early concepts of print; for them the teaching goal shifts to address more complex text conventions, including sentence and paragraph structure, table of contents, index, photographs, charts, and captions. During guided reading, the teacher selects books that enable the students to apply their knowledge of these text conventions with limited support.

Framework for Shared Reading

Shared reading occurs in a predictable context and includes five interrelated steps: (1) rereading of familiar or easy texts for fluency and orchestration; (2) orientation to a new text; (3) shared reading of the new text, (4) follow-up discussion and teaching points; and (5) literary extensions. These five work together to create a balance of easy and challenging work that promotes a smooth orchestration of reading elements. Let's take a closer look.

Practicing on the Easy or Familiar

Familiar texts provide an opportunity for fluent and expressive reading on easy materials. Types of texts that can be used to advantage include nursery rhymes, songs, poems, plays, chants, stories with repetitive or cumulative patterns, class-authored texts, and favorite stories. These familiar experiences enable children to sound like readers, making an imprint of language patterns in the mind that prepares them for reading a new text with greater fluency. After the shared reading, the teacher might quickly highlight a reading strategy or skill the students need to learn or practice.

Orientation to the New Text

With a model of successful reading in their minds, the children are now ready for the new text. An orientation to the text will aid their comprehension, and the teacher may, for example, guide the children to make predictions from the title, author, and cover illustrations before the text is read. As the pages are turned, the teacher stops from time to time to engage the children in discussing the pictures and making inferences about the story.

Shared Reading of the Text

Teacher and students then read the text aloud together with minimal interruptions, with the focus on fluency, expression, and comprehension. The teacher's role is to move the reading along while simultaneously working on comprehension and word-solving strategies. The children begin to develop metacognition, which is needed for comprehension, as the teacher explains and models strategies. During the reading, the teacher encourages and celebrates student participation and asks thought-provoking questions as needed to ensure understanding. To guarantee the involvement of all the children, the teacher provides an adjustable scale of help, scaling back support when children are doing well and increasing it when they begin to struggle. The goal is to make certain that the shared experience provides a model of successful reading.

Follow-Up Discussion and Teaching Points

After the reading, the teacher should always engage the students in an interactive and enjoyable conversation. This provides an opportunity for the children to deepen their understanding of the text. The teacher prompts the children to respond to the message, discussing what they learned or reacting to specific story elements. Here are some examples of prompts the teacher might use.

- Talk about the message in the story.
- What was the author trying to teach us?
- What do you think will happen next? Why do you think that?
- Does everyone agree, or does anyone disagree, and why?
- Did you enjoy the story? Why or why not?
- What was your favorite part of the story? Why?
- Which character did you like best? Which one did you like least? Why?
- Was there anything that confused you? Why?
- Will you read this story again? Why? Why not?

Following the discussion of the text, the teacher selects one or two teaching points that focus on strategies for problem solving and comprehending the text. For instance, at the emergent level, the teacher might use dry-erase marker boards or wikki sticks to help students examine text information in greater detail. For early and transitional readers, the teacher might model how to use sticky notes to flag favorite words or phrases to be added to a reading log. (See Section I of the Appendix for examples of how text tools can be used during shared reading.)

Shared reading provides a social context for scaffolding students' knowledge of literacy, with a special focus on the following literacy concepts:

- Aspects of language, such as structure, rhyme, rhythm, and alliteration.
- Concepts about print, such as where to start reading, directionality, special concepts, punctuation, words, and letters.
- Problem-solving strategies, such as monitoring, locating, checking, confirming, and self-correcting at the levels of letter, word, and full text.
- Comprehending strategies, such as questioning, inferring, summarizing, identifying the author's purpose, and making connections.
- Story elements, such as plot, character, setting, problem, solution, and theme.
- New vocabulary.
- Text structures to help students discern between, for example, fiction and nonfiction.
- Special features of nonfiction text that help readers access information, such as index, table of contents, glossary, headings, graphs, photographs, charts, and captions.

Literary Extensions

At the end of the shared reading activity, the teacher should create opportunities for the children to extend the shared reading to new levels of comprehension. They could, for instance, reread the book with peers, write a different version of the story, or respond through art or dramatic activities.

A Scale of Help in Prompting for Understanding

The important point is that literacy learning should be rhythmic, with one or two challenges placed within a stretch of smooth processing. The choice of book is critical, in that it should support fluent reading. The teacher's language is also a crucial factor. Teachers should know how to regulate their language prompts along a continuum of reading difficulty. At the highest level of support, the teacher provides explicit demonstrations; as the learner acquires more knowledge, the teacher relinquishes more control to the student (Dorn and Soffos 2001b). Our model is based on scaffolding theory as conceptualized by David Wood (1998) and is compatible with a gradual-release-of-responsibility model, as described by Duke and Pearson (2002). There are three degrees of language support:

- *High support:* Here, the teacher uses explicit language with accompanying actions.
- *Moderate support:* Here, the teacher gives reminders and focused prompts that present two or three choices for fast decision making.
- *Low support:* Here, the teacher listens and provides encouraging language that sustains the comprehending process, yet offers no direct assistance.

The degree of teacher assistance depends on two factors: (1) the goal of the problem-solving task, and (2) the student's ability to carry out the task with varying degrees of support. The problem-solving cycle must be completed for learning to be memorable; this means that the teacher must be sensitive to the learner's performance at all times. Furthermore, teaching should occur at the student's instructional level—in other words, in the student's area of potential literacy growth. (See Figure 3.1.)

To illustrate, let's take a look at what degree of help might be given to an early reader named Aaron at three points in time along the processing continuum (Figure 3.2). The context is a guided reading lesson, wherein the students are reading independently; the teacher is circu-

Figure 3.1 Scale of Help in Prompting for Problem Solving

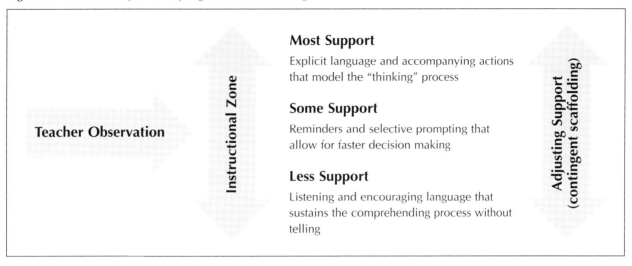

Most Support

Explicit language and accompanying actions that model the "thinking" process

Some Support

Reminders and selective prompting that allow for faster decision making

Less Support

Listening and encouraging language that sustains the comprehending process without telling

lating among the group, listening and prompting individual students as needed. In Aaron's case, the teaching goal of the reading conference is to help him develop strategies for solving unknown words. The teacher, Carla, understands the power of contingent scaffolding—specifically, the need to regulate her scale of help while focusing on her instructional goal at all times. When the learning is new, Carla provides the highest degree of support with explicit language and concrete actions, but her support diminishes over time as Aaron becomes more competent with the visual searching strategy he is learning.

Initially (Figure 3.2A), Aaron's running record indicates that he applies visual strategies for searching when he gets to the unknown word *river*, but he has difficulty with the word *down*. The first step in any new learning is the ability to monitor the problem—in this case, the word *down*. Carla prompts Aaron with the question "Is there a tricky word on this page?" Aaron immediately points to the unknown word. Since the word is *not* the goal here, but rather is the means for learning a strategy, Carla adjusts her prompts toward this learning goal. She provides two degrees of scaffolding. First, she says, "Go back

Figure 3.2A Providing Support for Aaron. First attempt.

High Support for Early Reader

Goal: Use meaning, structure, and cross-checks visually by searching through the unknown word (taking words apart using larger units of analysis).

Text: *Father Bear went fishing. He went down to the river.*

- C: Father Bear went fishing. He went d-d-d | A | to the r-river.
  down | | TS
- T: Where was the tricky part on this page?
- C: (Points to "down.")
- T: Go back and read it again and run your finger under that word and think of a word that would make sense, sound right, and look right.
- C: He went d-d-(hesitates)
- T: (Begins writing the word on the wipe board and prompts the child to blend the parts together in the word as she writes it *d-ow-n*.)
- C: Oh, *down*! (He returns and quickly rereads.)
- T: Are you right? So looking all the way through tricky words can help you, right? (Slides her finger under the word slowly.)

Plan of Action: Provide children with lots of opportunities to develop knowledge of this strategy through guided reading, shared reading, strategy-based mini-lessons, assisted writing, and writing workshop.

Figure 3.2B Providing Support for Aaron. Two days later.

Moderate Support for Early Reader

Goal: Use meaning, structure, and cross-checks visually by searching through the unknown word (taking words apart using larger units of analysis).

Text: *Father Bear looked up. "Here come the fish," he said.*
- C: Father Bear <u>look</u> up. "Here come the fish," he said.

     looked
- T: Can you read this page again and see if you can find a place where you need to do some work? Make sure it sounds right and looks right.
- C: Father Bear look up. (Returns to reread.) Father Bear <u>look (pauses)</u>

                 looked
- T: Can you run your finger under the word and think of a word that would make sense, sound right, and look right?
- C: Father Bear <u>look-ed</u> (running his finger under the word) up. "Here come the fish," he said.

     looked
- T: Good checking. You know a way to help yourself figure out those tricky parts, don't you?
- C: Yeah.

Plan of Action: Provide children with lots of opportunities to practice this strategy through guided reading, shared reading, strategy-based mini-lessons, assisted writing, and writing workshop.

---

and read it again and run your finger under that word and think of a word that would make sense, sound right, and look right." In response, Aaron rereads, articulates the first letter of the troublesome word, and stops. Carla at that point increases the scale of help to its highest degree. She pulls over a dry erase board, writes the letters of the word, and prompts Aaron to blend the sounds together and think about the story as the word is constructed. With this level of support, Aaron is able to figure out the word. Carla concludes the problem-solving cycle with explicit feedback: "So looking all the way through tricky words can help you, right?"

Two days later, Carla again adjusts the scale of help to accommodate what Aaron knows. Contingent scaffolding is provided by giving some support in the form of general reminders and selective prompting. In this case (Figure 3.2B), Aaron demonstrates greater independence with the strategy of visual searching into unknown words. According to his running record, he ignores the ending on the word *looked*. Carla prompts him to monitor his reading: "Can you read this page again and see if you can find a place you need to do some work?" Aaron rereads, pausing when he gets to the troublesome word. Carla increases her scale of help: "Can you run your finger under the word and think of a word that would make sense, sound right, and look right?" Aaron uses his finger to help his eyes move to the end of the word and immediately self-corrects. Carla provides feedback in her closing remarks: "Good checking. You know a way to help yourself figure out those tricky parts, don't you?"

In the final example, the scale of help is once again adjusted to reflect less teacher support and more student independence. Contingent scaffolding is provided by Carla's listening and using encouraging language to help Aaron apply appropriate strategies and sustain the comprehending process. This time (Figure 3.2C), when Aaron encounters a tricky word and needs to

Figure 3.2C Providing Support for Aaron. Less support.

Low Support for Early Reader

Goal: Use meaning, structure, and cross-checks visually by searching through the unknown word (taking words apart using larger units of analysis).

Text: *But Tabby stayed up at the top of the tree. "Meow," she said.*
- C: But Tabby—st-ay
                stayed
- T: What can you do to help yourself?
- C: But Tabby stay-ed | R at the top of the tree. "Meow," she said.. (Keeps reading.)
                stayed

Plan of Action: Provide the child with opportunities to practice this strategy and learn more about visual patterns through guided reading, shared reading, strategy-based mini-lessons, assisted writing, and writing workshop.

---

apply a visual searching strategy, Carla provides no direct assistance. She simply asks, "What can you do to help yourself?" With this vague prompt, Aaron is able to quickly self-correct his error and continue to read.

These examples illustrate how teachers must adjust their language scaffolds to match their students' literacy needs. How might this scale of help apply to book orientations during guided reading lessons? Would teachers provide the same degree of language support for the transitional or fluent reader as they do for the emergent reader? I've asked these questions of my graduate students, who proceeded to videotape their lessons and analyze their own scales of help as they work with readers at different points along the reading continuum. The findings are clear.

With emergent readers, the teacher's language is explicit, pointing out language patterns, specialized vocabulary, and unfamiliar words. The teacher and the children may rehearse specific language phrases and share responsibility for creating the reading event. At this level, memory of the text provides young readers with a scaffold for integrating meaning, structure, and visual cues. The teacher's language remains close to the language of the text, thus enabling the reader to orchestrate background and text knowledge into a meaningful experience.

At the early reading level, the teacher's language is adjusted to accommodate an almost equal balance between the explicit and the inferential. This is to be expected, as the literacy system of the early reader is still under construction (See Dorn and Soffos 2002). However, at the transitional and fluent levels, inferential talk is the dominant form of discussion. Students at this level adopt more of an inquiry stance and show evidence of self-reflective behavior. Here the teacher is more apt to be a participant in the book discussion, with the children making inferences and asking questions that indicate deeper comprehension. Thus, findings from actual examples of classroom reading instruction suggest that teachers adjust their language support to reflect changes in their students' reading comprehension.

Closing Thoughts

In this chapter, I've emphasized the link between language and literacy, specifically how language is a tool for shaping how we think and learn. From a teacher's point of view, language is our greatest teaching resource. Therefore, it is important to consider the distinction between two language forms: prompting and questioning.

- *Prompts* use language designed to mobilize strategies into action— for example, "You noticed something there. What can you do to help yourself?"
- *Questions* use language designed to elicit particular responses, such as "Where did the story take place?" or "How did the story end?"

Generally, prompting is more useful than questioning—as long as it leads students to effective searching and self-correcting. In the process of building meaning, readers acquire a toolbox of efficient strategies, but more important, they learn how to regulate these strategies according to the changing demands of the reading task. Questioning can have limited potential in fostering this development, particularly if the questions are simply designed to bring out an accurate response.

Recently I asked a group of teachers, "Can a question become a prompt, and thus lift the learner's comprehending to a higher level?" This led to an interesting discussion of the power of language as a tool for restructuring the mind of the learner. One teacher commented that a literal question, such as "What happened in this story?" places limited demands on the mind, as it only activates short-term memory. In contrast, a prompt—for example, "How did the story make you feel?"—activates a mental network of both short- and long-term (semantic) memories that work together to construct a simple story event into a new personal experience. The language teachers use is critical for stimulating the learner's mind to strategic activity—activating background knowledge, searching for links, building connections, and orchestrating varied information into new meanings.

Can questions be used to promote comprehension? Can questioning lead to deeper understandings? Of course there will be times when teachers should ask questions; but generally, questions are more beneficial when they come from the reader, not from the teacher. Teachers therefore should create conditions that foster student inquiry, such as reading and writing workshops, where students can learn the importance of self-questioning as they read for deeper meaning. Furthermore, students should be encouraged to bring questions to group discussions where, once again, language becomes the tool for promoting deeper comprehension.

The goal for teachers is to create varied opportunities that will enable young readers to develop flexible strategies for constructing deeper understandings. Literacy knowledge results from the dynamic interplay of teaching, prompting, and questioning—with language at the heart of the process.

Teaching for Strategic Processing

I learn to make meanings, to analyze meanings. I can do all of this at my own pace, re-reading, skipping, turning to the end, pausing for thoughts when I like. I can go in deep, as it were, when my interests are most engaged. Certain authors seem to be my friends, for all that they have been dead for centuries. Reading makes me excited about ideas as much as about events and people. Sometimes I grasp only part of what I know the writer has made quite plain. At other times, I feel I could have made it clearer for the writer. This isn't arrogance; most dialogues work in this way. I expect reading to be an adventure, with the possibility of surprises. Reading can be both a kind of day-dreaming and very hard work.

Being literate comes from knowing what reading is good for, from engaging in it so that we enlarge our understanding not only of books and texts, what they are about and how they are written, but also of ourselves. But none of this, not the power, enjoyment, understanding, nor the pursuit of knowledge that reading makes possible is available to those whose early experience of reading has been joyless, unplayful, lacking the pleasure of entering into stories or the reward of sustained effort.

Margaret Meek, On Being Literate

My work has been greatly influenced by the theories of Marie Clay, specifically her theories regarding the strategies readers use in constructing meaning. According to Clay, reading is a message-getting process, and comprehension takes place as the reader strives to create meaning. Comprehension moves from simple to deeper levels as the reader acquires greater knowledge, strategies, and experiences. In her book *Change Over Time in Children's Literacy Development,* Clay (2001) writes about a simple level of comprehension: "a word by word, sentence by sentence, and page by page understanding of a very simple story such that an ending would be anticipated by the young reader who has comprehended the strings of words for their collective meaning" (p. 107). She concludes that "comprehension is involved in all reading and writing of continuous texts, even a one-sentence message" (p. 107).

When readers read, they exhibit behaviors that indicate the strategies they use for solving problems and sustaining meaning. For instance, a reader who is puzzled by a passage might hesitate at the point of difficulty, turn back to the previous page, search for a clarifying connection, and reread a section in an attempt to clear up the confusion. Or the reader might jot a note in the margin of the text, flag a particular passage with a sticky note, and mention the passage in a discussion group in an attempt to seek clarification. Such behaviors represent critical moments in literacy learning, as they indicate the person's attempt to monitor confusion and search for meaning. An observant teacher can notice these processing patterns and make some assumptions about how the reader is working to comprehend the author's message.

Learning How to Problem-Solve

Problem solving is motivated by a desire to comprehend something. Developing efficient problem-solving strategies therefore will surely improve readers' level of comprehension. I suggested earlier that problem-solving actions in life share strategies with problem solving in literacy, and that both are driven by meaningful purposes and goals. I am especially intrigued by Don Holdaway's (1979) theory of rhythmic patterns, specifically the need to balance easy and challenging work to sustain "fatigueless" problem solving. In this chapter, I take these theories a step further, exploring how readers apply specific strategies to monitor, sustain, and extend their understanding.

Good readers constantly monitor their meaning; if they didn't, there would be no benefit to reading. Our minds are structured to construct meaning, for everyday happenings as well as literacy-related events. When meaning breaks down, the mind automatically begins searching and self-correcting to restore a sense of understanding. These strategic actions are part of a process, a cycle that is made up of problem solving constantly monitored with meaning. The cycle begins with a state of mental arousal: something that is known becomes the stimulus for initiating a problem-solving plan to deal with the unknown. As readers engage in continuous problem-solving cycles, their strategic actions form neural pathways in the brain, which eventually become automatic unconscious reactions to literacy situations (see Figure 4.1).

Strategies for Regulating Comprehension

Deep comprehension requires readers to plan, select, direct, and orchestrate the various cognitive structures and processes available to them in order to attain a particular goal. This involves readers' making deliberate choices, including about the selection of particular strategies for figuring out words and the amount of time to spend on particular aspects of reading. Two important signs of comprehending power might be fluent and expressive reading, and efficient and economical self-corrections. These external behaviors are signs of internal processing—that is, the quick and efficient orchestration of knowledge to comprehend a particular message.

Figure 4.1 Processing Cycle for Problem Solving

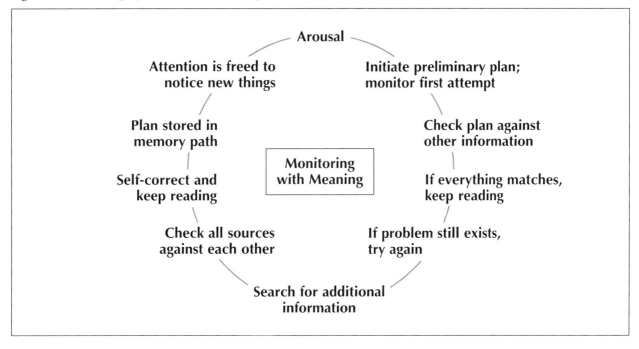

Reading with Fluency

The link between comprehension and fluency has been clearly documented. Fluency is directly linked to memory capacity, specifically the reader's ability to hold meaningful chunks of information in memory. Marie Clay has established that fluency has as much to do with thinking as it does with looking. This implies that fluency cannot be forced on a reader—in other words, telling someone "Read it fast" is not enough to ensure fluent reading. Instead, fluency develops as a result of a well-orchestrated system of knowledge whose elements work together to comprehend a message. Fluency consists of three interrelated elements: speed, rhythm, and flexibility (see Figure 4.2). *Speed* relates to retrieval rate, while *rhythm* relates to phrasing and orchestration. *Flexibility* implies that the reader understands how to self-regulate, or pace, his or her reading according to changing purposes and needs. This pacing can be heard in the reader's voice—for example, slowing down to determine the meaning of a passage, speeding up to cluster ideas or phrases, and using tone of voice to express meaning. For beginning readers, fluency can be encouraged with prompts, such as "Read that part like talking" or "Can you read the punctuation?" or "Read the dialogue like the character would say it." It is important to understand that speed is not necessarily an indication of comprehension. A reader who has good control of oral language structures and decoding skills can read a passage with speed and accuracy, but not necessarily with comprehension. A better indicator of comprehension might be how the reader self-regulates while reading, self-correcting when meaning breaks down, using punctuation as cues for constructing meaning, and parsing the text into natural units. Teachers can train themselves to listen to how students regulate their voices.

We have found the fluency scale from the National Assessment of Educational Progress (Rasinski 2003) to be helpful when studying

Figure 4.2 Three Elements of Fluency

Speed	Rhythm	Flexibility
• Speed of retrieval • Rapid word recognition • Fast decoding • Automaticity of item knowledge • Subroutine processes free working memory space for new information • Accuracy	• Large, meaningful groups of words • Intonation, stress, pitch, and expressive interpretation • Knowledge of book language (or author's syntax) • Knowledge of oral language structures • Meaning-driven responses	• Not context dependent • Able to transfer across different situations • Can apply similar strategies on range of material • Varies reading rate according to purpose • Displays depth of knowledge at highest level

change in reading fluency over time. This scale measures fluency according to three elements: (1) grouping or phrasing of words as revealed through intonation, stressing, and pauses exhibited by readers; (2) adherence to author's syntax; and (3) expressiveness—whether the reader interjects a sense of feeling, anticipation, or characterization when reading aloud. Students' fluency is measured on a scale of 1 to 4: students at levels 1 and 2 are nonfluent; those at levels 3 and 4 are generally considered fluent.

- *Level 1:* Reads primarily word by word. Occasional two-word or three-word phrases may occur, but these are infrequent and/or they do not preserve meaningful syntax.
- *Level 2:* Reads primarily in two-word phrases with some three- or four-word groupings. Some word-by-word reading may be present. Word groupings may seem awkward and unrelated to larger context of sentence or passage.
- *Level 3:* Reads primarily in three- or four-word phrases. Some smaller groupings may be present. The majority of the phrasing seems appropriate and preserves the syntax of the author. Little or no expressive interpretation is present.
- *Level 4:* Reads primarily in large, meaningful phrase groups. Although some regressions, repetitions, and deviations from text may be present, they do not detract from the overall structure of the story. Preservation of the author's syntax is consistent. Some or most of the story is read with expressive interpretation.

Self-Correcting

Self-correcting strategies may well be the most important factor in successful reading. They are the outcome of higher-level thinking; in other words, they reflect the mind's ability to orchestrate a range of cognitive processes to attain a particular goal. This is something all humans can do; without the ability to self-correct, we would not be able to learn. Consider the example in Chapter 1 of the toddler who is learning to button her shirt (Figure 1.1). Her self-correcting behaviors provide her with feedback that sustains her attention. The same process can be observed in talking: most conversations contain pauses, repeats, and self-repairs. In writing, self-correcting behavior is evident in the author's attempt to revise a message to better convey his or her meaning. In reading, self-correcting behavior is the ultimate act for constructing meaning. It shows that the reader is engaged in monitoring, searching, and decision-making, all with the goal of determining the meaning of a text. According to Clay, an absence of self-correcting reduces the learner's opportunities for initiating, forming, practicing, extending, and refining a network of strategies. Success is attained when the problem is solved, the strategies reinforced, and comprehension achieved.

From this point of view, self-correcting is related to fluency. As teachers, we might ask these questions: How often do our readers self-correct? What appears to trigger the self-correcting activity? How long does it take for a reader to solve the problem? Is there a change in the rate and efficiency of the reader's self-correcting behaviors? These questions are important because they provide us with a framework for exploring how our teaching may (or may not) be encouraging effective self-correcting strategies in our students' reading. An inquiry-based environment with language-rich activities provides a natural context for promoting self-correcting strategies, which in turn promotes deep comprehension and higher-level processing.

Strategies Versus Behaviors

In teaching for comprehension, we must keep in mind the difference between strategies, which are internal; and behaviors, which are external. Strategies are cognitive reactions that require the reader to activate prior knowledge and use multiple sources of information to think beyond the text. Strategies for deep comprehension include predicting, inferring, visualizing, connecting, analyzing, summarizing, synthesizing, skimming, critiquing, and reflecting. All are aimed toward enabling the reader to construct meaning for a given event. Behaviors, by contrast, are simply the outcomes of the strategy used. To illustrate, consider the example of a student's rereading, an observable behavior. As teachers, we might ask: What occurred in the reader's mind that activated the rereading of this particular passage? Remember, strategies are internal, and therefore unobservable (sometimes unconscious), actions the mind takes to resolve conflict and restore meaning. Although reading strategies cannot be observed, they can be inferred by studying reading behaviors, particularly changes in behavior over time and across literacy events. Therefore, it is critical for teachers to watch for behaviors that suggest particular reading strategies, as these overt actions provide evidence of the reader's comprehending process. Strategies and behaviors work together to produce what we call strategic behaviors—that is, the observable outcome of a reader's attempts to understand the author's message. Although the three types of action outlined below are related, their differences are important in understanding reading comprehension.

Reading Action	Characteristics	Example
Strategies	Cognitive processes; unobservable	Activating background knowledge
Behaviors	Observable	Turning pages and talking about the pictures
Strategic behaviors	Observable; indicates cognitive processing	Previewing a text to integrate background knowledge with text cues

Strategic Behaviors

At this point, we might ask a few questions: What sort of strategic behaviors do good readers exhibit? What do these behaviors tell us about the reader's comprehending process? How can we use this information in teaching for comprehension? Furthermore, can teachers develop these behaviors in their students? We have learned from Marie Clay how important it is to study the strategic behaviors of good readers, and how doing so can provide us with reliable information for teaching struggling readers. How logical—to learn from the experts, readers who have already figured out the process of comprehension!

Recently I asked a group of teachers to think of themselves as experts in reading and to identify the most common behaviors used by strategic readers for monitoring, sustaining, and expanding their comprehension. The following is their list of the ten most important strategic reading behaviors:

1. Rereading.
2. Previewing or surveying a text.
3. Asking questions before, during, and after reading.
4. Reading aloud to clarify thinking.
5. Using story structure, text genre, and writing conventions.
6. Using text aids to illuminate and extend meaning.
7. Marking texts and recording notes.
8. Using context and parts of words to infer meaning.
9. Writing in reading response logs.
10. Discussing ideas with others.

In the pages that follow, we'll consider each of these ten.

Rereading

Rereading is probably the most common behavior exhibited by strategic readers. When meaning breaks down, a strategic reader will reread particular passages to clear up the confusion. This behavior is the result of the mind's ability to monitor uncertainty and search for order. An emergent reader will generally reread a line or sentence to restore meaning; a more sophisticated reader might reread entire sections to clarify understanding. Teachers can prompt beginning readers to reread by saying something like, "Read that again and think of what would make sense there." As readers become more efficient, they are able to hold longer chains of meaning in their memories, and rereading becomes a more focused attempt to locate points of confusion and clarify meaning. Consider an example from my own reading. One of my favorite authors is Anne Rice, whose horror books often take the form of historical chronicles, with complex characters who appear in several books. Often I find myself stopping in the middle of one book, rushing to my bookshelf to locate another book I've read with the same character, and rereading entire sections to deepen my understanding. Series books for younger readers often include recurring characters; think of Cam Janson, Nancy Drew, and Harry Potter.

When reading for comprehension, a good reader will reread in order to deepen meaning. Teachers can observe how a student's rereading behaviors change over time as the comprehending process becomes more efficient. For instance:

- The child may move from rereading longer stretches of text, to rereading just a few words, to repeating the word as if to confirm the meaning (Dorn and Soffos 2001b).
- The child may employ selective rereading for a particular purpose, such as searching for specific information within a text, or across texts, to clarify or extend meaning.

Previewing or Surveying a Text

The process of comprehension begins the moment a good reader picks up a book—assuming the reader knows how to preview the text for important information. Imagine that you are in the library, looking for a new book to read.

How do you select the right one? How do you build knowledge for the text? The first step might be to look for a book by a particular author; choosing a book by an author you already know would lead you to expect a certain style of writing. You might use the book's title to make additional predictions about the text. You'll probably flip through the pages to check out the features of the book, such as the basic look of the page, the illustrations, the number and type of headings, and perhaps the writing style. In addition, good readers read the following elements of a book as a way of previewing it:

- The back cover and inside flap.
- Excerpts of reviews and information on awards the book may have won.
- The first page or lead paragraph.
- The table of contents.

Good readers can preview a book in this way in a short amount of time, surveying text features and making an appropriate selection. Previewing is central to learning; it relates to preplanning and promotes self-correcting strategies as the reader accumulates more information. Readers who lack the ability to preview texts for meaningful connections are likely to have impaired comprehension. Teachers can promote previewing skills in emergent readers by conducting interactive book orientations, pointing out such things as the book's title, author, pictures, language, and other text features. As young readers become more competent, they will begin to preview books on their own and, over time, will employ ever more sophisticated and efficient strategic behaviors.

Teachers must also provide children with opportunities to learn how to self-select books. Consider your own reading, and ask yourself: What would you do if you lacked the ability to pick out a book for yourself? One of the biggest barriers to comprehension is a reader's inability

Figure 4.3 Children learn how to choose books based on text types and other features.

to select a book. A well-designed classroom library is essential for developing this lifelong skill in young people. In such classrooms, teachers engage children in organizing the library according to genre, author, type, or other defining features of the books (Figure 4.3).

Asking Questions

Good readers know how to ask their own questions and how to set their own purposes for reading. They have an attitude of inquiry, which they need in order to transfer their problem-solving abilities to different contexts and for different purposes. Furthermore, good readers are always questioning the author's intentions, especially when the reader has trouble making meaning. Frank Smith (1994) notes that comprehension cannot occur if a reader is unable to ask questions of the author. Deep comprehension is dependent on the reader's ability to ask questions before, during, and after the reading. The reader and the writer share a common goal: supporting the reader's comprehension. After all, if a writer produces a text that is incomprehensible, the value of reading that text is negated.

Here are examples of questions that readers might ask as they read (Beck, McKeown, Hamilton, and Kucan 1997):

- What is the author trying to say here?
- What is the author's message?
- What is the author talking about?

Reading Aloud to Clarify

Reading aloud enables the reader to ponder more deliberately on any points of confusion; it brings the uncertainty out in the open for analysis and reflection. Reading aloud is similar to thinking aloud, a powerful technique for making one's thinking visible. Reading aloud helps readers regulate their actions and amplify their thoughts as they use sensory data to assist with the analysis of the text information. Think about your own reading behavior. If you are reading a difficult text, you are likely to subvocalize or read aloud the most difficult parts. This is a normal mental response: to involve additional sensory systems—mouth (tactile), ears (auditory), and eyes (visual)—to enable us to better analyze the troublesome passage. Teachers can promote this important behavior by prompting children to mark puzzling passages and read these pieces aloud during reading conferences or literature discussion groups.

Using Story Structure, Genre, and Writing Conventions

Good readers are analytical readers—they use their knowledge of text structures to assist with comprehending. Their repertoire of diverse experiences with books and authors provides them with reliable information for comprehending incoming information. They understand the conventions of how texts are organized, and they use this knowledge in comprehending new material. They use text maps (see Chapter 2 and examples in Section III of the Appendix) and graphic organizers to organize and regulate their thinking before, during, and after the reading event. In addition, readers can use their knowledge of text structures in comprehending different types of texts.

Here are two examples of charts a teacher and students have created as aids to understand how texts work.

What We Notice About Fairy Tales

- Begin with "Once upon a time " or "Long ago."
- End with "happily ever after."
- Magic
- Use sets of three (three wishes, three stepsisters).
- Take place in a faraway land.
- Good and evil (good always conquers over bad).
- May have animals that can talk.
- May have kings and queens.
- Teach a lesson.

Text Structures in Nonfiction Texts

- *Cause/effect:* accordingly, consequently, hence, so, therefore, thus
- *Chronological/sequence:* first, second, third, next, then, finally, after, afterward, meanwhile
- *Time order:* after, afterward, at last, before, currently, during, earlier, immediately, later, meanwhile, now, presently, recently, simultaneously, then
- *Problem/solution:* therefore, furthermore, as stated, thus, as a result, hence, then, likewise
- *Comparison/contrast:* also, in the same way, just as, so too, likewise, similarly, but, however, in spite of, on the other hand, while, nevertheless, nonetheless, whereas, notwithstanding, in contrast to, still, yet
- *Descriptive:* for example, namely, for instance, to illustrate, like, specifically

Using Text Aids to Illuminate and Extend Meaning

Good readers use pictorial information to support, clarify, and extend comprehension. Visual aids, such as pictures, diagrams, maps, graphs, charts, arrows, labels, headings, sidebars, and captions, are critical sources of information for understanding the author's message. Poor readers often skip over this valuable information, thus missing critical parts of the message. In his book *I See What You Mean,* Steve Moline (1995) provides teachers with excellent ideas for promoting students' visual literacy skills (Figure 4.4). Here are three ways to help young readers learn how to use pictorial aids in building strategic knowledge.

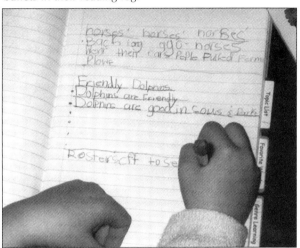

Figure 4.4 Children learn how to use headings, lists, and bullets in their reading log.

- During shared reading, use Big Books to demonstrate how readers attend to captions, diagrams, pictures, and other pictorial aids to support meaning.
- During writing workshop, demonstrate how writers can use pictorial aids such as captions, pictures, and charts to support their texts. Encourage students to include these visual aids in their own writing.
- During reading workshop, encourage students to include pictorial aids in their reading response logs.

Vicki Altland and her third graders created a chart of features from nonfiction texts with explanations of how these features can be used to comprehend the author's message:

Nonfiction Feature	How It Helps Us Find Information
Table of contents	Helps us find the main topics in the book in the order they are presented.
Index	Lists important words in the book in ABC order with the page number.
Glossary	Helps explain special words in the book and how to pronounce them.
Photographs and illustrations	Help us understand what something looks like.
Labels	Tell us about the photograph or illustration and its parts.
Captions	Tell us information about the picture.
Comparisons	Help us understand the size of something.
Cutaways	Show us what something looks like inside.
Maps	Tell us where things are in the world.
Close-ups	Help us see the details in something small.
Types of print	Signal important words.

Marking Texts and Recording Notes

Research has shown that students recall more information when they underline or highlight passages within a text. The act of highlighting requires the reader to decide which sections of the text are worth remembering. Strategic readers also write notes in the margins of the text or record specific information on sticky notes that they insert in appropriate places in the text. Teachers can help students to develop these strategic behaviors by prompting them to mark passages as they read and make notes on their reading. Simply put, note taking involves encoding written language with the intention of storing this information for the future. It is most useful for capturing information from nonfiction. Good readers take notes for different purposes: some notes simply paraphrase the text; some highlight key words and phrases; some include important sentences or short quotes; and some are drawings or diagrams. Good readers regulate their note taking according to the demands of the task. Teachers can promote effective note taking by demonstrating how to read a passage and record key words or ideas.

Using Context and Word Parts to Infer Meaning

Vocabulary knowledge is strongly related to reading comprehension. The very act of reading provides children with a context for learning new words. When readers encounter unknown words, their greatest tool for inferring meaning is found in the text that surrounds the word. Words that are only partially understood become better known through meaningful practice. Good readers are language collectors; they notice interesting words and record them in notebooks or on scraps of paper, simply because they like the sound of them. Good readers have developed a linguistic storehouse of word patterns, and they analyze unknown words by breaking them down into meaningful parts. Root words, compound words, prefixes, suffixes, and inflectional endings all contain units of meaning.

Teachers can provide opportunities for students to experiment with words, including writing activities that involve word play. To illustrate, here is a poem about words that Jenny, one of my former fourth-grade students, composed, using her knowledge of word parts—in this case, the suffix -*ation*:

A Poem of ATIONS

If you are thinking hard, that's concentration.
If you are watching stars in the sky, that's observation.
If you make plans to eat dinner somewhere, that's a reservation.
If you give life to something that's not living, that's personification.
If you take a short cut in adding, that's multiplication.
If your parents want you to clean up your room and you want to play, that's aggravation.
If you take a bus from Arkansas to Texas, that's transportation.
If you get your tonsils out, that's an operation.
If animals sleep during the winter, that's hibernation.
And that's all I have to say, and that's finalization!

In the classroom, putting together a display of words students have encountered from their reading and writing helps them learn about word meanings (Figure 4.5).

Writing in Reading Response Logs

Writing contributes to reading development, thus leading to deeper understanding. Mel Levine (2002) describes how writing is the greatest

Figure 4.5 A wall of words from children's reading and writing helps them learn about word meanings.

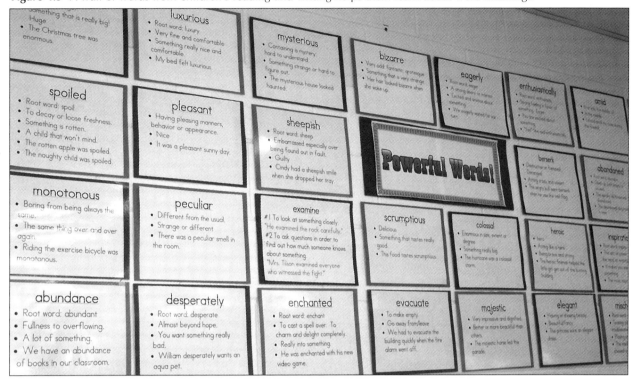

orchestra the mind will ever conduct; it involves integrating and coordinating multiple sources of information. Writing helps students learn how to organize their thinking more fluently and flexibly. Moreover, writing makes thinking visible and more tangible, thus promoting conscious awareness and deeper comprehension.

In early lessons, simple questions such as the following can provide a temporary scaffold for young readers:

- Was there a part that you really liked?
- Was there a part that you disliked?
- Was there a part that really puzzled you?
- Was there a part where you made an important connection?

Such prompts, if given, should be quickly discarded. If used too long, they can stifle comprehension by becoming the focus of reading.

When students write in response logs, they become more conscious of their thinking; they write to describe events, summarize information, formulate beliefs, and explore new ideas. A reading response log is designed to promote deeper understanding, and thus is personalized to support the reader's own thinking. Carla worked with classroom teachers to design a reading log that would contain meaningful categories related to comprehension. Figure 4.6 illustrates how they organized that reading log. It includes five sections: "My Thinking," "My Ideas," "Words and Phrases," "Beginnings and Endings," and "Genre Learning." Here are some examples of ideas that students might record under some of the categories:

- Descriptions of characters or events
- Connections to life, text, or world
- Comparisons or contrasting information

Figure 4.6 Reading logs can be divided into sections to help students organize their thinking.

- Summaries
- Memorable words or phrases
- Maps or visual displays
- Drawings or diagrams
- Author reviews
- Notes, questions, impressions

Teachers can promote this strategic behavior by sharing their own reading logs with students. I have kept reading logs for over twenty years, and they document important reading periods in my life. Each log is dated. For instance, a large period of my life was devoted to the arts, and I spent several years pursuing an art degree. Now when I revisit my reading logs, I can relive this part of my life. Furthermore, these literate experiences of my past continue to influence my thinking about life, even twenty years later. This type of behavior is characteristic of successful readers, and it reveals an ongoing habit of reading and comprehending.

Discussing Ideas with Others

The urge to discuss our ideas with others is part of our innate desire to confirm and clarify our thinking. Talking about their reading enables readers to consolidate information and store it in their semantic or long-term memory. During book discussions, readers have the chance to reflect on what they are interpreting as they read or listen to it. Teachers use inquiry-based language that invites reflection and tentativeness (Lindfors 1999), using such words and phrases as "I wonder . . . ," "Maybe . . . ," "If . . . ,"; "I think . . . ," or "Tell me more."

The talk in literature discussion groups is grounded in the reader's need to make sense of the author's message. Therefore, participants engage in collaborative language acts—they agree or disagree with each other, express confusion when puzzled, seek or give clarification, compare and contrast ideas, offer evidence, express opinions, generalize to new situations, and make connections (Figure 4.7). Literate knowledge is developed in social contexts, where language becomes the means for developing and expanding our minds.

Figure 4.7 The best way to understand a text is to talk to someone about it. Here, third graders engage in a book discussion.

Closing Thoughts

Here are some important principles that capture the essence of this chapter.

Strategies are cognitive processes, which means that they are unobservable. Strategic behaviors, however, can be observed and studied for evidence of students' power of comprehension. Teachers can use language prompts and teaching tools, such as reflection logs and sticky notes, to activate thinking processes; at the same time, they must take care that the tool itself does not become the reason for reading. Deep comprehension is the result of a well-orchestrated system of flexible decision-making strategies working together (most of the time, unconsciously) to construct meaning for the author's message.

Comprehension is directly related to fluency of thinking; both rely on efficient and meaningful self-corrections. When meaning becomes unclear, an active self-correcting system responds immediately to restore understanding and create order.

To understand the process of comprehension, we should study the strategic reading behaviors of expert readers, including how we ourselves employ specific behaviors to understand a text. If we can become more aware of our own process of comprehension, we will be better able to share this critical information with our students.

Understanding Language for Comprehending Texts

Remember the books you read . . . then you read again, maybe more than once . . . or from which you just reread particular lines or passages? What is it that pulls readers back to revisit a text? I know that for me it's the language—beyond the story line—that pulls me back. Sure, the story is great—but what makes it memorable? How does the writer use language to create the images that get stuck in my head? I try to remember how many times I've read *Beloved* by Toni Morrison, the story of Sethe, who escaped from slavery but can't escape from the horrors of her own past. The characters in the book are so mesmerizing that I can't stop thinking about them. I reread the words over and over, trying to make sense of the actions, yet lacking the experience to really understand them. Beloved, the ghost child, killed by her own mother; Denver, the living daughter, afraid to leave the house, afraid of the unknown, of the world outside that could cause a loving mother to murder her own child. I feel compelled to read the words again. "I'm afraid the thing that happened that made it all right for my mother to kill my sister could happen again." What horrible thing could have happened to Sethe that could justify—in the wildest stretch of human imagination—the killing of her own child? Morrison takes us inside Denver's mind: "I need to know what that thing might be, but I don't want to." Is it possible that knowing what caused this horrific action could be even more terrifying than the action itself? "I watch over the yard, so it can't happen again and my mother won't have to kill me too." What does Denver mean by "have to kill me"? Morrison's precision with language seems to remove the blame from Sethe, while simultaneously emphasizing a past so dreadful that it is hard for the reader to imagine. How does a writer take an abstract idea, one that is difficult to comprehend, and make it believable? Through written language, Morrison uses words to create images of beauty and horror, safety and fear, sorrow and ecstasy—opposite concepts existing side by side that tell a complex story of love and endurance. After reading the book, I watched the movie. The book helped me to make sense of the gaps in the movie; I could hear Morrison's words, lingering in the back of my head, reminding me of the thoughts in the minds of the actors on the screen. Toni Morrison is a master at crafting language to help her readers look deeply within themselves, seeing harsh reality in imaginary events and helping them move to deeper levels of comprehension. I am reminded of Vygotsky's theory of language and thought: written language that becomes the tool for influencing the reader's thoughts. I'll also never forget another book of Morrison's—*The Bluest Eye*. I first read that novel eight years ago, and it has stayed with me ever since. *The Bluest Eye* tells the story of eleven-year-old Pecola Breedlove, a black child raped by her father, growing up in the 1960s in an America that idolizes blond, blue-eyed children. In a child's way of thinking, Pecola believes that if her eyes would only turn blue, she would be beautiful and all her problems would disappear. At the end of the story, Morrison writes: "So it was. A little black girl yearns for the blue eyes of a little white girl, and the horror at the heart of her yearning is exceeded only by the evil of fulfillment." In the afterword to this book, Morrison describes the challenge of moving her readers to deeper levels of self-questioning, taking them beyond simple pity for the character to a self-interrogation of society for the part it played in destroying her. A writer's ultimate goal is to use language that moves readers to self-reflection, creating a memorable reading experience with long-lasting potential—in other words, a book you can't forget; words that stay with you; images and passages that become embedded within your thoughts. The connection between language and deep comprehension is indissoluble, and requires the writer to understand how language works in precise and reliable ways so as to help the reader comprehend the written message.

Language and Reading Comprehension

This book is as much about language as it is about reading. After all, reading is a use of language. Skilled writers understand how language works, and will use this knowledge to craft language in creative and flexible ways. Sometimes a writer will deliberately defy the rules of conventional language in order to speak more precisely to the reader. For instance, a good writer will know when a sentence fragment might be more effective than a complete sentence or when an adjective in an odd position might better convey the intended meaning. However, it is only when writers understand the conventions of language that they can understand when these conventions can be broken. That is, knowledge of the language system is the foundation on which flexibility and creativity with language are built. It is part of the writer's craft to manipulate language in order to enhance the reader's comprehension. For example, in the opening to *The Bluest Eye*, Toni Morrison begins with short, simple, repetitive sentences that create a textbook image of the perfect blond, blue-eyed family from the Dick-and-Jane era.

> Here is the house. It is green and white. It has a red door. It is very pretty. Here is the family. Mother, Father, Dick, and Jane live in the green-and-white house. They are very happy. See Jane. She has a red dress. She wants to play.

Chapter 5 Understanding Language for Comprehending Texts

Who will play with Jane? See the cat. It goes meow-meow. Come and play. Come and play with Jane.

Within these images of the perfect family, there exists an unsettling, almost surreal quality that disturbs the reader. In the next passage, notice how Morrison dishonors the language rules, omitting punctuation, forcing the reader to process the text in a rapid, nonsensical tone, treating every element, including names, with the same flat, meaningless identity.

Here is the house it is green and white it has a red door it is very pretty here is the family father dick and jane live in the green-and-white house they are very happy see jane she has a red dress she wants to play who will play with jane see the cat it goes meow-meow come and play come and play with jane

Morrison's deliberate use of run-on sentences interferes with the natural rhythms of language, creating an artificial, unnatural setting for telling her story. In her next passage, she defies the very foundation of the language system by eliminating the spaces between words, forcing the reader to treat the words as one long, meaningless phrase.

Hereisthehouseitisgreenandwriteithasareddoor itisveryprettyhereisthefamilymotherfatherdickandjanelivethegreenandwhitehousetheyareveryhappyseejaneshehasareddressshewantstoplaywhowillplaywithjaneseethecatitgoesmeowmeowcomeandplaycomeandplaywithjane

In these examples, Morrison uses the conventions of written language to provide the skeleton for an intentional manipulation of the system. This stimulates the reader's imagination, prompting a thoughtful analysis of the writer's message.

Here are two examples from children's books that illustrate how authors manipulate conventions in another way, by using sentence fragments to highlight specific information. The first is from *Pictures of Hollis Wood* by Patricia Reily Giff (2002):

Quick sketches, one after the other: hat down over his eyes in the first, standing in front of the river in the next, sleeping in the hammock in the third. His beard and the way he leaned forward, listening. I was trying to capture what he looked like so I'd have it to take back with me. To remember.

And here's another example, from *A Time for Angels* by Karen Hesse (1997):

Hesitating a moment in the dark stairwell, I breathed in the odors from the other apartments. Ham. Bacon. Smells that made my mouth swim with hope. But in our apartment only the foul stink of weeds waited for me.

Good readers are usually good writers. Students who understand and enjoy what they read can almost always communicate their ideas clearly on paper. When readers read, they try to follow the writer's ideas; when writers write, they try to communicate their ideas to someone else. Frank Smith (1994) calls this the reader/writer contract—a two-way communication process that is coordinated through the structures of the language system. Words are simply the tools used by the writer to stimulate the reader's imagination, activate memories, and promote deeper understanding. Good communication is grounded in knowledge of how language works.

What does this mean for us as teachers? First of all, we know that language is learned in meaningful contexts, and that the meanings of words depend on the syntactic relationships between them. The best resources for learning about the language system are found in good writing; an abundant classroom library is therefore a valuable tool for building this knowledge. Still, we should not assume that just because children are reading a lot of books they will automatically notice how writers are communicating with readers. This kind of complex understanding requires explicit teaching and guided analysis. Teachers can incorporate language studies into the reading workshop, providing students with the necessary foundation for thinking at deeper levels. Language studies are simply in-depth investigations of language conventions, wherein students use books from the classroom library to examine how writers use these conventions to communicate with readers.

Language-Based Behaviors That Influence Comprehension

All of what I've said up to now implies that a reader's knowledge of the language system can influence his or her depth of comprehension. We might say that structural knowledge is the very architecture on which creativity is shaped; without this basic foundation, writing is built on a faulty framework and can interfere with the reader's comprehension. What are some language-based strategies that can aid reading comprehension? Furthermore, how can these strategies be taught in meaningful ways that support reading and writing? Here are ten strategic behaviors that good language users employ:

1. They manipulate forms of speech to express meaning.
2. They make good word choices that communicate clear messages.
3. They use pronouns to stand for nouns.
4. They use punctuation to clarify meaning and regulate fluency.
5. They combine simple sentences into more complex ones.
6. They organize related ideas into paragraphs, chapters, texts, and genres.
7. They use dialogue to carry and extend meaning.
8. They use figurative language to symbolize meaning.
9. They build vocabulary through word relationships and patterns.
10. They use transitional words and phrases.

Manipulate Forms of Speech to Express Meaning

The building blocks of language are composed of eight basic speech forms that come together in a conventional order to communicate clear and precise messages. These eight, known as the parts of speech, are: nouns, verbs, adjectives, adverbs, pronouns, prepositions, conjunctions, and interjections. Although comprehension is derived from the semantic structures within the text, meaning is created by the syntactic relationships between the parts of speech. Readers approach written materials as language users and thinkers. If students understand how language works, they will use their sense of oral language structure to anticipate words within the written structure when reading. The parts of speech are best learned in meaningful contexts, and grammatical functions can only be applied within the context of language.

So, you might wonder, should teachers bother to teach students the names of the parts of speech? The answer is yes, simply because names provide us with precise labels for discussing how language works. For instance, if a reader comments on the way a writer uses words to describe something, the teacher might respond by saying, "Yes, these words are called adjectives. Adjectives are words that describe a person, place, or thing." As students develop a deeper understanding of the conventional forms of language—in this case, for example, that an adjective precedes a noun—they can begin to notice how good writers sometimes deliberately defy this rule in order to communicate a particular message. To illustrate, let's take a closer look at one of my favorite books, *My Mama Had a Dancing Heart*, by Libba Moore Gray (1999), an uplifting tale of how a mother and daughter welcome each season with a ballet. Gray's creativity with words and her manipulation of the language convey an atmosphere of playfulness. Look at how she defies language rules by reversing the noun and adjective in the phrases "drink hot tea spiced" and "cut snowflakes paper-white delicate." To convey a feeling of dancing, Gray invents new words—for instance, an adjective composed of a noun and a verb—and puts them together to create rhythmic patterns: "We'd dance/a frog-hopping/leaf-growing/flower-opening/hello spring ballet." She creates new verbs by adding inflectional endings to nouns: "shawling the earth," "satin-ribboning my feet." She uses verbs to create rhythmic movements: "the waves would come plash-splashing," "I'd slip-swish behind Mama." And she infuses life into nouns, creating moving images from concrete objects: "we'd sea-shell pile the windowsill." In every case, Gray's manipulation of language is intentional, grounded in a deep understanding of how language works. For a text to be effective, writer and reader must have a mutual understanding of how language is used to convey meanings; only with such mutual understanding can bridges be built between the writer's craft and the reader's comprehension.

Teachers can help students develop an understanding of the parts of speech. As each form is introduced, it can be added to a class language chart, and students can be encouraged to examine its usage in meaningful contexts. Using the classroom library, students can search through familiar books (texts already read and enjoyed), locate specific parts of speech, and record favorite examples in their reading logs.

Make Good Word Choices That Communicate Clear Messages

The reader's comprehension is directly influenced by the precision of the author's words. A good writer uses distinctive nouns that create clear images and active verbs that bring the nouns to life. One or two vivid, clearly focused details are more effective than nine or ten vague ones. Good writers use concrete words—that is, words that refer to specific things that can be seen, touched, or heard. Take, for instance, a simple sentence such as *The white, flowery tree stood outside my window.* Here, the adjectives *white* and *flowery* could describe several types of trees, thereby creating an ambiguous image in the reader's mind. Consider what happens when the adjectives are eliminated and the noun becomes more concrete: *The magnolia tree stood outside my window.* Writers always keeps their readers in mind, searching for the most precise words, the ones that will stimulate the clearest images.

Vygotsky notes that words are simply the tools people use to express ideas—clearly defined words that are sequenced in a logical order—yet words work together to create a holistic image for communicating a message. In his book *Thought and Language,* Vygotsky (1986) describes it this way:

> When I wish to communicate the thought that today I saw a barefoot boy in a blue shirt running down the street, I do not see every item separately: the boy, the shirt, its blue color, his running, the absence of shoes. I conceive of all this in one thought, but I must put it into separate words. (p. 251)

The point here is that the mind does not remember in words; instead, the words are clustered to represent larger chunks of meaning. The writer's responsibility is to find the right combination of words and place them in the right places within the sentence, so that the reader will process them as ideas rather than individual words. Take, for instance, the following passage from *Bridge to Terabithia* by Katherine Patterson (1977). As with Vygotsky's example, the reader does not recall each word individually; rather, the image of May Bell's ugliness is communicated by the collective power of the words working together:

> May Bell was as scrawny as Brenda was fat. She stood a moment in the middle of the floor in her underwear, her skin white and goose-bumpy. Her eyes were still drooped from sleep, and her pale brown hair stuck up all over her head like a squirrel's nest on a winter branch. That's got to be the world's ugliest kid, he thought, looking her over with genuine affection.

Good verb choices are critical to comprehension. Immature writers will sometimes use adverbs, for example, *slowly*, with a weak verb, such as *walk*. In contrast, good writers will find a stronger verb to describe the action of walking slowly, for instance, *amble, saunter, mosey,* or *meander*. Using strong, vivid verbs helps make a character come alive. In the following examples, notice how the authors use active verbs that describe precise movements.

From *A Taste of Blackberries* by Doris Buchannan Smith (1973):

> Jamie up-and-overed the fence and started across the field. My eyes skimmed the field until they bumped into the house.

From *Sable* by Karen Hesse (1994):

> I crept up the stairs, careful to skip the creakers. My heart hammered against my throat. Mam would sure explode if she caught me giving Sable one of Grandma Betts's quilts, even a ruined one.

From *Bud, not Buddy* by Christopher Paul Curtis (1999):

> Herman E. Calloway's pipe dropped out of his mouth and he stumbled and fumbled into Grand Calloway Station, feeling his way like he'd been struck blind.

Use Pronouns to Stand for Nouns

If a reader does not understand that pronouns represent nouns, his or her comprehension will be severely impaired, perhaps even nonexistent. To help students understand the relationship of pronouns to nouns, the teacher can use cloze activities. That is, the teacher takes a familiar text (one that the students have already read and enjoyed) and deletes the pronouns, thus requiring the students to infer the corresponding noun. In the following example, the teacher uses a passage from *Charlotte's Web* (White 1952) to help students understand the relationship of nouns and pronouns in reading comprehension.

> Everybody heard the song of the crickets. Avery and Fern Arable heard ___ as ___ walked the dusty road. They knew that school would soon begin again. The young geese heard ___ and knew that ___ would never be little goslings again. Charlotte heard ___ and knew that ___ hadn't much time left. Mrs. Zuckerman, at work in the kitchen, heard the crickets, and a sadness came over ___, too. "Another summer gone," ___ sighed. Lurvy, at work building a crate for Wilbur, heard the song and knew ___ was time to dig potatoes.

Use Punctuation to Clarify Meaning and Regulate Fluency

Readers must understand punctuation in order to understand the writer's message. In speaking, comprehension is aided by the speaker's inflections, and sometimes also by hand and body gestures. In written language, the conventions of punctuation take the place of the speaker's inflections: question marks are akin to an upturn in voice, issuing an invitation to respond; commas indicate a pause, used, for example, to separate items in a series; exclamation marks reveal excitement. Meaning can be altered or diminished if punctuation is misused or ignored. A classic example of the influence of punctuation on reading comprehension is found on the jacket of the best-seller *Eats, Shoots, and Leaves* by Lynne Truss (2003):

> A panda walks into a café. He orders a sandwich, eats it, then draws a gun and fires two shots in the air.
>
> "Why?" asks the confused waiter, as the panda makes towards the exit. The panda produces a badly punctuated wildlife manual and tosses it over his shoulder.
>
> "I'm a panda," he says, at the door. "Look it up."
>
> The waiter turns to the relevant entry and, sure enough, finds an explanation. "Panda. Large black-and-white bear-like mammal, native to China. Eats, shoots and leaves."

How can teachers design meaningful investigations of punctuation for their students, using the classroom library as a valuable resource? From a language-to-literacy perspective, children should *hear* the language first. Reading aloud provides them with a context for learning how language sounds. As the children become accustomed to the rhythms of language, teachers can guide them to notice the various forms and functions of punctuation in written texts. Let's consider the diverse punctuation used by Lisa Rowe Fraustino in her book *The Hickory Chair* (2001). First, an example of a semicolon:

> Her purse clicked open; I knew what it was because leather and peppermint smells jumped right out.

Quotation marks, dashes, exclamation point:

> "You'd poked this hole right here,"—her fingernail scratched wood—"and made a ball of batting in your little fist!"

Commas in a series, question mark:

> "Remember how Gran used to surprise us with notes hidden under pillows, between book pages, in pockets, and anywhere else she could connive?"

Commas to separate noun clauses, hyphens, apostrophe to show possession:

> I loved Gran's smell, and her warm face when we played touch-your-nose at the gold mirror, and salty kisses when we sat on Gramps' old army truck in the attic and listened to the wind sing on the roof.

Combine Simple Sentences into More Complex Ones

Using language effectively involves putting the various parts of speech together so that they form meaningful units of communication—sentences. The sentence is the basic unit of expression. For writing to have a rhythm that pleases the reader or enhances the content in some way, authors balance their sentences to include a variety of lengths and structures. For some readers, complex sentences can be difficult to comprehend, especially when the reader is not used to seeing or hearing them. The reason for this is fairly simple. Longer sentences contain a density of idea units—that is, several small ideas are made to work together to represent the author's larger message. Take, for instance, the following example from the text *Sounder* (1969) by William H. Armstrong:

> The shattered shoulder never grew together enough to carry weight, so the great hunter with the single eye, his head held to one side so he could see, never hopped much farther from the cabin than the spot in the road where he had tried to jump on the wagon with his master.

For deep comprehension to occur, the reader must deal with the idea units in the order in which they are written, simultaneously integrating the smaller ideas into a larger meaning. If children are not familiar with complex sentence structures, they will have a hard time comprehending deeper ideas. To facilitate children's handling of complex sentences, teachers can provide opportunities for children to combine sentences, followed by guided practice, where children use the classroom library to investigate how writers use this technique. Consider how the following example might be used during a study on sentence combining:

> Karen was in the house.
> Karen was running.
> Karen fell down.
> Karen hurt her knee.
> Karen will not run in the house again.

Reading aloud to children exposes them to language patterns, including complex sentences, structural patterns, and figurative language. Spoken language, phrased at meaningful breaks, creates a rhythmic pattern that is easier to recall. Children need to learn how to focus on chunks of meaning in speech. One way to help students think about such chunks of meaning (idea units or phrases) is to read aloud a sentence from a familiar story and ask students to raise their hand each time they hear a chunk of meaning.

Language is built on a framework of predictable language conventions. Writers must understand these conventions in order to use them effectively; at the same time, readers must understand how writers use these grammatical functions in order to comprehend the writer's intentions. An effective technique for learning about language structure is through sentence transformations—the act of using the syntax of a sentence as the framework for creating a semantically correct, new sentence. As with any language study, the text is first read and enjoyed. Later, during a mini-lesson, the teacher selects a particular sentence from the text and guides the children to substitute new words to create a new sentence, while maintaining the structural framework of the original. For instance, using a sentence from *Because of Winn-Dixie* (DiCamillo 2000), the teacher prompts the children to think about the parts of speech as they occur within the sentence. Utilizing the framework of the original sentence, the teacher guides the students to create new sentences that are both syntactically and semantically correct.

> He/put/down his pencil/and/scratched/ Winn-Dixie/behind/the ears.
> She/raced/up the hill/and/hid/the book/ under/the tree.
> The car/ran/off the road/and/hit/a haystack/by/the barn.

Organize Related Ideas into Sentences, Paragraphs, Texts, and Genres

Language is organized according to established conventions of print that increase in complexity, beginning with words and moving into greater size and complexity. At the most elemental level,

Chapter 5 Understanding Language for Comprehending Texts 59

Figure 5.1 Layers of Language Expectations for Written Text (Smith 1994: Layers of Prediction in Reading a Book)

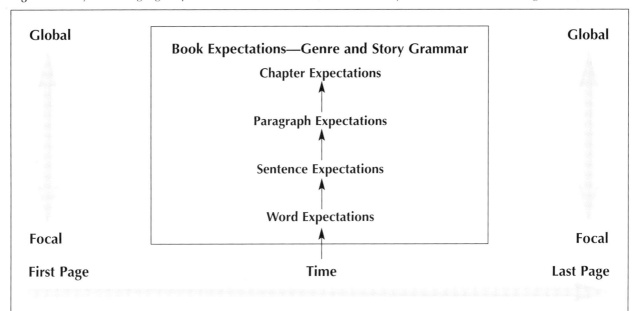

students must understand that a word is the simplest idea unit. They can be shown that the structure of language is a kind of continuum that moves from simpler to more complex elements: words are organized into sentences, sentences are organized into paragraphs, paragraphs come together to form chapters, chapters are organized into books, and books are organized into genres (see Figure 5.1). At each level, language is regulated according to traditional conventions of print.

Good readers understand how writers organize smaller ideas (sentences) into larger ideas (paragraphs). In the elementary grades, some teachers have found it helpful to provide students with a framework for writing a paragraph, including a topic sentence that expresses the main idea, details that develop the idea, and a closing sentence that summarizes or restates the idea. Although this structure can provide a basic awareness of paragraphs, it does not apply to all well-written ones. Sometimes a main idea may be implied rather than specifically stated in a topic sentence; an author may take two or three paragraphs to develop just one idea; or a single sentence may make up an entire paragraph. I have demonstrated how expert writers may deliberately manipulate written language conventions for a given purpose, but this ability depends on a solid knowledge of those conventions. Simply put, you can break the rules with style only if you know what the rules are. This same notion applies to paragraph structure. Students therefore must learn the basic structures of written language as they gain numerous experiences with good writing.

At the global level, certain features are common in particular text types, as follows:

Picture Books (grades K–4)

- Include pictures and text that work together to convey a message.
- Represent a range of genres—for example, fairy tales, folktales, fiction, informational text, or poetry.
- May include complex patterns and figurative language, which can be used as a read-aloud text.

- Some examples: *Owl Moon* by Jane Yolen, *The Hickory Chair* by Lisa Rowe Fraustino, *Molly Bannaky* by Alice McGill, *Wilfrid Gordon McDonald Partridge* by Mem Fox, *My Great Aunt Arizona* by Gloria Houston, *Thunder Cake* by Patricia Polacco, and *Nettie Jo's Friends* by Patricia McKissack.

Easy Readers (grades K–3)

- Small-book format, divided into sections that resemble chapters.
- Simple illustrations to break up the text and promote comprehension.
- Simple plot with one main event and one main character.
- Lots of dialogue to move the plot along.
- Some examples: series books such as *Frog and Toad* books by Arnold Lobel, *Nate the Great* books by Marjorie Sharmat, and Peggy Parish's *Amelia Bedelia* stories.

Chapter Books (grades 2–4)

- Include many short chapters, but do not rely as heavily on illustrations as easy readers do.
- Characters are children with everyday problems and issues that relate to a child's world.
- Contain lots of dialogue to move the action along.
- Contain a variety of sentence structures and more complex vocabulary.
- Stories are fast paced and may include a complicated plot and several characters.
- Examples: series books such as *Junie B. Jones* books by Barbara Park and *The Kids of Polk Street* by Patricia Reily Giff. Higher-level chapter books include *Charlotte's Web* by E. B. White and *Ribsy, Henry Huggins,* and *Ramona* titles by Beverly Cleary.

Beginning Novels (grades 4–7)

- Plots are often more complex than chapter books, usually built around issues that students at this age are concerned with, including family and peer relationships.
- Illustrations are rarely seen, and there's not much white space on the page.
- Lots of dialogue, complicated plot, and several characters.
- Variety of sentence structures, figurative language, and complex vocabulary.
- Some examples: *Crash* by Jerry Spinelli, *Bud, not Buddy* by Christopher Paul Curtis, and *The Pinballs* by Betsy Byars.

Use Dialogue to Carry and Extend Meaning

Authors make their writing more interesting, as well as more complex, by inserting dialogue in different places within their texts. Good writers will use dialogue in strategic places to sustain the reader's attention, promoting a nice rhythm between their descriptions of their characters and the characters' own voices. Authors also use descriptive phrases or clauses to describe the dialogue, such as the speaker's body movement, facial expressions, and tone of voice. Young readers should be exposed to dialogue patterns in various language structures, in order to learn appropriate strategies to use when they encounter unfamiliar phrases or clauses. In the following examples, notice how the authors move the dialogue and the dialogue carrier (the accompanying action) to different positions within the sentences. Also notice that in the last example there is no dialogue carrier, requiring the reader to infer the characters and logical actions.

First, from *Aunt Nancy and Cousin Lazybones* by Phyllis Root (1998):

> "Shoo, shoo!" Cousin Lazybones flaps at the chickens. "Reckon I'll go gather the eggs after all."

From *Thank You, Mr. Falker* by Patricia Polacco (1998):

As they walked, Trisha said, "Gramma, do you think I'm different?"

From *Nettie Jo's Friends* by Patricia McKissack (1989):

"What?" Miz Rabbit asked. "A wedding? A dress?" She was a mess of nerves, talking fast and hopping from foot to foot.

And from *Pictures of Hollis Wood* by Patricia Reily Giff (2002):

"Where are we going? I asked.
  "To the movies."
  "What will we use for money?"

Use Figurative Language to Symbolize Meaning

Imaginative expressions that compare things unlike in reality but alike in the writer's imagination are called figurative language. Good writers will use figurative language to build layers of meaning for a particular concept, stimulating the reader to think at deeper levels. To illustrate, consider the following passage from *The Watsons Go to Birmingham, 1963* by Christopher Paul Curtis (1995):

It was one of those super-duper-cold Saturdays. One of those days that when you breathed out your breath kind of hung frozen in the air like a hunk of smoke and you could walk along and look exactly like a train blowing out big, fat, white puffs of smoke.

It was so cold that if you were stupid enough to go outside your eyes would automatically blink a thousand times all by themselves, probably so the juice inside of them wouldn't freeze up. It was so cold that if you spit, the slob would be an ice cube before it hit the ground. It was about a zillion degrees below zero.

In this passage the author used figurative language to convey the idea of coldness. Can you imagine being so cold that your breath hung frozen in the air and your eyes would blink a thousand times to keep from freezing, or your spit would become an ice cube before it hit the ground? Even the phrase "super-duper cold" creates an image of coldness that is extraordinary. And exaggerations, such as a "zillion degrees below zero," communicate a degree of coldness that stretches beyond the human imagination. A reader gets a clear image of an extreme type of cold—a cold that can only be explained through figurative language.

A reader must be able to go beyond an author's surface language and infer deeper meanings through implied relationships. Figurative language is symbolic language, requiring the reader to think in images. Metaphor, simile, onomatopoeia, and imagery are common examples of figurative language. A metaphor expresses a relationship between two things that are not commonly associated with one another—for instance, *The night sky was a cool blanket that covered us.* A simile is a type of metaphor, but it includes the words *like* or *as*—for example, *I ran like the wind was chasing me.* Onomatopoeia is the use of words that imitate the sounds associated with them or an action they refer to—as Patricia McKissack does in describing the force of the wind in *Mirandy and Brother Wind* (1988):

Swish! Swish!
  It was spring, and Brother Wind was back. He came high steppin' through Ridge Top, dressed in his finest and trailing that long, silvery wind cape behind him.
  Swoosh! Swoosh! Swoosh!

Imagery uses language to provoke rich images. To help children understand imagery in texts, teachers can have students create anchor charts that highlight various types of figurative language (see Figure 5.2). Children can also use the classroom library as a resource for investigating how good writers use figurative language to communicate their messages. For instance, Vickie Altland and her third graders conducted a language study around several Patricia Polacco books. They created an anchor chart of language phrases, many of which use figurative language (Figure 5.3). As a result of these investigations, students will begin to use these techniques in their own writing. For example, Jonathan, one of my former fourth-grade students, used imagery to create a poem that reflected his impressions of nature:

> Spring on its way
> With the wind softly behind
> Washed by the rain.
> Rain beating on my windowpane
> Beneath a blurry sky
> Singing me a lullaby
> Listen to the wind
> Blowing the storms away
> Whispering spring in

Build Vocabulary Through Word Relationships and Patterns

One of the greatest resources for comprehension is a good vocabulary. Good readers understand that the meanings of words do not exist in isolation; rather, they are constructed through relationships. In other words, a strong vocabulary is the result of understanding how language works. Although a word can have a standard meaning (the dictionary version), its true meaning is developed over time and across different contexts. A reader's understanding of a word can range from mild familiarity to deep knowledge. The depth of a word's meaning to a reader is influenced by his or her experiences with the

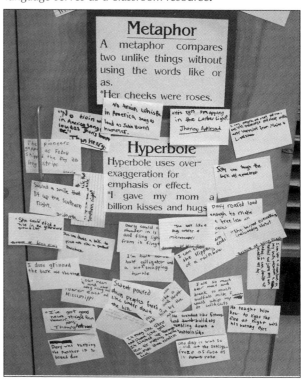

Figure 5.2 An anchor chart illustrating figurative language serves as a classroom resource.

Figure 5.3 Third-grade students examined language phrases used in Patricia Polacco's books.

word and the ability to utilize the word for communicating a message in varying circumstances. Consider a simple example. A beginning reader is reading a patterned text with the repetitive line "Clever little car." How much does the reader need to know about the word *clever* to understand its function in communicating a certain message in a particular context? Can the reader gather enough information from text cues to infer that *clever* is just another word to describe the smart little car? What is the difference between knowing the word and having a conceptual understanding of the word? Some years ago, Michael Graves (1985, p. 8) described four types of words; I have found his list helpful for thinking about how word knowledge influences reading comprehension.

- *Sight words*—Words that are in students' oral vocabularies, but that they cannot yet read.
- *New words*—Words that are in neither students' oral nor their reading vocabularies, but for which a concept is available (in known words) or for which one can be built fairly easily.
- *New concepts*—Words that are in neither students' oral nor their reading vocabularies, for which they don't have a concept, and for which a concept is not easily built.
- *New meaning*—Words that are in the students' reading vocabularies with one or more meanings, but for which additional meanings need to be learned.

Not surprisingly, comprehension of a word will be easier if the reader has some background knowledge of the word concept; similarly, comprehension may be harder to attain if the concept is new and difficult. Language users need many experiences with a word—in different contexts—to develop their conceptual understanding.

Use Transitional Words and Phrases

Transitional words act as signals. They give directions. They tell where the paragraph is going. They also serve to hold sentences together. Transitional words serve as language aids to support the meaning-making process. Good writers place transitional words at strategic points to assist their readers; likewise, good readers recognize that transitional words are important for understanding the author's message. The following is a list of several kinds of transition, with the words commonly used for each:

- To restate: *also, furthermore, in fact, likewise, moreover, in other words*
- To emphasize: *indeed, that is to say, to be sure, without a doubt*
- To illustrate: *for example, for instance, that is, namely*
- To conclude: *as a result, in summary, consequently, simply put, hence, so, therefore, whereby, thus, thereafter*
- To give directions: *at the top, further down*

Closing Thoughts

This chapter has described the role of language in reading comprehension. Here are some key points of this chapter.

Awareness of language is a prerequisite to becoming literate. Children should hear language before becoming involved with the written word.

Oral language and the written word are inseparable. The more we know about oral language, the more we know about written language. At the same time, the better we understand the writing process, the better we are at comprehending what we read.

A classroom literacy program should include language studies that make use of authentic, mean-

ingful literature. The teacher can design focus units about language and provide guided opportunities to help students understand how language works.

Students must acquire a solid understanding of the forms and functions of language. This is the foundation—the architecture—for good writing. When a writer understands the basic structures of language, the writer will know when to break the rules and reinvent the system for literary purposes.

A Workshop Approach to Literacy Learning

I opened my e-mail to find an intriguing message with the heading "Making a difference—one stall at a time." The message was from a literacy coach who was working in a high-poverty school that had recently implemented a reading workshop approach in the classroom. The story began with the teacher going into the girl's bathroom to wash her hands. As she looked in the mirror, she noticed two feet dangling behind the door of the bathroom stall. From the direction of the tiny feet the teacher heard a soft murmur with a hint of giggle. The teacher finished washing her hands, but could not take her eyes off the swinging feet. Several minutes passed. The teacher was about to tell the child to return to class when the bathroom door opened and the youngster emerged with a chapter book in her hands. She held the book out to the teacher and exclaimed, "This book is so good I just couldn't put it down to come to the bathroom!" As I read the teacher's e-mail message, I thought, "This little girl has developed a reading habit—a necessary prerequisite for literacy. How can teachers enable *all* children to develop this habit?" I am reminded of the power of the reading workshop—a memory of my own third-grade workshop of years before. On this particular day, a group of university students had dropped by, and the children were discussing books with one another. Nicole, a passionate reader, was standing alone, a Beverly Cleary book clutched to her chest. Her eyes searched the room and settled on one of the visitors. Nicole approached the visitor and asked timidly, "Have you read *Dear Mr. Henshaw*? It is a great book, and I really want to talk with someone about it." As readers, we can all relate to Nicole's story—

we've just finished a great book and desperately need to share the experience with someone. As I think back on Nicole and the other young readers in her class, I wonder whether they are still reading and discussing books with the same passion and determination; and I realize what an awesome responsibility teachers have in teaching reading.

Developing Reading Habits

What exactly is a habit? Why are habits so difficult to break? How long does it take for a behavior to become a habit? We know that habits develop through repeated practice over time, and that they are automatic reactions of the brain to engage in particular behaviors. Helping children develop the habit of reading is probably a teacher's most important goal, because a reading habit is a tool for lifelong learning. So we might ask: How can teachers create learning conditions where children develop lifelong habits of reading?

Creating a Reading Environment

Creating an environment conducive to reading is a necessary step in developing motivated learners who read for pleasure and purpose. The environment should be designed to guarantee every child's success in reading. To achieve this goal, teachers need to differentiate their instruction in order to meet the diverse needs of their students. The reading curriculum should include a blend of whole-group, small-group, and individual instruction, as well as opportunities for students to read independently, without teacher assistance. Differentiated instruction also applies to the degree of assistance provided to learners. A one-to-one conference with the teacher, for example, provides a higher degree of support than a small-group conference. To promote deeper comprehension, students must be given opportunities to apply their knowledge, skills, and strategies in different contexts and for different purposes. In Chapter 3, I described how teachers apply a scale of help (similar to a gradual release model) that enables readers to assume more responsibility in completing a task. Earlier I discussed how successful learning is characterized by rhythms of easy and challenging work and pointed out that too much challenging work can interfere with smooth processing. A workshop approach allows for differentiated instruction, providing a supportive context that allows teachers to meet the literacy needs of all students.

The Workshop Framework

The ultimate goal of a workshop approach is to enable learners to acquire strategies for self-regulating their learning. The workshop is based on a conceptual framework that includes five components, which work together to scaffold student knowledge. Once teachers understand the framework, they can use workshops in all areas of the curriculum, including reading, writing, science, social studies, and math. In this chapter I focus on the reading workshop, which, like all types of workshop, has five components:

1. *Mini-lessons.* A mini-lesson is an explicit teaching demonstration that, in the reading workshop, focuses on a critical component of the reading process—for instance, comprehension strategies, workshop procedures, vocabulary investigations, or language studies. Mini-lessons are generally 10–15 minutes long and include an opportunity for students to engage in guided practice. Each workshop block begins with a whole-group mini-lesson; later, in small-group instruction,

Chapter 6 A Workshop Approach to Literacy Learning **67**

teachers can provide mini-lessons tailored to the instructional needs of specific groups of students (Chapter 8 focuses on how to design such mini-lessons).

2. *Small-group instruction.* In the reading workshop, the teacher meets with small groups of students, organized around guided reading and literature discussion. In guided reading, the teacher selects a common text for a group of students with similar needs. Each student reads the entire text; the teacher circulates among the group, prompting individual students to apply various comprehending strategies (Dorn, French, and Jones 1998). In literature discussion groups, small groups of students read and discuss a common text. During the group discussion, the teacher is a participant-observer, allowing the students to assume the major responsibility for talking about the book (see Chapter 7).

3. *Independent practice or working with peers.* To promote transfer, teachers need to give students opportunities to apply their knowledge without guidance. Independent activities can include teacher-assigned tasks, such as recording reflections in a reading log, creating a story map, analyzing characters, writing to an author, doing Internet searches, reading other books by the same author, and other projects that support reading comprehension. Peer projects can also be undertaken; these include such activities as buddy reading, paired reading, peer discussion groups, reader's theatre, and literature extensions.

4. *One-to-one or small-group conferences.* Reading conferences are a critical aspect of the workshop, as they allow the teacher both to observe how well students are comprehending the text and to help the reader think at deeper levels. The conferences can be either one-to-one or small-group, made up of two to four students with similar needs. Conferences take place while the rest of the class works on independent or peer projects. A typical reading conference lasts approximately three minutes; given the time frame, a teacher can generally conduct seven or eight conferences daily. (See Chapter 7 for more on conferences.)

5. *Share time.* During share time, generally around ten minutes long, the students meet with the teacher in a large circle for a whole-group discussion. They bring any projects they are currently working on, as well as their books and reflection logs. Share time provides a social context for students to share their work with the teacher and their peers.

Each workshop component has a built-in assessment piece that allows the teacher to observe students across different contexts and with varying degrees of support. The aim of the workshop is to encourage students to develop positive, constructive habits of thinking and, in doing so, refine their strategies, deepen their comprehension, and expand their knowledge. The basic workshop structure can be applied equally well across the curriculum.

Figure 6.1 shows two typical schedules for a classroom using the workshop approach. Notice that the daily schedule includes five types of workshops:

1. Reading workshop Phase 1 (guided reading/ literature discussion groups).
2. Reading workshop Phase 2 (language studies/ author studies/genre studies).
3. Writing workshop.
4. Math workshop.
5. Content workshop.

In each workshop, demonstrations, guided participation, engagement, and assessment are dynamically linked to facilitate student learning. Also, workshop blocks are designed to promote an integrated curriculum. For instance, during

Figure 6.1A Typical schedules for elementary classrooms. First grade.

Morning Block
Morning Hours: 8:10–12:10

- **Shared Reading, Poetry, or Read-Aloud** (10 minutes) 8:10–8:20

- **Spelling/Phonics** (15 minutes) 8:20–8:35

- **Reading Workshop Phase 1** (95 minutes) 8:35–10:10
  T: Read-Aloud, Mini-Lesson and Guided Practice, Shared Reading or Explicit Teaching from Shared Text (10 minutes)
  T & S: Small-Group Instruction: Guided Reading, Book Discussions, and/or Assisted Writing (25 minutes each)
  S: Work in Corners
  Share Time (10 minutes)

- **Reading Workshop Phase 2: Language Studies/ Author and/or Genre Studies** (45 minutes) 10:10–10:55
  T: Read-Aloud, Mini-Lesson and Guided Practice, Shared Reading or Explicit Teaching (10 minutes)
  T: One to One Conferences, Small-Group Conferences and Assessment (running record)
  S: Familiar Reading (2 books)
  S: Choice Reading: Classroom Library, Buddy Reading, Pair Reading, Choral Reading, Recorded Reading, Peer Book Discussions (20 minutes)
  Share Time (15 minutes)

- **Math Workshop Part 1** (20 minutes) 10:55–11:15
  T: Read-Aloud, Mini-Lesson and Guided Practice, Shared Reading (10 minutes)
  S: Begin Practice and T: Conferences (10 minutes)

- **Lunch/Recess** (50 minutes) 11:20–11:40, 11:40–12:10

Afternoon Block
Afternoon Hours: 12:10–3:10

- **Math Workshop Part 2** (40 minutes) 12:10–12:50
  S: Finish Practice and T: Finish Conferences
  Share Time (10 minutes)

- **Specials** (40 minutes) 12:50–1:30

- **Writing Workshop** (45 minutes) 1:30–2:15
  T: Read-Aloud, Mini-Lesson and Guided Practice, Shared Reading or Explicit Teaching from Shared Text (10 minutes)
  S: Independent Writing and T: Conferences (25 minutes)
  Share Time (10 minutes)

- **Content Workshop** (45 minutes) 2:15–3:00
  T: Read-Aloud, Mini-Lesson and Guided Practice, Shared Reading or Revisiting Shared Text (10 minutes)
  S: Independent Reading/Writing and
  T: Conferences (25 minutes)
  Share Time (10 minutes)

- **Read-Aloud** (10 minutes) 3:00–3:10

- **Dismissal** 3:10

reading workshop, teachers can introduce nonfiction texts that relate to the content workshop; and during writing workshop, teachers can provide mini-lessons that focus on the reading-writing connection, including an analysis of how writers craft texts to support readers' comprehension.

Anchor Charts for Scaffolding Students' Learning

Anchor charts are an important part of the reading workshop. These are class charts, created by the teacher and the students, that highlight

Figure 6.1B Typical schedules for elementary classrooms. Second through fifth grades.

Morning Block Morning Hours: 8:10–12:25	Afternoon Block Afternoon Hours: 12:25–3:10

• **Shared Reading, Poetry, or Read-Aloud** (10 minutes) 8:10–8:20
 	
• **Spelling/Word Study** (15 minutes) 8:20–8:35
 	
• **Reading Workshop Phase 1** (90 minutes) 8:35–10:05
  T: Read-Aloud, Mini-Lesson and Guided Practice, Shared Reading or Explicit Teaching from Shared Text (10 minutes)
  T&S: Small-Group Instruction: Guided Reading, Book Discussions, Assisted Writing, One to One Conferences, and/or Small-Group Conferences (70 minutes total)
  S: Choice Reading: Classroom Library, Buddy Reading, Pair Reading, Choral Reading, Recorded Reading, Peer Book Discussions
  Share Time (10 minutes)
 	
• **Reading Workshop Phase 2: Language Studies/ Author and/or Genre Studies** (40 minutes) 10:05–10:45
  T: Read-Aloud, Mini-Lesson and Guided Practice, Shared Reading or Explicit Teaching from Shared Text (10 minutes)
  S: Independent Reading/Writing (20 minutes)
  Share Time (10 minutes)
 	
• **Writers' Workshop** (50 minutes) 10:45–11:35
  T: Read-Aloud, Mini-Lesson and Guided Practice, or Explicit Teaching from Shared Text (10 minutes)
  S: Independent Writing and T: Conferences (30 minutes)
  Share Time (10 minutes)
• **Lunch/Recess** (50 minutes) 11:35–11:55, 11:55–12:25
	• **Specials** (40 minutes) 12:25–1:05
	
	• **Math Workshop** (60 minutes) 1:05–2:05
	  T: Read-Aloud, Mini-Lesson and Guided Practice, Shared Reading or Explicit Teaching from Shared Text (10 minutes)
	  S: Independent Practice and T: Conferences (35 minutes)
	  Share Time (15 minutes)
	
	• **Content Workshop** (50 minutes) 2:05–2:55
	  T: Read-Aloud, Mini-Lesson and Guided Practice, Shared Reading or Explicit Teaching from Shared Text (10 minutes)
	  S: Independent Reading/Writing and T: Conferences (30 minutes)
	  Share Time (10 minutes)
	
	• **Read-Aloud** (10 minutes) 2:55–3:10
	
	• **Dismissal** 3:10

specific guidelines or behaviors for performing a particular literacy task. The idea is to document the thinking processes related to a particular learning experience. For example, an anchor chart called "Strategies Used by Good Readers" would contain only the strategies the class had learned up to that point. As students learn new strategies, these are added to the anchor chart. Generally, the charts are created during mini-lessons and are referenced as needed throughout the reading workshop. For instance, prior to a book discussion, the teacher might direct students' attention to an anchor chart labeled "Guidelines for Literature Group Discussions" (see Chapter 7). The charts are placed in prominent spots in the room, serving as temporary scaffolds (or reminders) for students. Most charts remain posted all year, though students will use them with less frequency as they internalize the information from the chart.

In planning an anchor chart, the teacher should focus on topics that relate to the needs of the students. Here are a few examples of anchor charts that might be useful.

- Procedures for reading workshop
- Guidelines for independent reading
- Guidelines for peer discussions
- Guidelines for buddy reading
- Preparing for a reading conference
- Guidelines for using a reading log
- Preparing for share time
- Guidelines for book talks
- Organizing books in the classroom library

Teachers can also guide students to create anchor charts that provide evidence of how writers use language in expressing meaning. Here, the students use the classroom library as an ongoing resource for collecting language examples, such as the following:

- Examples of figurative language
- Examples of good leads
- Examples of parts of speech
- Examples of punctuation

In summary, anchor charts can provide teachers with a tool for scaffolding students' learning. They are deliberately designed to spotlight an important concept while providing students with an immediate resource when the teacher is unavailable.

Reading Workshop

A question I hear frequently from teachers relates to classroom management: How do you organize the workshop to include guided reading, literature discussion groups, free choice, and language studies? Adding to the complexity, instruction must be tailored to meet the diverse needs of all children, requiring a myriad of reading experiences, from whole groups, small groups, and peer groups to one-to-one conferences and independent work. The schedules in Figure 6.1 provide examples of how a range of language-based experiences can be managed across two reading phases, or blocks. Consider the two blocks as complementary, overlapping language experiences that fall within the larger framework of the reading workshop. Remember, written text is simply spoken language written down, so it is important for students to understand how language works in general. In the schedules shown in Figure 6.1, the two reading blocks work together to provide students with necessary experiences and strategies for learning about written language.

Let's take a closer look at the schedules in Figure 6.1. You'll notice that the entire reading workshop is 130–140 minutes, with the first phase consisting of a 90-to-95-minute period. The workshop begins with a 10–15 minute mini-lesson that focuses on problem solving and comprehending strategies (see Chapter 4), with an expectation that children will apply this learning to their independent or group work. The mini-lesson is followed by instruction provided through guided reading, literature discussion groups, and individual or small-group reading conferences with the teacher. While the teacher meets with students, the others are engaged in a variety of reading activities, such as independent reading, buddy reading, paired reading, recorded reading, peer discussion groups, research projects, response logs, or literature extensions. Phase 1 of the reading workshop concludes when the teacher gathers the students in a circle and guides them to share learning from independent activities.

The next phase of the reading workshop, lasting 40–45 minutes, focuses on opportunities for children to learn about language, including focus units that investigate the language strategies discussed in Chapter 5. This part of the reading workshop begins with a 10–15 minute mini-lesson that sets the tone for the subsequent work, which could, for instance, focus on sentence, paragraph, and text structures; the writing style of a particular author; the forms and functions of speech, such as concrete nouns and strong verbs; the functions of punctuation in regulating fluency and meaning; the various ways writers use dialogue; word choice; new vocabulary; and other features of language that influence reading comprehension. After the mini-lesson, the teacher guides the students to use the classroom library as a resource, having them examine books by favorite authors to locate specific examples of language usage. The students become language investigators, collecting and analyzing language and recording this information in reading logs for use in later reading and writing workshops. Language studies are the outgrowth of book discussions and read-aloud sessions—literate experiences that provide students with the raw materials for language investigations. The language studies portion of the reading workshop can also include in-depth author and genre studies, with students building a language base for subsequent investigations. Throughout, the teacher meets with individual or small groups of students as needed to observe and scaffold their learning. This phase of the reading workshop, like the previous one, ends with share time, wherein children share their response logs or language projects with the teacher and classmates.

The various types of reading experiences in the reading workshop provide students with opportunities to increase their reading volume—that is, the number of books they read. During explicit mini-lessons, the teacher introduces four types of reading experiences and then explains how children can select one reading option from the Reading Workshop Option Board while the teacher works with small groups of students. (The option board is described later in this chapter.) Each of these reading experiences is designed to promote fluent reading and comprehending strategies.

- *Independent reading.* In independent reading, as the name suggests, a reader reads a text alone. At the emergent and early levels, students might keep their own basket, or tub, of familiar books for use in independent reading; or they can select a book from the classroom library.
- *Paired reading.* In paired reading, two students at different reading levels sit side by side and read a text together. The teacher generally determines the pairs, having the more skilled reader support the lower-level reader at points of difficulty, and keeping the focus on fluency and comprehension.
- *Buddy reading.* In buddy reading, two students at similar reading levels read together. They can alternate pages, read in unison, or echo each other. Unlike paired reading, where the teacher pairs the students, in buddy reading students select their own pairs. Buddy reading can be an extension of a guided reading or literature discussion group.
- *Recorded reading.* In recorded reading, a student listens to a prerecorded text at instructional level and reads aloud with the recording.

The two parts of the reading workshop complement each other, ensuring that students' reading opportunities are balanced, and include instructional grouping with leveled texts and literature studies with some free choice. As with any new learning, the children will need an apprenticeship period. The workshop approach follows a gradual release model, where children are presented with clear demonstrations and guided practice for learning a specific task. During reading workshop, students are expected to self-select books and engage in sustained periods of independent reading. This implies that students must possess the knowledge and strategies to maintain their attention for long spans of time. A preparation period might be needed in order to scaffold students toward greater independence. Carla and Vicki Altland, a third-grade teacher, developed a phase-in structure that allows them to apprentice students for independent and peer work. As Vicki introduces each reading component, she places the corresponding icon on the Reading Workshop Option Board (Figure 6.2), and students are told to select one of these options for independent or peer activity. To illustrate, let's look at three options: learning how to self-select books, learning how to participate in buddy reading, and learning how to conduct good book talks. The process is similar for all the activities in the reading workshop, including paired reading, recorded reading, text analysis, and research.

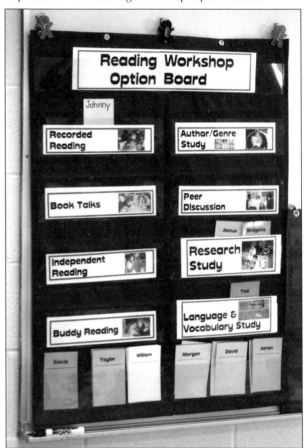

Figure 6.2 After each component is introduced, the icon is placed on the Reading Workshop Option Board.

Self-Selecting Books

In order to attain independence in reading, children must be able to self-select books. The teacher models self-selection with three or four books, adding these behaviors to an anchor chart called "Guidelines for Self-Selecting Books." The teacher continues to model the process over an extended period of time (usually two or three weeks) until he or she feels the students have acquired a repertoire of strategies for self-selecting books from the classroom library. At the same time, the teacher provides students with guided practice, wherein they select books from the classroom library and reflect on their performance based on criteria from the anchor chart. As students acquire more experience with book selection (including perhaps reasons for abandoning books), the additional criteria are added to the anchor chart. Here, for example, are two anchor charts created by Vicki Altland's third graders:

Guidelines for Selecting Books
- Look at the pictures
- Favorite authors
- Favorite characters
- Series we like
- Recommendations from others
- Books we have heard or read about
- Interesting title

- Read the back
- Read the first page
- Read the book jacket
- Genres we like

Some Reasons to Abandon Books

- Too hard
- Too easy
- Boring
- Not enough action
- Too sad
- Too confusing
- Not what we expected
- Want to read something else

Buddy Reading

The teacher introduces buddy reading by explaining and modeling how pairs of readers can read in unison or read alternate pages to each other. The students and teacher may construct an anchor chart listing the guidelines for buddy reading. The teacher then sets up pairs of students who are at similar reading levels and has them share the reading of a familiar text. As the students read, the teacher circulates among the groups and observes their reading behaviors. The students then reconvene to the whole-group circle and, under the teacher's guidance, reflect on their performance, using the anchor chart as a self-reflection tool. This routine is continued until the teacher is confident that the students understand the process of buddy reading. At this point, the Buddy Reading icon is placed on the Reading Workshop Option Board.

Here is an example of an anchor chart listing guidelines for buddy reading, created by third-grade students.

- Choose a partner who has read the same text.
- Negotiate how the two of you will read the text (chorally, alternate pages, echo fashion).
- Discuss the text during and after reading.
- Check out the text and read it at home.

Book Talks

To model the process of book talks, the teacher selects two or three books from a current author study and engages the students in creating an anchor chart that describes the guidelines for conducting good book talks. The students then choose a favorite book and engage in a knee-to-knee book talk, enticing their partner to read the book. As the students introduce books to one another, the teacher observes the process, making mental notes of how well the students are doing. Then the group reconvenes, and the teacher guides the students to use the anchor chart to reflect on their book talks. The teacher continues to model and provide guided practice until it is clear that the students understand the process. At this point, the Book Talk icon is placed on the Reading Workshop Option Board.

Here are two examples of anchor charts related to book talks.

Preparing for Book Talks

- Select a text that you want to recommend to the group.
- Outline important information needed to hook the audience:
  - Character traits
  - Problems encountered
  - Interesting information learned
  - Blurb on the back of the book, inside flap, table of contents and/or favorite part

Presenting Book Talks

- Look at your audience.
- Read the title of the book and show the front cover.
- Speak loudly and clearly.
- Invite your friends to read the text.

Reading Volume

Research indicates that volume reading is a critical condition of reading success. Foertsch (1992) found that the amount of reading that students do in and out of school is positively correlated to their reading achievement. McBride-Chang and colleagues (1993) concluded that volume reading was correlated to reading comprehension in both disabled and normally achieving students. In addition, volume reading can lead to the development of a habit for reading. This implies that students should be given the chance to read as often as possible.

The Role of the Classroom Library

Research shows that students read better when they have greater access to books and other materials (Rasinski 2003). Furthermore, the ability to locate and preview reading materials is a critical condition of success in reading (see Chapter 4). A well-organized classroom library is an important factor in promoting children's ability to access texts with efficiency. In order to self-select books, children must understand that books are generally organized according to specific features or categories. This implies that children benefit from being involved in the process of classifying and organizing books in the class library.

To help children understand how books can be organized in meaningful categories, teachers can share models from personal experiences. A few years ago, I visited the Library of Congress in Washington, D.C., where I learned how Thomas Jefferson designed his home library. His books were organized by three categories: memory, reason, and imagination. Later, when I shared this information with colleagues, we wondered what types of books Jefferson placed under each category. We shared information on how we organize our own personal libraries, identifying some meaningful classifications we have used to organize our own books. It became clear through our conversation that each of us had a specific system for organizing our books in meaningful and helpful ways. For example, the groupings (with subgroupings under major topics) that I have used are these: professional texts (research books, theory books, literacy topics), adult novels (fiction, nonfiction, particular authors), historical books (history, art, philosophy), and children's books (picture books, ABC books, chapter books). Think about how bookstores organize their books to attract readers. They usually, for instance, exhibit best sellers in prominent positions, cluster topics together in related areas, place books on shelves in a way that displays their covers, and create cozy nooks that entice readers to pick up and delve into a good book.

Teachers can help students notice how libraries are organized by bringing in pictures of libraries and guiding students to discuss specific features (see Figure 6.3). The students can then be encouraged to create a design for their own classroom library, including arrangements of books in various locations of the classroom.

In reading workshop during mini-lessons, the teacher can prompt students to identify various ways that books can be classified. Then the teacher and students can create anchor charts with logical classifications for books, which can be used as helpful resources in locating books. The categories are written on a chart and hung on the wall as a reference tool. Children learn that books can be placed in more than one category, and teachers guide children to regroup the books in other categories throughout the year.

Some logical classifications are the following:

- books written by particular authors
- books written in particular genres
- book themes
- chapter books
- picture books

Figure 6.3 Some views of classroom libraries. Left: In Vicki Altland's third-grade classroom, books are organized in logical categories and displayed in tubs to promote browsing. Right: Intervention specialist Rebecca Keith has created a cozy reading nook with book displays.

- series books
- books on a particular topic—for example, pets, space, friends, and so on
- books about writing
- books about reading

During share time, teachers can prompt students to talk about the characteristics of particular books and where these texts might be found in the library. These experiences will provide students with critical knowledge for accessing literacy tools with greater ease.

Creating the Classroom Library

How do books get in the classroom library? Here are some suggestions that we have found helpful for building a classroom library with the children.

With students who are at the emergent level of literacy, teachers can read a book aloud to the students, then guide them as they decide where the book should go in the class library. The students then deposit the book in the appropriate book tub or on the shelf in the appropriate section of the library.

For students at the early to transitional levels, teachers should model how to preview a book, reading the back cover and looking for information on awards and excerpts of reviews. The teacher then places a collection of books on the table and divides students into groups. The students categorize the books into stacks using such categories as specific themes, authors, favorite series, and so forth. The teacher and children discuss the categories and make additional decisions about book placement. The teacher continues to bring in books throughout the year, and teacher and students preview the books and place them in the appropriate sections of the library.

Teachers can introduce three or four tubs of books from the classroom library, with the discussion focused on the organization of the tubs. The children are placed in groups, each with a tub, and are invited to browse through the book tub. Then the children reconvene as a group and talk about the contents of the tub they explored.

Teachers can also give book talks for any new book being introduced to the classroom library.

(A book talk is a brief two- or three-minute preview of a book, similar to a commercial.) With assistance, the students then decide where the new book should be placed in the class library. Later, children are invited to give their own book talks when books are added to the classroom library.

Four Types of Libraries

A school can contain several types of libraries. Four are described below.

Classroom Library

The classroom library is organized according to features of books, not including gradients of difficulty. The children work with the teacher in developing a classification system for organizing books. The categories are recorded on anchor charts that are hung in the classroom as a handy reference for locating books. Books are kept in tubs, baskets, or other containers, all of which are clearly labeled to help children in locating materials. Spotlighted books are placed on shelves with covers facing outward to attract children's attention. (Figure 6.4 shows one arrangement for a useful classroom library.)

Curriculum Library

The curriculum library is a schoolwide book room that includes a range of reading materials, including Big Books, sets of leveled texts for guided reading, sets of trade books for literature discussion groups, poems, plays, literacy task cards, and other curriculum materials that support reading. Teachers work together to organize the curriculum library, coordinating books into class sets and designing a schoolwide system

Figure 6.4 This U-shaped classroom library is the centerpiece of Vicki Altland's third-grade classroom at Sallie Cone Elementary in Conway, Arkansas.

Chapter 6 A Workshop Approach to Literacy Learning

Figure 6.5 In Sedalia, Missouri, the teachers at Skyline Elementary have organized their curriculum library to include thousands of leveled texts with a teacher checkout system for schoolwide use.

for checking out books. Each year the teachers should evaluate the library and decide on new materials to add to it. (Figure 6.5 shows a photo of a well-designed curriculum library.)

Guided Reading Library
The guided reading library is a collection of leveled texts kept in the classroom (generally behind the teacher's desk or reading table) for purposes of guided reading groups. The teacher checks out the guided reading sets from the curriculum library and returns them when they are no longer needed. It is important to emphasize that information on book levels are for the teacher only; children must check out books by literary category, *not* level.

Professional Library
A professional library is a collection of teacher books and materials, including both single copies of titles and multiple sets for literacy team meetings. These are usually kept in a separate section of the curriculum library.

Closing Thoughts

This chapter has described how the reading workshop can provide a context for learning about books, thus increasing students' reading comprehension. Here are the key points of the chapter.

A reading habit is a critical condition of reading achievement. Volume reading and reading habits are directly related. The classroom schedule must include large blocks of time for reading.

The reading workshop is an ideal way to provide differentiated instruction. The format allows teachers to address the diverse needs of learners, and encourages small-group, whole-group, and individual instruction.

In order to attain deep comprehension, children must learn how to select books. A classroom library is an important resource for learning about books. Children should be involved in organizing and managing their classroom library.

Creating Literature Discussion Groups

In preparing to write this chapter, I reread James Britton's book *Language and Learning: The Importance of Speech* (1970). It's been a couple of years since I last read the book, and I am surprised to find that it feels like I'm reading it for the first time. In a sense I am, because the last time I read this book, I read it differently. (I had a similar experience when I reread *The Grapes of Wrath*). Today, as I reflect on Britton's words, I find myself interpreting his work through a new lens—a new goal—that is, how his theories of participant and spectator might apply to my beliefs about literature discussion groups. Consider this example from Britton's work—a conversation between friends as they wait for the morning train:

> From time to time a friend and a neighbor of mine catches the same train as I do in the morning. We meet on the platform and the whole body of past experience of each of us offers to each of us a vast area from which to choose a topic to start the conversation. Since neither of us is a complete bore, we shall not choose what currently preoccupies us unless it happens to be something that would be likely to interest the other. Initial silence probably indicates that our individual preoccupations were not in an area of common interest. In that case, we are likely to cast our minds back to the last time we met: as a result of this, he may say to me, "How did your date with X go? Did you find him in the end?" and I shall embark on the story of my meeting with X, perhaps bringing out all the difficulties and frustrations I had in tracking him down.

Britton's example implies that several underlying rules guide a productive discussion. The discussion between these friends is a joint responsibility; each member works to maintain the attention and interest of the other. As I think about this, I am reminded of how Barbara Rogoff (1990) describes conversation as a language dance—a set of well-orchestrated moves that are regulated by the desire to construct meaning. Neil Mercer (1995) calls this the co-construction of knowledge, implying that meaning is negotiated through group interactions. In Britton's example, the two friends shared a common set of experiences, thereby providing the raw material for choosing a relevant topic to discuss. Their silence was a signal that a new topic was needed. This makes me think about the social side of talking, and how the desire to communicate with others about a common event is a human response. As I reflect on these theories, I wonder how they support teacher-student interactions during literature discussion groups. Britton's concept of participant and spectator applies to the shifting roles of teacher and student as they negotiate meaning for a particular text. From Britton's perspective, the spectator is an observer—the listener; the participant is the speaker—the language user. Yet in reality the roles are not so clearly defined, because the participant is also a spectator, listening and reflecting on his or her own language as it represents the intended message. As participants in a literature discussion group, teachers must be observant of how much they add to the group's understanding. As in any good discussion, the dynamic interplay between listening and responding is a critical component of constructing deeper meaning.

Literate Language

In Chapter 4, I discussed how talking about books is a crucial behavior for shaping reading comprehension. This type of talk is called literate talk—discourse for talking about literacy. In his book *A Mind at a Time,* Mel Levine (2002) explains how children acquire two types of language: automatic language and literate language. Automatic language is the language we use in everyday life, whereas literate language is the language of books. Levine describes literate language as a type of "verbal craftsmanship" that includes "sophisticated classroom talk as well as academic reading and writing" (p. 122). Literate language is full of complex patterns and literary devices, including symbolic and metaphorical language that requires the reader to think in images. If children do not acquire literate language, they may have difficultly comprehending texts at higher levels.

As children progress through school, they are required to remember increasingly longer chains of verbal discourse, simultaneously orchestrating this information with new, incoming information. This is a complex process, whereby "readers must be able to extract meaning from a particular sentence without forgetting the information or events that led up to it" (Levine 2002, p. 142). The process is especially evident during book discussions, where children must hold extended chains of discourse in their memories as they contemplate how to add their own ideas into the meaning-making chain. These conversations represent the raw material on which deeper comprehension is built. Literate discourse is most effective when the teacher is available to monitor students' understanding and to guide the dialogue to higher levels. However, the teacher's role is not that of instructor, but rather that of active participant—one who also understands scaffolding theory and has acquired more experience and knowledge about literacy learning.

In *Questioning the Author,* Isabel Beck and her colleagues (Beck, McKeown, Hamilton, and Kucan 1997) make a distinction between the dynamics of question-driven and inquiry-driven discussion. They describe how teacher questioning might result in one-word answers, which often consist simply of the precise words of the text. By contrast, inquiry-based discussions prompt students to use longer, more elaborate language. Consider the difference in response when a teacher prompts a child to "tell me more" and when the teacher asks a direct question aimed to yield a response to the text at a literal level. Donnie Skinner, a literacy coach, analyzed the language development of her third-grade students during book discussion groups. She found that when she assumed the role of active participant in the discussion, as opposed to her being the leader of the discussion, her students used longer and more elaborate discourse. Donnie also noted that when she said such things as "Do you agree?" or "Tell us more" the students built on one another's ideas, which resulted in sustained chains of discourse that clarified and extended meaning. Talk became the tool for building conceptual chains of meaning, thus deepening the reader's comprehension and promoting self-reflection.

Literature Discussion Groups

If we believe in the power of language for literacy learning, then classrooms should burst with opportunities to talk about literacy. One of the most powerful language experiences can occur during literature discussion groups.

What are literature discussion groups? Simply put, they are small-group conversations about books. They emerged from the literature-based era of the 1980s; over the years, they have been adapted to fit the goals and philosophies of individual teachers. There are numerous ways to organize literature discussion groups, but the biggest issue relates to whether the groups should be led by the students or by the teacher. I first began using literature discussion groups over twenty years ago with my third- and fourth-grade students; and during the past ten years, Carla and I have been using this framework in training literacy coaches and classroom teachers. The following are the theories that have most influenced my thinking on how to present literature discussion groups in a reading workshop.

Rogoff's Theory of Apprenticeship Learning

Barbara Rogoff's apprenticeship theory implies that learning takes place in a social context with a more knowledgeable person who understands how to scaffold a novice toward learning a new task (Rogoff 1990). In a cognitive apprenticeship (see Dorn and Soffos 2001a), the teacher presents the learner with problem-solving opportunities, thus encouraging the learner to think at deeper levels. Two important principles of apprenticeship theory are the notions of guided participation and leading from behind. During literature discussion groups, the teacher creates an environment where students learn how to talk about books. As a sensitive observer, the teacher determines when (and when not) to join the discussion, all the while working toward the goal of deeper comprehension for the students.

Vygotsky's Theory of the More Knowledgeable Other

From Lev Vygotsky's point of view, a teacher, as the more knowledgeable person, possesses the ability to lift a student's learning to a higher psychological plane (Vygotsky 1987). To do this, the teacher must understand how to use language as an instructional tool for activating thinking. In other words, the teacher must be an expert at observing student behavior and regulating language prompts, so that students are kept at the cutting edge of their learning. How might this look in a literature discussion group?

When learning is new, the teacher assumes more responsibility, prompting students to think at higher levels; as students acquire more knowledge, the teacher's role shifts from mediator to participant-observer. Here the teacher sits with the group, but mainly to observe and, if needed, to interject a thought-provoking prompt to lift the discussion to a higher level. In these social contexts, language becomes the tool for shaping deeper comprehension.

David Wood's Theory of Contingent Scaffolding

David Wood (1998) has described how teachers can make complex learning more manageable by providing students with an adjustable scale of help aimed toward completing a particular task. Here, language becomes the tool for activating student thinking for completing specific actions. Decision making is grounded in three types of teacher knowledge: knowledge of the student, knowledge of the task, and knowledge of language prompts along a scale of help. During literature discussion groups, teachers use a scale of help, including modeling, guided participation, and adjustable prompts that provide varying degrees of support. (See Chapter 3 for information on the scale of help.) Teachers should also be aware of the importance of teaching for transfer—that is, guiding students to develop conceptual knowledge as evidenced by their ability to comprehend relationships across changing circumstances. I believe that teachers are experts at contingent scaffolding, but that students may not possess the same degree of expertise for lifting the group discussion to higher levels.

Theory of Differentiated Instruction

The theory of differentiated instruction is critical when organizing the framework for literature discussion groups. This theory simply calls for students to be provided with varying degrees of support according to their individual needs across changing contexts. This notion is linked to theories of self-regulation and transfer (see Dorn, French, and Jones 1998). Reading workshop provides a structure for differentiated instruction, including whole-group, small-group, individual, and independent opportunities. Each provides a different degree of teacher support, adjusted to promote the students' transfer of knowledge, strategies, and skills across different situations. The structure should allow for the gradual reduction of teacher assistance in a familiar area, with an increase of support for unfamiliar concepts.

Building the Background: Providing a Model for Students

When students are first introduced to literature discussion groups, it is helpful for them to have models provided by the teacher. Without such models, children can find it hard to grasp the goal of a book discussion. Book discussions may be too abstract a concept for students who have no experience with them. Literacy coaches and classroom teachers have devised ways to provide students with authentic models for learning how to talk about books. Three examples will show how this is done.

In one case, the literacy coach videotaped a book discussion with small groups of teachers during a literacy team meeting. She also videotaped the follow-up session, where the teachers assessed their level of participation in the group discussion; and she collected copies of teacher reflection logs and rubrics for assessing the discussion group. She then distributed copies of the tapes to the classroom teachers and developed an observation protocol with the aim of focusing students' attention on important behaviors. Some questions that served as observation prompts included the following:

- Were the teachers prepared to discuss the book?
- Did the teachers bring their reflection logs and use these as a reference tool?
- Did they flag particular passages for discussion?
- Did all teachers contribute to the discussion?
- Did the teachers look at one another as they talked?

Later, when the teachers in the group returned to their classrooms, they would use a mini-lesson to describe to their students the purpose of book discussions, explain the observation guide for noticing particular behaviors, and share the videotape. After the viewing, the teachers and students discussed what they had seen on the tape; and over the following few days, the teachers introduced book discussions into the reading workshop.

In another case, during a literacy team meeting the teachers discussed how their students needed a good model of a book discussion. The third-grade teacher volunteered to bring her students to different classrooms and model the process. The third graders became known as the "traveling book club," and for two weeks they visited different classrooms to demonstrate book discussions to other students. Prior to each visit, the classroom teachers presented mini-lessons on good book discussions, producing a chart entitled "Guidelines for Conducting Good Book Discussions" (see Chapter 6). The students used these guidelines as an observation protocol to look for specific behaviors. At the end of each discussion group, the classroom teacher and students discussed their observations. Here, too, book discussions were gradually introduced into the reading workshop.

In a third case, teachers used professional videotapes (Dorn and Soffos 2001b; Dorn and Soffos 2003) as a means of providing their students with a model for good literature discussions. On the tapes, Donnie Skinner, literacy coach at Boone Park Elementary in North Little Rock, Arkansas, conducted a literature discussion group with her third graders on two books, *Secret Signs* (Riggo 1997) and *Flossie and the Fox* (McKissack 1986). As was done in the two examples just mentioned, the students were given an observation protocol; after they viewed the video, the teacher guided the discussion, focusing on how each student built on the ideas of the others.

Framework of Literature Discussion Groups

Literature discussion groups consist of seven predictable, yet flexible, components, with the discussion running over several days depending on the length of the book being discussed. Within the framework, teachers constantly make decisions about how best to support students in developing deeper comprehension.

Component 1: Introduction and Selection of a Book

Choice is an important factor in reading success; however, this does not mean that students can select any book without some teacher guidance. To allow for choice within a framework, a teacher can introduce several books within a particular genre, author, or theme, provide a brief book talk on each text, then ask students to rate their top three choices. The most popular choice becomes the book for the literature discussion group. The remaining texts are placed in the classroom library for other reading experiences, including read-aloud, choice reading, or a literature discussion group at a later time.

Before the students go off to read independently, the teacher provides them with guidance in using specific tools to support their reading—for instance, using sticky notes to highlight passages for discussion or making a text map to organize story elements. The teacher should also refer to the appropriate anchor charts (described in Chapter 6) to support independent learning. Here are two examples of anchor charts that can help students engage in constructive literature discussion groups.

Preparing for Literature Discussion Groups
- Read assigned text.
- Flag your thinking with sticky notes.
- Respond to your thinking in reading log.

Guidelines for Engaging in Literature Discussion Groups
- Prepare for group meeting ahead of time (log section is marked and thinking is visible).
- Quickly come to group meeting excited and ready to begin discussion.
- Actively participate in book discussion by sharing thinking.
- Support thinking using evidence from text.
- Stay on topic.
- Listen carefully to others' thinking.
- Make eye contact with person talking.
- Offer opinion and build on ideas at appropriate times.
- Respect the thinking of other students and react using appropriate language.
- Ask questions when needed to clarify understanding.
- Achieve deeper understanding through discussion.

Component 2: Silent Reading

After students have a copy of the book they have selected, they find a comfortable spot to read independently. Depending on the length of the text, the silent reading block may last over several days. For short chapter books, the teacher generally does not assign specific chapters, but rather instructs the students to read the entire book. With some longer texts, the teacher might choose to break the reading into sections, bringing the students together at important points in the text for a group discussion. As the students read, they use comprehension tools, such as story maps, sticky notes, and response logs, to monitor their thinking and prepare for group discussion. During mini-lessons and reading conferences, students learn to assess their reading. (Section IV of the Appendix contains a rubric for assessing independent reading.)

Component 3: Teacher Conference

As the students silently read their books, the teacher conducts one-to-one conferences with each student in order to check students' comprehension and guide their thinking to a higher level. Each conference lasts about three or four minutes, which means that the teacher can meet with approximately eight students daily. The student brings the book being read, his or her response log, and, if requested, a story map. The conference begins with the teacher prompting the student to talk about the reading, perhaps beginning with an open-ended question, such as "Is there any part of your reading that you would like to talk about?" Or the teacher might choose to focus the conference with more specific questions. Here are some examples of prompts in three areas: responding to the story, questioning the author, and assessing comprehension.

Responding to the Story
- What did you like or dislike about the story?
- How did the story make you feel?
- Who was your favorite (or least favorite) character? Why?

- Did any of the characters remind you of anyone you know?
- Has anything similar to this ever happened to you?
- Would you recommend this story to a friend? Why or why not?

Questioning the Author

- What does the author mean here?
- Why do you think the author wrote this story?
- What is the author trying to tell us here?
- Does the author tell us why this happened?
- Does this make sense given what the author told us earlier?
- How does the author let us know that something has changed?
- How does the author use words to help us see what he (or she) is describing?
- What are some of your favorite phrases or words used by the author?
- How would you describe the author's style of writing?
- Would you recommend this author to a friend? Why or why not?

Assessing Comprehension

- Tell me about the story in your own words.
- What was the theme of the story?
- Did the story have a strong message?
- What do you think the main character learned?
- Was there a moral to this story?
- How would the story change in a different setting?

In the following example, a group of third graders are silently reading *The Story of Ruby Bridges* by Robert Cole (1995), and today is the day for one-to-one conferences. Carla calls one student, Teal, for her conference, and begins by asking her, "Where are you in your reading?" Teal responds that she has just completed the book. "How did you feel about the book?" Carla asks. Teal enthusiastically responds that she loved the book. Carla then prompts her to talk about her feelings. "Share your thinking with me," she encourages. Teal opens her book to a page she has flagged for the conference.

Teal: I could see this scene in my mind—the way Ruby walked in the school. She just sat down in the class and started doing her work.
Carla: Tell me more about why this scene was so important to you.
Teal: Well, because there were no other kids there and it didn't seem to bother Ruby. She just kept on going—learning and praying. I don't think I would have felt that way. I would have been upset, cried, and wanted to quit.
Carla: That helps me to understand your thinking. I agree with you. Ruby was certainly courageous. Would you like to add that part to your log?
Teal: Yes, it tells me more about my thoughts.

Reading logs are important tools for aiding students' comprehension. Figure 7.1 shows three examples of log entries students have made in response to their reading of *The Story of Ruby Bridges*. (Section IV of the Appendix contains a form for assessing students' reading logs).

Component 4: Group Discussion

The teacher periodically convenes the class for a group discussion of the book. These conversations can occur after the students have completed the text or several times during the reading, depending on the length and complexity of the text. The students have ready their response logs and books flagged with sticky notes for sharing particular sections. In this setting, the students are apprentices; the teacher's role is to mentor them to conduct good literature discussions on their own; the needs of

Figure 7.1 Three examples of reading response log entries for *The Story of Ruby Bridges*.

> Ruby Bridges   2-23-05
>
> In this book Ruby Bridges moves to a new house and school. It reminds me of when I lived with my mom Sarah and we moved to a different house and school. We were poor too and everyone treated me mean.
>
> I think the message is no matter what color you are you can still do good things and learn.

> The Story of Ruby Bridges   2-23-05
> This book touched my heart because she was black and she went to an all white school. A long time ago black people didn't go to white people's school. This hurts me. I think I know the author's message is it doesn't matter if your color is black or white. What really matters is that deep down inside you are nice and friendly to other people.

> The Story of Ruby Bridges
> I think the massage was in this book is it doesn't matter if you are black or white you should treat others the way you want to be treated.
>
> In this book Ruby was treated bad by white people she prays to Jesus twice a day an I bet Jesus led her through bad things.

the group should regulate the degree of support the teacher gives. Early on, when students are just starting to learn how to engage in literature discussions, the teacher provides a high to moderate degree of support, using language designed to help students find constructive strategies for comprehending the message. The teacher should be sensitive to how the children are responding to one another and prompt them to build discourse chains within the group, by asking, for instance, "Can someone tell us more about that? Does anyone disagree with what Josh said? Can anyone think of another solution?" The teacher monitors the students' comprehension and redirects the dialogue if the talk becomes off-task. The goal is to support the text discussion by scaffolding and offering assistance as needed—while promoting independent thinking within the group. Table 7.1 presents examples of language prompts to help students attain greater independence. The ultimate goal is that children will develop analytical and reflective strategies for comprehending at deeper levels. Students can also learn to assess their own performance in literature discussion groups. (Section IV of the Appendix contains a form for assessing literature discussion groups.)

The teacher's role should quickly move to that of participant-observer, sitting on the outside of the group as the students assume more responsibility for regulating the discussion. When this occurs, the students become both participants and spectators in the literature discussions. On a scale of help, the teacher's scaffolding is low (see Chapter 3).

To illustrate how literature discussions might sound at this level, here is a transcript of third graders talking about *The Story of Ruby Bridges*. Carla begins the discussion by asking, "Who would like to share your thinking about the Ruby Bridges book?" Marcus speaks up: "I love this book because I owe her a lot. She demonstrated bravery—she went to school when white people

Chapter 7 Creating Literature Discussion Groups

Table 7.1 **Supporting Text Talk by Scaffolding and Offering Assistance** (Slightly adapted from Pearson and Duke 2002)

Goal: Participants to internalize language for discussing text		Teacher scaffolds: prompting and offering assistance in achieving the goal
Restating	Repeats and adds to previous contribution	Can someone say that in a different way?
Inviting	Invites others to contribute	Do you want to invite anyone else to add to what you said?
Acknowledging	Confirms response without agreeing or disagreeing	Do you all get what _____ is trying to say here?
Focusing/refocusing	Making a comment about the course of the conversation	I think we have lost track of the question we were trying to answer. Can anyone help us here?
Agreeing/disagreeing	Confirming or disconfirming an opinion or thinking	Does everyone agree with _____? Does anyone want to disagree, or does anyone see it another way?
Elaborating	Building on someone else's thinking	Does anyone want to say something more about that? Can anyone think of another solution or another reason?
Providing evidence	Supporting one's own or another's thinking; examples can be inside or outside the text	Can anyone else give an example of _____ from the text? Has anything like this ever happened to you or someone you know?
Requesting clarification	Confused or needs additional information for someone else's thinking or about this part	Does anyone want to raise any questions about _____'s thinking here? Did anyone find anything confusing in this part of the text?
Posing questions for the group	Questioning text information, their own thinking, or someone else's thinking about something	Does anyone have a question for the group?
Goal: Participants to share and/or question their comprehending processes before, during, and after reading		**Teacher scaffolds: prompting and offering assistance with getting the participants to share their thinking and learn from each other**
Making connections	Connecting text to a personal experience, to other texts, to the world, to the writer, or to other parts of the text	Did anyone make a connection to this part of the text? Does this text/part remind any of you of another text we've read? Would anyone like to discuss: • The theme of the text? • What the text was mostly about? • What the author was trying to teach us?
Making predictions	Using background knowledge and text information to predict what the reader thinks is coming next or how the problem might be solved	Would anyone like to share their prediction or what they think might happen next? Would anyone like to predict how the problem might be solved? Why did the author put that part in the text?
Recalling	Paraphrasing or summarizing the text	Who would like to tell the group what the text was about?
Inferring	Using prior knowledge with new information gained from text in an effort to construct meaning	So, you think _____ because . . .
Visualizing	Using the author's language to create mind pictures—to feel, see, touch, taste, and/or hear	Would anyone like to share how the author created mind pictures here?

threatened her with her life and she didn't let that stop her—she got an education anyway." Marcus's comment becomes the initiating event for building a chain of reasoning among the group.

Taylor: I agree with you, Marcus. I think she opened the door for black kids to go to school with white kids so they could get a better education.

Teal: Yeah, the white kids went to the best schools.

David: Why do you think that, Teal?

Teal: Well, on the page where they are in court (*waits for everyone to find page*), the author says, "The black children were not able to receive the same education as the white children. It wasn't fair. And it was against the nation's law."

Alexius: But Ruby kept going and that changed our schools. I love her for that.

Matthew: I was wondering why the whites were so mean and did not want her to go to their school.

Taylor: Well, I think it was because they thought they were better.

David: Yeah, back a long time ago during the slave days they thought they were better. That is why they made them work for them and treated them so mean.

Teal: But Ruby made it through those hard times because she prayed for the people who were being mean. Remember on the page where Mrs. Henry asked Ruby what she was saying to the people (*waits for everyone to locate that page*) and Ruby said, "I wasn't talking, I was praying for them."

David: I am like Ruby in ways because I pray for people when they are mean to me, too.

Alexius: I think the author's message in this book is (*checking log*) it doesn't matter if you are black or white, you should treat others the way you want to be treated.

Carla: I wonder if we need to look beyond these events and think more about how Ruby demonstrated love and forgiveness even when she was mistreated.

Taylor: I think that is how Ruby Bridges wants us to look at it. She is still living. I would love to talk to her and see if she is still helping people today.

Two students, David and Matthew, contribute questions that bring the conversation to a new level. Throughout the discussion, the students provide evidence to support their thinking, and they use their response log as a resource. Carla's role is minimal; she is a participant-observer here, primarily observing, but available to redirect the discussion if needed. Near the end of the discussion, Carla asks the students to think about the character of Ruby Bridges—specifically, how her actions exemplify love and forgiveness. The closing comment shows Taylor's understanding of Ruby's desire to help other people. Carla was delighted to note that the students used many of the same prompts that their teacher had used in earlier discussion groups. This suggests that the students have learned appropriate language for literature discussions from previous conversations and are now utilizing these prompts to help one another construct meaning. Figure 7.2 shows a similar discussion group of third graders.

Component 5: Peer Discussions

Peer discussions are an extension of literature discussion groups with the teacher. Students are encouraged to continue discussing texts after they leave the group. As with all new learning, the teacher provides a scale of help to ease the students into the situation. Students must learn to self-assess the peer discussion at two levels: at the individual level and at the group level. The teacher acts as an outside observer, dropping by

Chapter 7 Creating Literature Discussion Groups

Figure 7.2 Vicki Altland and third graders hold a literature discussion group.

to listen in on segments of the conversation. At the end of the peer discussion, the teacher gathers the students together and invites them to share their self-assessments. The teacher also shares his or her own observations of the group, citing specific examples of how students interacted with one another.

Component 6: Text Mapping and Focus Groups

When students read literature, the teacher's goal is always to prompt the students to think analytically about the text or engage in a focused examination of a particular element in the text. Two successful techniques for promoting deeper comprehension are text or story mapping and focus groups.

Text or Story Maps

In text or story mapping, the teacher prepares a map that covers the essential features of the book type. Students use the map to analyze the book. This can occur in small groups, independently, or in a teacher-guided group. (Some examples of text maps are provided in Section III of the Appendix.) In Figure 7.3, Vicki and her third graders created a story map for *Because of Winn-Dixie* (2000) by Kate DiCamillo. As they read, the children developed questions and predictions about both the characters and the setting for each chapter, then they met with Vicki and as a group added information to the story map. In Figure 7.4, Regina Logan, a second-grade teacher, collaborated with her students on creating text maps for the Marc Brown series; they rated each book on a scale of 1 to 5. Teachers can also have students read different books within a theme, then compare the books according to common text features.

Focus Groups

Focus groups can also develop students' reading comprehension. Here, the teacher identifies a

Figure 7.3 A text map of *Because of Winn-Dixie*.

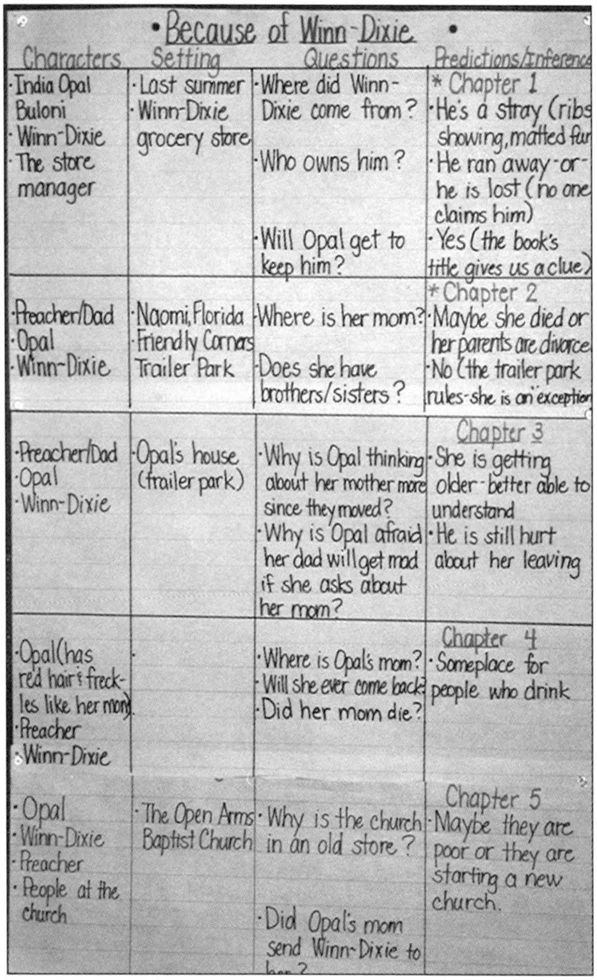

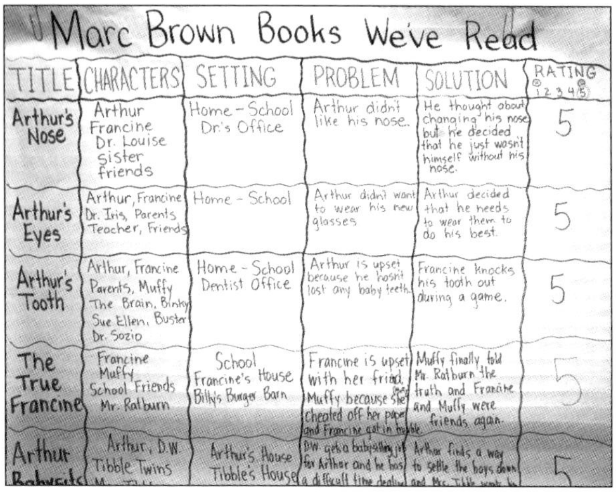

particular element for analysis and focuses the students' attention on a deep analysis of that one element. Some subjects for focus groups include the following:

Author's Style	Text Features
Leads and ending	Settings
Types of punctuation	Episodes
Figurative language	Theme
Use of dialogue	Time
Sentence structures	Multiple problems
Voice	Resolutions
Words that grab our attention	Character analysis

Component 7: Literature Extensions

After reading a book, students can be encouraged to work alone or in teams on extending the text. The teacher might choose to give guidance (e.g., listing various extension activities on the board) or she might encourage the students to come up with their own extensions. Some ways to extend the text include the following:

- Continue book discussions in peer groups.
- Read another book by the same author.
- Conduct an Internet search on the book's topic or theme.
- Write a letter to the author.
- Rewrite the text into a play, assign parts to classmates, and perform it for class.
- Interview the main character in the book.
- Research the author or illustrator.
- Write a poem related to the reading.
- Carry out a character analysis of several characters.
- Create a timeline of events.

Genre and Author Studies

In previous chapters, I discussed the relationship between reading and writing—specifically, how

Figure 7.4 A text map of five books from the Marc Brown series.

authors write texts that readers can comprehend and how readers use their knowledge of text conventions and style to assist their comprehending. If readers understand how texts are organized and how writers write, and if they have an understanding of the author's topic, they can use this information to predict and infer the author's intentions. If readers lack experience with authors and texts, however, their reading comprehension is likely to be impaired. Therefore, because it is so important for students to have some knowledge of the organization of the texts they read, we as teachers must introduce our students to genre and author studies. Texts often fall into a specific genre—that is, they are organized according to a specified set of criteria for a particular written form. For instance, a book in the mystery genre is characterized by the standard conventions of fiction: it has characters, a setting, a problem or problems, and a resolution; but it also includes characteristics peculiar to mysteries, such as unexplained events and clues that enable the reader to solve the problem. (Section III of the Appendix contains more information on genre.) In the reading workshop, students should be given many opportunities to become familiar with various genres. They can develop their knowledge of text features through diverse experiences with books, such as read-alouds (remember the six types of books for daily read-alouds mentioned in Chapter 3), shared reading, literature discussions, and book talks. Although a genre study can take several weeks, it can be integrated into these other literacy activities.

Here is a sample ten-step format for a genre study:

1. The teacher introduces the genre to be studied and shares the text characteristics for the particular genre.
2. The teacher reads aloud a book that typifies the genre.
3. The teacher revisits the text characteristics and fills in a blank chart with the students.
4. The teacher collects several texts in the genre and provides a brief book talk on each one.
5. The students rate their top three choices; the most popular choice becomes the group book.
6. The students read silently, fill in a text map, and record their thoughts in their response logs. The teacher holds individual conferences as the students read.
7. The group meets with the teacher to fill in a group text map.
8. The students read other books in the genre.
9. The students engage in literature extension activities, perhaps writing their own texts using the text map as a preplanning guide.
10. The students share their projects with the class during group share time.

Author studies are similar to genre studies, but here the focus is on a particular author rather than a specific genre. Having students focus on books by a particular writer helps them understand how different authors craft their writing to communicate their intended message. Author studies are best introduced in an apprenticeship setting along a supportive continuum that is adjusted according to students' needs. Here are some examples of how author studies might be conducted for students at various levels:

Emergent to Beginning Readers

- The teacher and the students select an author to study.
- The teacher shares the author's biographical information.
- The teacher displays several titles by the author, and students select one to be read aloud.
- The teacher reads the text aloud; students draw or record their impressions and ideas on sticky notes to be shared and discussed later.

- The teacher and the students together construct a chart that focus on one of the following: theme, language, biographical information, special features, and other information.
- The students read, reread, and enjoy the author's text during independent reading.
- The students discuss the text with others during share time.

Late Early to Transitional Readers

- The teacher and the students choose an author to study.
- The teacher displays the author's texts.
- The teacher conducts book talk on several of the texts.
- The teacher supplies multiple copies of several titles.
- The students select a text to read independently.
- The students form peer discussion groups with other students who have read the same text.
- During share time, students describe their favorite parts, quotes, and reflections, encouraging other students to read the text.
- The teacher and the students continue this cycle until all the titles in the author study have been read.
- The teacher and the students construct a chart or table as a way of considering all the texts by the author, taking into account, for example, theme, language, biographical information, and other special features (see Table 7.2).

Fluent Readers

- The students select an author to research.
- The students research and write a biographical sketch of their chosen author in their reading log.
- The students read independently and record their notes, ideas, questions, insights, quotes, and reflections in their reading log.
- The students read several different titles by the same author.
- The students compile a bibliography and list of resources that they used in their study.
- The students write a brief summary or review of the texts they read.
- The students compile their research, reviews, and reflections and give an oral presentation of their author to their class.
- The students may choose a multimedia presentation to showcase their work and entice others to read works by this author.

Closing Thoughts

My goal in this chapter has been to show how literature discussion groups provide children with a social context for developing literate talk. Here are three key points of this chapter.

Talk is a necessary condition of literacy learning. Literate talk is developed through reading and discussing books. Literature discussions help children learn how to hold discourse chains of meaning in their memories, while they consider how their ideas fit into the meaning-making chain. The teacher participates in the book discussions, prompting children to deeper levels of understanding.

Literature discussion groups are grounded in the theory of apprenticeship learning, including the role of scaffolding for regulating assistance in accomplishing a literate task. Teachers mentor students in how to talk about books. The goal of literature discussion groups is to move students toward deeper levels of comprehension.

Genre and author studies provide a context for comprehending texts at deeper levels. The connection between reading and writing is emphasized as students learn the techniques and styles of their favorite writers and use this knowledge to predict and infer messages. As readers acquire

Table 7.2 **Author Study of Eric Carle Books**

Feature	*The Very Hungry Caterpillar*	*The Very Busy Spider*	*The Very Quiet Cricket*	*The Grouchy Ladybug*
Characters	A caterpillar.	Spider, horse, cow, fly, sheep, goat, pig, dog, cat, duck, rooster, owl.	Little cricket, big cricket, girl cricket, locust, praying mantis, worm, spittle bug, cicada, bumblebee, dragonfly, mosquitoes, luna moth.	Grouchy Ladybug, Friendly Ladybug.
Interesting language, new words	"In the light of the moon . . . " Swiss cheese, salami, stomachache.	"A thin silky thread trailed from her body." Meadow, pesty fly.	Whizzed. "Disappeared silently into the distance"	"If you insist" Aphids, stag beetle, laughing eerily, encountered, tusks.
Connections	I was so hungry that I ate a whole pizza! It made me feel really sick!	Last fall there was a beautiful spider web with a garden spider on it on my back porch. The animals reminded me of when I was a girl growing up on a farm.	When I had laryngitis I really wanted to talk, but I couldn't. It was very frustrating.	One time after basketball practice a girl asked me if I wanted to fight. Then she laughed and drove off.
Wonderings	Did the caterpillar know he was going to become a butterfly?	I wonder how long it really takes a spider to make a web?	Do crickets make that sound to attract a mate? How do they make that sound?	Why wasn't the grouchy ladybug willing to share the aphids?
Theme	Hope. When you grow up you can spread your wings and use your talents.	If you work hard, you will be rewarded.	Love. When he saw the girl, she was just right for him and he was able to make the sound.	It is better to be friendly than greedy and grouchy.

knowledge of text patterns, they build a cognitive framework for expecting structures and events to occur in certain kinds of books. This knowledge fosters deep comprehension, because it enables the mind to bypass lower-level expectations and focus on higher-level thinking.

Designing Mini-Lessons for Deep Comprehension

It's a two-hour drive to Wynne, Arkansas. Carla and I are on the way to visit a school, and the drive is providing us with much-needed time to talk about our book. We are down to the last chapter—this one, on mini-lessons. Lately, we have been preoccupied with concerns about scripted programs and their disempowering effect on teachers. The script mentality seems to be creeping into our schools. Even some publishers of professional materials have fallen under the spell of providing teachers with supposedly foolproof scripts that are said to guarantee success with students, though in fact they simply ignore the complexity and uniqueness of student learning. I tell Carla about a conversation I recently overheard at a reading conference. I was sitting at a table with some elementary teachers, and they were discussing a popular author who had just published a program for teachers. The program includes a teacher script for each lesson. One teacher laughed as she said, "I always wanted to sound just like her, and now I can. All I have to do is read her script." Carla and I discuss the teacher's comment. We wonder whether a model can become a barrier to learning. Our theories of learning have always included modeling, yet the models are always personalized—not standardized—to meet the needs of students. We discuss the need to move beyond models into guided practice, which allows students to immediately apply the knowledge gleaned from the demonstration, with guidance and support from the teacher. This framework for learning exceeds the model—which is, after all, only an example—because it allows students to transfer their learning to personal application. As we enter Wynne, our trip nearing an end, we talk about how this theory will shape the final chapter in our book; and we make a conscious decision to avoid providing a script for each mini-lesson. Instead, we will focus on outlining the conceptual framework that we believe will allow teachers to take the lessons and provide their own language to engage their students. Thus, our final chapter uses the framework of mini-lessons to present ten strategic reading behaviors; we trust you, the teacher, to make personal decisions on what to say based on the strengths and needs of your students.

The Framework of a Mini-Lesson

The success of a mini-lesson is grounded in the teacher's knowledge of the reading process as it relates to the students' ability to apply strategic behaviors for comprehending the author's message. The purpose of a mini-lesson is to enable students to accomplish a particular goal with assistance from the teacher. The teacher closely observes the group, makes mental notes of students who need extra help, and plans for ways to scaffold these students in small groups or individual conferences (Dorn and Soffos 2001a, p. 48).

The first step in conducting a reading workshop is to introduce a mini-lesson. The teacher uses books from the classroom library to demonstrate how authors craft their texts to support the reader's comprehension. Prior to any mini-lesson, the students should have heard the book during read-aloud time; this previous experience with the book will give them a meaningful context for studying the strategy that will be introduced. Teachers should use a variety of texts in mini-lessons so that students can learn how to apply strategies for different types of texts.

The teacher gathers all the students in a group and presents a brief and explicit teaching demonstration, usually making use of good literature, which provides the basis for thinking out loud and demonstrating the strategy being taught. Typically, mini-lessons are approximately fifteen minutes long; longer mini-lessons run the risk of degenerating into a focus on items instead of a strategic process for problem solving. A mini-lesson should leave memorable traces in the minds of the students, enabling them to recall the important points of the lesson with ease. The mini-lesson follows a pattern within the workshop format. The workshop begins in a small group with the mini-lesson, proceeds to independent practice, and ends with a time for sharing. This framework is compatible with a gradual release model, which begins with a high degree of teacher support and ends with a high degree of student independence (see Figure 8.1).

Step 1: Review anchor chart of comprehension strategies. The workshop mini-lesson begins with a review of comprehension strategies from the anchor chart. As comprehension strategies are introduced and discussed, they are added to the anchor chart. In Figure 8.2, Donnie Skinner, a third-grade literacy coach, adds a new strategy to the class anchor chart. This part of the workshop generally takes two or three minutes.

Step 2: Model the process. The second step of the mini-lesson is to model the comprehension strategy being introduced. To do this, the teacher uses a think-aloud process with a mentor book—an appropriate text, generally from a previous read-aloud, that will help students notice and apply a particular comprehending behavior. The teacher preselects a particular segment from the mentor text to use as the think-aloud model, then reads the text aloud in class, stopping at three or four strategic points to describe his or her thought processes. At appropriate places, the teacher might solicit brief comments from the class, maintaining the focus on the strategy at all times. This step generally lasts eight to ten minutes.

Step 3: Provide guided practice. The third step is to have the students apply the strategy with

Figure 8.1 The gradual release of responsibility model and how it relates to mini-lessons (*source:* adapted from Pearson and Gallagher 1983)

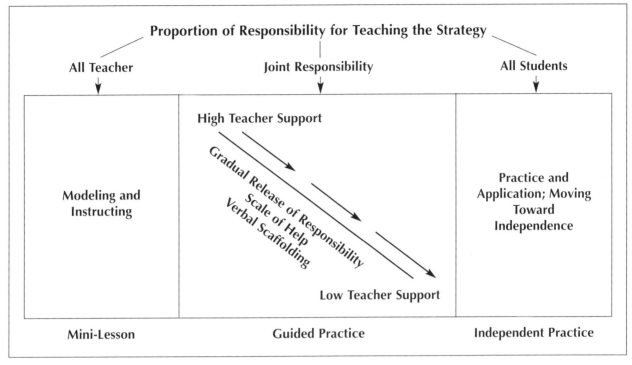

Figure 8.2 During a mini-lesson, Donnie Skinner adds a new point to the anchor chart on comprehension strategies.

teacher guidance. Without guided practice, students might find the model useless; in any case, it would be quickly forgotten. Guided practice is the step that makes the model meaningful and enables students to see the connection to their own learning. This step generally takes about ten minutes.

Step 4: Provide independent practice. Next, the class moves beyond the mini-lesson to independent practice. Students must have opportunities to transfer their knowledge to different problem-solving situations; otherwise, they become dependent on a specific context for activating a strategy. Although guided practice and independent practice are complementary processes, they involve different degrees of processing power. During guided practice, students apply a specific strategy with the goal of testing it in context; during independent practice, students must apply the single strategy in concert with other strategies, thus promoting deeper comprehension.

Step 5: Sharing. The fifth step, sharing, occurs at the end of the reading workshop. Allowing a time for sharing serves two purposes: (1) it gives students a chance to share their comprehending processes with the class, and (2) it allows the teacher to assess the students' learning. This part of the reading workshop generally lasts about ten minutes.

Building a Mental Toolbox of Effective Strategies

During each mini-lesson, teachers can focus on a single strategy. This enables students to acquire a cognitive toolbox of meaningful strategies that they can use as needed. Good readers know which strategy to use for a solving a particular reading problem; they apply a range of strategies in order to attain meaning. In contrast, poor readers are more likely to view strategies as skills and make the skill itself the reason for reading. For instance, if a mini-lesson has focused on visualization, the poor reader may perceive visualization as the goal of reading. This narrow viewpoint can inhibit the reader's comprehension, interfering with the ability to practice the orchestration of multiple strategies—a prerequisite to deep comprehension. Mini-lessons can introduce students to problem-solving strategies, but the comprehending process requires that readers coordinate a range of comprehending strategies as they work to construct deep meaning.

In determining the focus of a mini-lesson, the teacher must know what the students need at a particular time. The focus must change as the students change. Here are five types of mini-lessons:

1. *Procedures and organization.* Mini-lessons are used to establish the workshop format—for example, creating guidelines for book discussions or procedures for buddy reading (see Chapter 6).
2. *Comprehension strategies.* Mini-lessons may introduce comprehension strategies, such as ways to visualize and make connections (see the ten comprehension strategies in Chapter 4).
3. *Strategic behaviors.* Mini-lessons may also focus on specific behaviors, such as rereading and previewing.
4. *Language strategies.* Mini-lessons can help children understand how the language system works—for example, how writers use figurative language or how texts are organized according to writing conventions (see the ten language strategies in Chapter 5).
5. *Comprehension skills.* Mini-lessons can also help children learn inferential, literal, and critical thinking skills, including the following:
   - Inferential skills (reading between the lines) regarding such things as:
     - Mood of the selection
     - Author's purpose
     - Conclusions
     - Implied locations
     - Implied times
     - Character motivation and actions
     - Meaning of figurative language
     - Vocabulary meanings
     - Pronoun referents
     - Adverb referents
     - Omitted words
     - Implied main ideas
   - Literal skills (directly stated ideas), including recognition of the following:
     - Details
     - Cause and effect
     - Sequence of events
     - Problem of the story and its solution
   - Critical skills (reading for evaluation), such as:

Recognizing whether a piece of text is fact or opinion
Identifying point of view
Critiquing
Making value judgments
Assessing writing style and tone

The rest of this chapter applies the five-step format to ten mini-lessons for shaping deep comprehension, following the ten strategic reading behaviors listed in Chapter 4.

Type of Mini-Lesson: Strategic Behavior #1
Rereading When Meaning Breaks Down

Materials

The following materials should be organized for the learning before the lesson begins:

- Text to use in the mini-lesson, with a specific portion identified that is somewhat complex and could possibly confuse the reader
- Text that students are currently reading
- Comprehension strategies anchor chart

Step 1: Introduce the Lesson (during the whole-group session)

Tell the students that reading is a message-getting, meaning-making process. Explain that when readers are reading and something doesn't make sense they must reread and try to clear up the confusion. Inform them that sometimes readers reread just a couple of sentences to figure out the meaning, but at other times they have to reread a whole section or chapter.

Step 2: Model the Process (during the whole-group session)

Begin reading aloud from a text. Think aloud as you model your confusion about a particular character. Who is this character? Show the students how you turn back to the chapter where the character is first introduced and reread. Through modeling and thinking aloud, make sure the students clearly notice how rereading assists you when you become confused.

Step 3: Provide Guided Practice (during the whole-group session)

Tell the students to select the text they are currently reading from their independent reading box. Ask them to begin reading the text and flag places where they become confused. Suggest that when that happens, they go back as far as they think they need and reread the text to help get their thinking back on track. Circulate among the students and listen, observe, and document how they are monitoring their reading based on meaning and how well they are initiating the rereading strategy. Bring the students back together as a group and have several share their successes. Add the strategic behavior to the class comprehension strategies chart. Bring the lesson to a close by engaging the students in a discussion of how reading must make sense and how they should go back and reread when and if meaning breaks down. Remind them that if they can't figure it out on their own, they can bring their confusions to share time, book discussions, or guided reading time and elicit help from others.

Step 4: Provide Independent Practice (during reading workshop)

Provide students with ample time for reading and applying the rereading strategy across meaningful contexts.

Step 5: Share Time (bringing the workshop to closure by learning from others in a community environment)

Allow students to share their thinking from the reading they just did. Listen carefully as they share and informally assess their comprehending processes (any comprehending process is fine to discuss here). Offer praise, provide feedback, and elicit peer support or suggestions.

Type of Mini-Lesson:
Strategic Behavior #2
Previewing or Surveying a Text by Using the Blurb on the Back Cover, the Inside Flap, and the Table of Contents

Materials
- Several texts that include one or two of the following features (depending on the students' background knowledge):
    - Blurb on back cover or inside flap (goal of this lesson)
    - Table of contents (goal of this lesson)
    - Favorite author or series
    - List of recommendations and awards
- Classroom library
- Comprehension strategies anchor chart

Step 1: Introduce the Lesson
Tell the students that when readers are trying to decide what text to read they often read the blurbs on the back cover and inside flap. They can also scan the table of contents for information about the chapters or sections in the text. Applying this surveying and previewing strategy before reading helps readers decide what text they might enjoy.

Step 2: Model the Process
Think aloud as you model the strategies you use when choosing a text to read. Show how the first thing you do is read the blurbs on the back cover and the inside flap (point to these sections as you describe your thinking). Think aloud about the new information you are acquiring about the text as you read these features of the cover or book jacket. Finally, direct students' attention to the table of contents and show how the table of contents can help you make predictions about the text and set a purpose for your reading.

Step 3: Provide Guided Practice
Have the students visit the classroom library, browse through the book boxes, and locate a text that looks interesting to them or that grabs their attention. Remind them to read the back cover and the flaps (if the book cover or jacket has these features) and to scan the table of contents. Suggest that they use this information to help them decide whether they do or do not want to read the text. Break the students into groups and have each group member share with the others their chosen text and how the modeled features assisted them with text selection. Circulate among the students and listen, observe, and document how they use the previewing and surveying strategy. Bring the students back together as a group and have one or two students share their successes. Add the strategic behavior to the class comprehension strategies chart. Bring the lesson to a close by engaging the students in a discussion about the importance of using these features to assist with text selection.

Step 4: Provide Independent Practice
Provide students with ample time for applying the previewing and surveying strategies across meaningful contexts on their own.

Step 5: Share Time
Have students share their thinking from the reading they have done during this workshop. Listen carefully and informally assess their comprehending processes. Offer praise, provide feedback, and elicit peer support or suggestions.

Type of Mini-Lesson: Strategic Behavior #3
Asking Questions Before, During, and After Reading

Materials
- A new or unseen text
- Students' independent reading boxes
- Comprehension strategies anchor chart

Step 1: Introduce the Lesson
Tell the students that they are asking themselves good questions before reading by reading the blurbs on the back of the text, reading the inside flaps, skimming the table of contents, and thinking about the author's writing style. Explain that as they read they should also be asking themselves questions, such as: "What is a ——?" or "Who is this character?" Explain that after reading they might still have questions. If the questions they had during reading are just not answered, they have to infer the answers—that is, they must use background knowledge and the information from the text to help them answer their questions or think beyond the text. This question asking during and after reading requires thinking. Readers must think while they read or they will have difficulty understanding the text.

Step 2: Model the Process
Use the text and model some questions you ask yourself before reading. Think aloud about how these questions help you set a purpose for reading. As you read through the text, model deep-level questioning in two or three places, and mark these places using sticky notes. After reading, return to the flagged areas and think aloud about whether your questions were answered or not. As you think aloud, support your answers from the text. If some of your questions remain unanswered, make inferences based on the text information and your background knowledge.

Step 3: Provide Guided Practice
Tell the students to select the text they are currently reading from their independent reading box. Suggest that as they are reading and they ask themselves questions or wonder about something, they should place a sticky note on the page and keep reading to see if they find the answer. Circulate among the students and listen, observe, and document how they are applying the process. Bring the students back to the group. Allow several students to share the questions they generated during and after reading; have them make inferences. Add the strategic behavior to the class comprehension strategies chart. Bring the lesson to a close by engaging the students in a discussion around the importance of asking questions before, during, and after reading and how asking questions can help them think more deeply about their reading.

Step 4: Provide Independent Practice
Provide students with ample time for reading and applying the questioning strategy across meaningful contexts.

Step 5: Share Time
Allow students to share their thinking from the reading they have done during independent practice. Listen carefully as the students share their thinking and informally assess their comprehending processes. Provide feedback and elicit peer support.

Type of Mini-Lesson: Strategic Behavior #4
Reading Aloud to Clarify Thinking

Materials
- Text, either familiar or not previously seen, with a portion identified that is somewhat complex and could cause some confusion

- Classroom library
- Students' independent reading boxes
- Comprehension strategies anchor chart

Step 1: Introduce the Lesson
Tell the students that sometimes as they read they may become confused or forget what is going on in the text. Explain that when this happens, they can read aloud to help get their thinking back on track. This reading aloud is similar to thinking aloud and is a powerful technique for making one's thinking visible.

Step 2: Model the Process
Read aloud a text (or part of a text) and in one or two places, model some confusion. Use the reading-aloud strategy to show how sometimes just hearing the text read aloud helps a reader clarify misunderstanding.

Step 3: Provide Guided Practice
Tell the students to select a text from their independent reading box or from the classroom library. Tell them that when they become confused as they read, they should try reading aloud and see if it helps clarify their thinking. Ask them to flag the places in the text where they've tried this; then bring them back to the group meeting. Circulate among the students and listen, observe, and document how they are applying the strategy. Bring the students back to the group. Allow one or two students to share their successes. Add the strategic behavior to the class comprehension strategies chart. Bring the lesson to a close by engaging the students in a discussion about the importance of reading aloud when they are confused in their reading.

Step 4: Provide Independent Practice
Provide students with ample time for reading on their own and applying the reading-aloud strategy across meaningful contexts.

Step 5: Share Time
Allow students to share their thinking from the reading they did during the reading workshop. Listen carefully and informally assess the students' comprehending processes. Offer praise, provide feedback, and elicit peer support or suggestions.

Type of Mini-Lesson: Strategic Behavior #5
Using Knowledge of Text Structure, Text Genre, and Writing Conventions

Materials
- Fairy tales
- Fairy-tale text map (see Section III of the Appendix)
- Comprehension strategies anchor chart

Step 1: Introduce the Lesson
Tell the students that readers understand and comprehend texts at deeper levels when they are familiar with how specific kinds of texts are organized. Explain that writers use these text structures to help readers comprehend their texts.

Step 2: Model the Process
Show the students several fairy tales that you know they have read or heard. Then think aloud about how fairy tales are organized and/or how they contain specific language.

Step 3: Provide Guided Practice
Read aloud a fairy tale to the students. After reading, construct a chart with the students using a text map format (see Section III of the Appendix) to help them understand the text structure. Listen carefully and observe how well the students are learning about the text structure of a fairy tale from reading and focusing on its literary elements. Add the strategic behavior to the class compre-

hension strategies chart. Bring the lesson to a close by engaging the students in a discussion around the importance of reading many fairy tales and how understanding the language and organization of this genre increases comprehension.

Step 4: **Provide Independent Practice**
Provide students with ample time for reading fairy tales and learning about their structure.

Step 5: **Share Time**
Allow students to share their thinking from the reading they have done during the reading workshop. Listen carefully and informally assess the students' comprehending processes. Offer praise, provide feedback, and elicit peer support or suggestions.

Type of Mini-Lesson: Strategic Behavior #6
Using Text Aids to Illuminate and Extend Meaning

Materials
- A familiar nonfiction text
- Classroom library
- Students' independent reading boxes
- Text aids; anchor chart of text features

Step 1: **Introduce the Lesson**
Tell the students that readers of nonfiction use photographs or illustrations to help them understand specific concepts within the text (point to such a feature in the text you are showing them). Explain how this text aid helps readers see the details in something and how it provides them with extra visual information in order to comprehend at a deeper level.

Step 2: **Model the Process**
Revisit a page from a familiar text that includes photographs or illustrations. Using the think-aloud strategy, model how this particular nonfiction text aid helps you to see the details in something. Think aloud about how these details from the photograph help you understand what you have read. Explain further how authors include this technique to facilitate deeper understanding about a particular concept.

Step 3: **Provide Guided Practice**
Tell the students to select a nonfiction text from their independent reading box or from the classroom library. Ask them to identify and flag photographs, examine the details that they provide, and bring their examples back to the group. Circulate among the students and listen, observe, and document how they are applying the process. Bring the students back to the group. Allow one or two students to share their successes. Add the strategic behavior to the class text aids/features anchor chart for understanding nonfiction. Bring the lesson to a close by engaging the students in a discussion about the importance of using text aids to assist with comprehension when reading nonfiction.

Step 4: **Provide Independent Practice**
Provide students with ample time for identifying and using text aids across meaningful contexts.

Step 5: **Share Time**
Allow students to share their thinking from the reading they have done in reading workshop. Listen carefully and informally assess their comprehending processes. Offer praise, provide feedback, and elicit peer support or suggestions.

Type of Mini-Lesson: Strategic Behavior #7
Marking Texts and Recording Notes

Materials
- A text marked with sticky sheets and recorded notes (to use as an example)

- A nonfiction Big Book, a nonfiction poster, or an article
- Classroom library
- Students' independent reading boxes
- Comprehension strategies anchor chart

Step 1: Introduce the Lesson
Tell the students that readers often mark the text and record notes as they read (open up your book and point to the places you have marked). Explain that readers do this because it spotlights important information that they think is worth remembering. It might be a part that grabs their attention or it might be a question that occurred to them as they read. Readers highlight passages and make notes to help them remember and understand what they are reading.

Step 2: Model the Process
Begin reading the text and model how a specific part is important information worth remembering. Place a sticky slip on the page and record a word or phrase in reference to that part. Continue to show the students how you identify important information by writing down a word or phrase and/or sketching a picture, and explain that this also helps readers deepen their comprehension.

Step 3: Provide Guided Practice
Tell the students to select a text from their independent reading box or from the classroom library. Suggest that when they are reading and encounter a part of the text that they think is worth remembering, they should place a sticky slip on the page and record key words or ideas to help them recall the information. Ask them to bring their examples back to the group meeting. Circulate among the students and listen, observe, and document how they are applying the process. Bring the students back to the group. Allow one or two students to share their successes. Add the strategic behavior to the class comprehension strategies chart. Bring the lesson to a close by engaging the students in a discussion of how marking text and recording notes will help them remember and understand what they read.

Step 4: Provide Independent Practice
Provide students with ample time for reading and applying the marking text and recording notes strategy across meaningful contexts.

Step 5: Share Time
Allow students to share their thinking from the reading they have done during reading workshop. Listen carefully and informally assess their comprehending processes. Offer praise, provide feedback, and elicit peer support or suggestions.

Type of Mini-Lesson: Strategic Behavior #8
Using Context and Parts of Words to Infer Meaning

Materials
- A text to be read aloud
- Classroom library
- Students' independent reading boxes
- Comprehension strategies anchor chart
- Reading log

Step 1: Introduce the Lesson
Tell the students that when they encounter words they don't know how to pronounce or words they don't understand, they should simply ask themselves "What do I already know about this word? Do I know the meaning of the root word? Can I get the meaning from rereading and using context clues?" If not, then they should flag the word and use other resources, including talking with others, to help them.

Chapter 8 Designing Mini-Lessons for Deep Comprehension

Step 2: **Model the Process**
Begin reading aloud a text and model how you identify unknown words. Think aloud as you do so, using parts of the word and context cues to help you figure out the meaning of the word. Flag one or two places where you were not able to figure out the word this way; at the end of the read-aloud session, engage the students in a conversation about possible meanings. Model how to use both the dictionary definition and the sentence from the book to learn more about the word and its meaning. Write the word in your reading log for future use.

Step 3: **Provide Guided Practice**
Tell the students to select a text from their independent reading box or from the classroom library. Suggest that when they are reading and encounter a word they don't understand or know how to pronounce, they should first reread the sentence, section, or chapter and ask themselves: "Do I know the root word? What do I know about this word?" If they can't figure out the word this way, ask them to highlight both the word and the relevant section from the book to discuss with the group later. Circulate among the students and listen, observe, and document how they are applying the process. Bring the students back to the group. Allow one or two students to share their successes. Add the strategic behavior to the class comprehension strategies chart. Bring the lesson to a close by engaging the students in a discussion of how using word parts and context clues helps readers infer meaning as they read.

Step 4: **Provide Independent Practice**
Provide students with ample time for reading and applying the strategies for learning new words across meaningful contexts.

Step 5: **Share Time**
Allow students to share their thinking from the reading they have done during reading work-shop. Listen carefully and informally assess their comprehending processes. Offer praise, provide feedback, and elicit peer support or suggestions.

Type of Mini-Lesson: Strategic Behavior #9
Writing in Reading Logs

Materials
- Text that is marked with sticky slips and recorded notes
- New text for reading aloud
- Students' independent reading boxes
- Reading log
- Comprehension strategies anchor chart

Step 1: **Introduce the Lesson**
Tell students that readers often mark the text and record notes of things from their reading that they think are worth remembering. After reading, they record their responses in reading logs. This helps them remember things for group discussion and for their own later writing.

Step 2: **Model the Process**
Read a short text and think aloud as you read. Use sticky slips to mark the text and record notes if necessary. After the reading, revisit the marked sections. Respond to the text at the theme level by recording your unanswered questions and making inferences about them, noting your personal opinion of the text, describing and responding to one or more characters, making connections, or creating maps, drawings, or diagrams for future reference. The modeling must represent the teacher's true thinking and it must be deep and authentic.

Step 3: **Provide Guided Practice**
Tell the students to select a text from their independent reading box that is already marked with sticky slips. Ask them to revisit their marked

passages and respond to one such passage in their log. Ask them to bring their examples back to the group meeting for sharing. Circulate among the students and listen, observe, and document how they are applying the process. Bring the students back to the group. Allow one or two students to share their successes. Add the strategic behavior to the class comprehension strategies chart. Bring the lesson to a close by engaging the students in a discussion of how responding in your log provides you with information worth remembering and thoughts for sharing with the group.

Step 4: **Provide Independent Practice**
Provide students with ample time for reading, marking texts, recording notes, and responding in their logs across meaningful contexts.

Step 5: **Share Time**
Allow students to share their thinking from the reading they have done during reading workshop. Listen carefully and informally assess their comprehending processes. Offer praise, provide feedback, and elicit peer support or suggestions.

Type of Mini-Lesson:
Strategic Behavior #10
Discussing Ideas and Impressions with Others

Materials
- Short book for read aloud
- Classroom library
- Comprehension strategies anchor chart

Step 1: **Introduce the Lesson**
Tell the students that when people read a good book or text, they have an innate desire to share their thoughts about it with others. This talk helps readers confirm or reshape their thinking based on others' opinions and input. People naturally want to talk, discuss, and learn from each other.

Step 2: **Model the Process**
Read aloud a short text and engage in a conversation with the students about the book. Think aloud as you confirm and/or reshape your thinking from the discussion. Model how there are no right or wrong answers—our thinking is grounded in our background knowledge and experiences. Talk about how we all view experiences differently. What we remember about something has to do with what we are thinking about at that time.

Step 3: **Provide Guided Practice**
Ask the students to select their favorite book from the classroom library. Put the students into small groups and allow them to share their thinking about the book with the group. Suggest that as they listen and discuss books together, they can record on a sticky note any new book they now want to read. Circulate among the students and listen, observe, and document how they are applying the process. Bring the students back to the group. Allow one or two students to share their experience. Add the strategic behavior to the class comprehension strategies chart. Bring the lesson to a close by engaging the students in a short discussion about how talking about books can get others interested in a book you like and can aid your own comprehension.

Step 4: **Provide Independent Practice**
Provide students with ample time for reading and discussing ideas and impressions of books they have read with others across meaningful contexts.

Step 5: **Share Time**
Allow students to share their thinking from the reading they have done during reading work-

shop. Listen carefully and informally assess their comprehending processes. The teacher and the students can offer praise, provide feedback, and elicit peer support or suggestions.

Closing Thoughts

The material contained in this chapter seems an appropriate way to end a book on comprehension. A theme throughout the book has been the role of language in shaping literacy. Following the philosophy of teaching involving apprenticeship, a mini-lesson provides a language model for arousing a reader's attention. Students learn from the experts—their teachers—about the comprehending process. The teacher spotlights particular strategies used by good readers, then provides students with both guided and independent practice. The whole process is a kind of cognitive apprenticeship, whereby a more knowledgeable language user mentors students into the world of literacy.

APPENDIX SECTION 1

Shared Reading Aids

Change Over Time in Shared Reading and Guided Reading for Emergent Readers of Fiction Texts

Emergent Readers *Identifying/Setting Goals*	**Shared Reading** *Becoming Aware/Increasing Awareness of Reading Strategies*	**Guided Reading** *Developing and Gaining Control of Reading Strategies*
Enjoy the rhythm and rhyme of language (phonological awareness)	Teacher and students chant poems, text, songs, and raps fluently with expression and intonation	
Develop phonological and phonemic awareness	Teacher engages students in developing phonological awareness skills by inviting students to engage in word play, i.e., alliteration, rhyme (onset and rhyme), segmenting sounds, deleting sounds, adding sounds, substituting sounds, and blending sounds together to form new words	
Learn about and use book and print conventions (i.e., concepts about print) when reading	Teacher models and invites student participation in learning about and using book and print conventions, i.e., where to begin reading, directionality, one-to-one matching, locating a word (understanding word concept and identifying known/unknown words), locating known letters (seeing known letters embedded in print), locating capital and lowercase letters, identifying, highlighting, and learning about specific punctuation and high-frequency words	Reads text using knowledge of text conventions, i.e., where to start, which way to go, one-to-one matching, and monitoring and self-correcting using known letters and words
Build a small core of high-frequency words	Teacher/students highlight high-frequency word(s) and use magnetic letters or wipe board to practice building, dismembering, and rebuilding words	Reads high-frequency words quickly, fluently, and automatically

Teaching for Deep Comprehension: A Reading Workshop Approach by Linda J. Dorn and Carla Soffos. Copyright © 2005. Stenhouse Publishers.

Change Over Time in Shared Reading and Guided Reading for Emergent Readers of Fiction Texts *(continued)*

Emergent Readers *Identifying/Setting Goals*	**Shared Reading** *Becoming Aware/Increasing Awareness of Reading Strategies*	**Guided Reading** *Developing and Gaining Control of Reading Strategies*
Develop concept knowledge, internalize more complex language structures, and gain vocabulary knowledge through listening, reading, and interacting with text	Teacher supports the development of more complex oral language structures, background knowledge, and concepts by reading to and with students while enjoying the sounds of language Teacher supports vocabulary knowledge by defining words for students, providing examples other than ones in text, encouraging students to think of other examples, and charting new learning for future reference	Begins to use background knowledge (schema) before and during reading, reads more complex text (1–2 lines of print) with fluency, expression, and intonation, and increases concept and vocabulary knowledge by interacting with text and other group members
Begin to develop reading fluency, i.e., reads with phrasing, intonation, and expression	Teacher and students read text together fluently with phrasing, intonation, and expression	Reads text fluently with phrasing, intonation, and expression
Become aware of how to use text features such as title and illustrations to activate background knowledge and make predictions in text	Teacher models, supports, and encourages students to activate background knowledge by reading the title, examining illustrations on the cover, and making predictions	Begins to use title and illustrations to activate background knowledge and make predictions
Become aware of how to think and act like readers, i.e., learn about plot, characters, setting, and theme	Teacher and students read text fluently, talk about characters, discuss setting in story, identify the plot, and participate in drama activities and literature extensions	
Learn how readers think, question, connect, infer, identify themes, and comprehend text	Teacher reads text, models using metacognitive processes (thinking about thinking) before, during, and after reading, and invites student participation in all of these processes	

Change Over Time in Shared Reading and Guided Reading for Emergent Readers of Fiction Texts (continued)

Emergent Readers *Identifying/Setting Goals*	**Shared Reading** *Becoming Aware/Increasing Awareness of Reading Strategies*	**Guided Reading** *Developing and Gaining Control of Reading Strategies*
Become aware of the importance of using all sources of information together in an orchestrated way, i.e., using meaning, structure, and visual information simultaneously while reading	Teacher reads text fluently and invites students to join in and when appropriate invites participation in cloze procedures, i.e., predicting words based on meaning and structure, using letter-sound relationships to confirm/disconfirm predictions, and engaging in phonics skills (segmenting and blending) to problem-solve and read word accurately	Uses background knowledge (schema) and syntax to predict, uses letter-sound knowledge to confirm/disconfirm predictions, and if needed uses phonics skills to problem-solve or self-correct
Become aware of punctuation and how it shares a relationship with reading fluency	Teacher and students fluently read text and teacher invites students to flag a selected form of punctuation; uses the punctuation to read text appropriately with phrasing, intonation, and expression	Reads 1–2 lines of text with fluency, expression, and intonation, demonstrating some beginning knowledge of punctuation (end-of-sentence punctuation)
Develop a love for reading	Teacher and students read text for enjoyment and the pleasure of reading	Reads for pleasure inside and outside of the school setting

Change Over Time in Shared Reading and Guided Reading for Early and Transitional Readers of Fiction Texts

Early and Transitional Readers *Identifying/Setting Goals*	Shared Reading *Becoming Aware/Increasing Awareness of Reading Strategies*	Guided Reading *Developing and Gaining Control of Reading Strategies*
Enjoy the rhythm and rhyme of language	Teacher and students chant poems, text, songs, and raps fluently with expression and intonation	Reads a wide variety of text with fluency, expression, and intonation, demonstrating more fluent knowledge of the three language systems (meaning, structure, and visual)
Increase phonological knowledge (sounds of language) and phonics skills and efficiently apply this knowledge when reading for meaning	Teacher and students read texts, chant poems, songs, raps, and engage in word play, i.e., alliteration, rhyme/rime (onset and rhyme/rime), segmenting sounds/letter sounds, deleting sounds/letter sounds, adding sounds/letter sounds, substituting sounds/letter sounds, and blending sounds/letter sounds together to form new words	Reads more complex texts with fluency; uses meaning and language structures to predict. At the point of difficulty, initiates more efficient and fluent word problem-solving strategies: —within word parts —prefixes, suffixes, and base words —syllable juncture
Develop new concepts, internalize more complex language structures, and increase vocabulary knowledge through interacting with text and group members	Teacher supports the development of more complex oral language structures, background knowledge, and concepts by reading to and with students while enjoying the sounds of language Teacher supports vocabulary knowledge by defining words for students, providing examples other than ones in text, encouraging students to think of other examples, and charting new learning for future reference	Reads more complex texts and questions at the word level (word meanings), sentence level, or phrase level and/or at the text level (theme); flags and records questions and favorite parts; discusses text with group members after reading
Increase knowledge of how to use text features such as title, illustrations, chapter titles, and blurb on back cover to construct meaning	Teacher invites students to build meaning for text by reading title, examining illustrations on cover, scanning chapter titles, reading back cover blurb, activating prior knowledge and making predictions, and questioning	Uses text features to build meaning and make predictions before reading, i.e., reads title, examines illustrations on cover, scans chapter titles, and reads back cover blurb

Change Over Time in Shared Reading and Guided Reading for Early and Transitional Readers of Fiction Texts *(continued)*

Early and Transitional Readers *Identifying/Setting Goals*	**Shared Reading** *Becoming Aware/Increasing Awareness of Reading Strategies*	**Guided Reading** *Developing and Gaining Control of Reading Strategies*
Increase knowledge of the importance of using meaning, knowledge of language structures (to predict), word meanings, and more complex letter-sound relationships as text is read	Teacher reads text fluently and invites students to join in and when appropriate invites participation in cloze procedures, i.e., predicting words based on meaning and structure, using more complex letter-sound relationships to confirm/disconfirm predictions, and initiating more complex visual searching (within-word patterns, syllable juncture) to problem-solve and self-correct	Uses all sources of information fluently when reading and at the point of difficulty; initiates complex visual searching actions to problem-solve and self-correct fluently
Learn how readers think, question, connect, infer, identify themes, and comprehend text	Teacher reads text, models using metacognitive processes (thinking about thinking) before, during, and after reading, and invites student participation in all of these processes	Uses comprehension strategies while reading, i.e., flags thinking while reading and makes thinking visible by recording in log; continues to learn after the reading by sharing and discussing text with other group members
Learn to think and act like readers, learn about plots, characters, settings, and themes	Teacher and students read text fluently, talk about characters, discuss setting in story, identify the plot, participate in drama activities and literature extensions	Uses knowledge of story elements, i.e., analyzes characters, setting, plot, and theme, thus resulting in a deeper level of comprehension
Build an extensive and more complex core of high-frequency words	Teacher and students highlight high-frequency word(s) and use magnetic letters or wipe board to practice building, dismembering, and rebuilding words	Reads high-frequency words quickly, fluently, and automatically
Develop structural knowledge of words, i.e., compound words, contractions, prefixes, suffixes, and base words	Teacher and students highlight, analyze, build, and categorize words; students record words in word study notebook	Reads text fluently and with understanding

Change Over Time in Shared Reading and Guided Reading for Early and Transitional Readers of Fiction Texts *(continued)*

Early and Transitional Readers *Identifying/Setting Goals*	**Shared Reading** *Becoming Aware/Increasing Awareness of Reading Strategies*	**Guided Reading** *Developing and Gaining Control of Reading Strategies*
Learn about punctuation and how reading punctuation promotes fluency and comprehension	Teachers and students read text with fluency; teacher invites students to flag a selected form of punctuation for deeper analysis to understand its relationship to fluency and comprehension	Uses punctuation to read with fluency, expression, intonation, and comprehension
Develop a love for reading	Teacher and students read text with fluency, intonation, and expression	Reads for pleasure inside and outside of the school setting

Change Over Time in Shared Reading and Guided Reading for Emergent Readers of Nonfiction Texts

Emergent Readers *Identifying/Setting Goals*	**Shared Reading** *Becoming Aware/Increasing Awareness of Reading Strategies*	**Guided Reading** *Developing and Gaining Control of Reading Strategies*
Develop inquiry of real-world topics	Teacher models inquiry about real-world topics and invites student participation	Reads nonfiction texts to satisfy curiosity, shares and discusses new learning, and questions further
Become aware of strategic ways to build or activate prior knowledge and understand its relationship to comprehension	Teacher encourages and invites student participation in developing a "KWL" chart (what I *know*, what I *want* to know, what I *learned*) and discusses the importance of building and activating background knowledge	Begins to use background knowledge to support comprehension in learning new information
Become aware of text features, i.e., illustrations, photographs, specialized vocabulary, labels, captions, and table of contents in nonfiction texts	Teacher models and invites student participation in locating nonfiction text features, i.e., illustrations, photographs, specialized vocabulary, labels, captions, and table of contents and creates a chart along with pictures of features and their roles in text	Begins to recognize text features to assist with organization of information, thus leading to deeper comprehension
Become aware of ways to use text features, i.e., illustrations, photographs, specialized vocabulary, labels, captions, and table of contents when reading nonfiction	Teacher models and invites student participation in using nonfiction text features, i.e., illustrations, photographs, specialized vocabulary, labels, captions, and table of contents when reading text	Begins to use text features when applicable to assist with comprehension
Become aware of strategic ways to read nonfiction text and understand how this process is different from reading other genres	Teacher models and invites student participation in reading and discussing nonfiction texts, develops strategic ways to navigate through text, and creates chart on how to read nonfiction text	Begins to apply strategies for reading nonfiction text when reading independently

Change Over Time in Shared Reading and Guided Reading for Emergent Readers of Nonfiction Texts (*continued*)

Emergent Readers *Identifying/Setting Goals*	**Shared Reading** *Becoming Aware/Increasing Awareness of Reading Strategies*	**Guided Reading** *Developing and Gaining Control of Reading Strategies*
Become aware of how inquiry of a topic (setting a purpose for reading) affects how to navigate through the text, i.e., skim and scan to locate specific information	Teacher models and encourages student participation in how setting a purpose for reading determines how to navigate through text, i.e., skim and scan to locate specific information	Begins to use skim and scan strategies to locate specific information for reading
Develop a love for reading nonfiction texts	Teacher and students engage in using inquiry of real-world topics to motivate learners to read, study, and learn from nonfiction texts	Reads, enjoys, and learns from nonfiction texts; reads nonfiction inside and outside of the school setting

Change Over Time in Shared Reading and Guided Reading for Early and Transitional Readers of Nonfiction Texts

Early and Transitional Readers *Identifying/Setting Goals*	**Shared Reading** *Becoming Aware/Increasing Awareness of Reading Strategies*	**Guided Reading** *Developing and Gaining Control of Reading Strategies*
Develop inquiry of real-world topics	Teacher models inquiry about real-world topics and invites student participation	Reads nonfiction texts to satisfy curiosity, shares and discusses new learning, and questions further
Develop strategic ways to build or activate prior knowledge and understand its relationship to comprehension	Teacher encourages and invites student participation in developing a "KWL" chart (what I *know*, what I *want* to know, what I *learned*) and discusses the importance of building and activating background knowledge	Develops strategic ways to activate and use background knowledge to support comprehension
Identify and use more complex text features, i.e., headings, specialized vocabulary, photographs, diagrams, labels and captions, table of contents, index, and glossary when reading nonfiction	Teacher models and invites student participation in identifying, locating, and using nonfiction text features, i.e., headings, specialized vocabulary, photographs, diagrams, labels and captions, table of contents, index, and glossary, thus leading to deeper comprehension	Uses text features to assist with organization of information, thus leading to deeper comprehension
Identify specific text structures associated with nonfiction texts, i.e., enumeration, sequence or time order, compare-contrast, cause-effect, and problem-solution, and use cue words for basis of identification	Teacher models, introduces, or revisits texts and invites student participation in identifying nonfiction text structures using cue words for basis of identification, and develops charts for future reference	Uses knowledge of cue words to identify text structure, thus leading to deeper comprehension
Increase awareness of how inquiry of a topic (setting a purpose for reading) affects how to navigate through the text, i.e., skim and scan text to locate specific information	Teacher models and encourages student participation in using the table of contents and index for locating specific parts for reading, i.e., skim and scan text	Uses skim and scan strategies to locate specific information for reading

Change Over Time in Shared Reading and Guided Reading for Early and Transitional Readers of Nonfiction Texts *(continued)*

Early and Transitional Readers *Identifying/Setting Goals*	**Shared Reading** *Becoming Aware/Increasing Awareness of Reading Strategies*	**Guided Reading** *Developing and Gaining Control of Reading Strategies*
Become aware of the "why and how" of recording in their logs, i.e., making their thinking visible; sharing and discussing with others leads to deeper comprehension	Teacher develops an understanding of the "why and how" of recording in their logs, i.e., making their thinking visible; sharing and discussing with others leads to deeper comprehension	Records new learning and questions in log, i.e., makes thinking visible; shares, discusses, and learns from group
Develop strategic ways to read nonfiction text and understand how this process is different from reading other genres	Teacher models and invites student participation in reading and discussing nonfiction texts, develops strategic ways to navigate through text, and creates chart on how to read nonfiction text	Applies strategies for reading nonfiction text when reading independently
Develop a love for reading nonfiction texts	Teacher and students engage in using inquiry of real-world topics to motivate learners to read, study, and learn from nonfiction texts	Reads, enjoys, and learns from nonfiction texts; reads nonfiction inside and outside of the school setting

Tools for the Teacher

- Storage areas for books
- Highlighter tape (translucent, in different colors and widths)
- Wikki Stix
- Sticky notes (different sizes)
- Correction tape
- Framing cards or tools
- Flags to mark text
- Sentence strips
- Pocket charts
- Blank index cards (word cards)
- Magnetic boards
- Marker board
- Chart paper
- Pointers
- Magnetic letters
- Transparencies of poems or texts

Uses of Sticky Notes and Flags

Emergent readers

- Draw picture of favorite part from story.
- Draw illustrations to match text.
- Cover chosen word/s and have students supply missing word/s (cloze procedure).
- Cover ending punctuation and elicit predictions.
- Flag favorite words, phrases, and repetitive phrases and add to classroom chart.
- Flag specialized vocabulary for in-depth study.
- Synthesize and summarize information using the sketch-to-stretch strategy.
- Cover specific nonfiction features of text and elicit predictions (bold words, captions, words or definition in glossary, table of contents).

Early and transitional readers

- Cover specific nonfiction features of text and elicit predictions (bold words, captions, words or definition in glossary, table of contents).
- Cover words and have students supply missing words (cloze procedure).
- Synthesize and summarize text at the end of the page/chapter of text (nonfiction and fiction).
- Read selected text and have students illustrate on sticky notes.
- Cover captions and write predictions to match photographs.
- Flag parts of text for questioning and clarifying.
- Flag favorite words/phrases to add to students' reading/writing log to be used as a resource for writing.
- Flag specialized vocabulary for in-depth study.

Uses of Framing Cards and Highlighter Tape

Framing cards and highlighter tape can be used to highlight specific language features for in-depth study.

Emergent readers	*Early and transitional readers*
• Whole-group and small-group shared reading	• Whole-group and small-group shared reading
• Specialized vocabulary (favorite words or phrases)	• Specialized vocabulary (favorite words or phrases)
• Where to begin reading	• Parts of speech (verbs, adjectives, nouns)
• Spaces between words	• Rhyming words
• Word (concept of word)	• Contractions
• Letter (concept of letter)	• Compound words
• Letter in student's name or friend's name	• Suffixes
• Known letters (uppercase and lowercase)	• Prefixes
• Letter with the sound of ———	• Synonyms, antonyms, homonyms, homophones
• Upper- or lowercase letter	• Pronouns
• Word that begins like student's name	• Repetitive text patterns
• Word that begins with ———	• Root words
• Word that ends with ———	• Word endings
• Word with one or two parts (syllables)	• Vowel patterns
• Rhyming words	• Transition words
• Known words	• Letter clusters
• Beginning letter of word	• Digraphs
• Ending letter of word	• Definitions
• Ending punctuation	• Bold words
• Repetitive text patterns	• Italicized words
• Bold words	• Cue words (indicate text structure)
• Italicized words	• Punctuation (beginning and ending punctuation, comma, quotation marks)
	• Capitalization

Uses of Sentence Strips, Pocket Chart, Word Cards (Index Cards)

Emergent readers
Whole-group and small-group

- Reread text for enjoyment.

- Rebuild easy familiar text (poems, stories, nonfiction).

- Match text on top of text.

- Match text underneath text.

- Match text to illustrations.

- Match illustrations to text.

- Match high-frequency words on top of words in text.

- Use cut-up sentence strips or word cards to fill in missing word from text.

- Write or highlight a word from the text—invite students to generate other words that begin the same, rime, or end the same; write words on cards and have students sort words in pocket chart.

Early and transitional readers
Whole-group and small-group

- Reread text on sentence strips for enjoyment.

- Rebuild texts in pocket chart (poems, stories, nonfiction texts).

- Use cut-up sentence strips or word cards to fill in missing word from text.

- Write a word from the text—invite students to generate other words that begin the same (blends, consonant clusters, diagraphs, prefixes), rhyme, or end the same (diagraphs, suffixes, rime patterns).

- Write generated words on cards and have students sort words in pocket chart (visual, sound, meaning).

- Highlight word in text and match to definition.

- Match charts, maps, sidebars, headings, labels, and/or captions to written text on sentence strips.

- Use highlighter tape or colored transparency to highlight special nonfiction features, i.e., bold words, italicized words).

- Highlight cue words from text that indicate text structures (example: cause/effect—so, therefore).

- Locate a word and generate synonyms, antonyms, or homophones for the word.

Uses of Wipe-Off Board and Chart Paper

Emergent readers	*Early and transitional readers*
• Rewrite favorite poems on charts to be read, reread, and enjoyed.	• Rewrite favorite poems on charts to be read, reread, and enjoyed.
• Record favorite words, phrases, and repetitive phrases on classroom chart.	• Record favorite words, phrases, and repetitive phrases on classroom chart.
• Chart an in-depth study of specialized vocabulary (i.e., record word from text, from teacher, from students) and record student-friendly definition.	• Chart in-depth study of specialized vocabulary (i.e., record word from text, from teacher, from students) and record student-friendly definition.
• Chart genre studies, i.e., fairy tales, poetry, nonfiction, and folktales.	• Chart genre studies, i.e., fairy tales, poetry, nonfiction, and folktales.
• Chart authors' names and titles of favorite books including nonfiction text to be revisited, enjoyed, and recommended.	• Chart authors' names and titles of favorite books including nonfiction text to be revisited, enjoyed, and recommended.
• Chart nonfiction features and their role in text.	• Chart nonfiction features and their role in text.
• Draw a Venn diagram and compare and contrast information from reading.	• Draw a Venn diagram and compare and contrast information from reading.
• Chart predictions from text when using cloze procedure.	• Chart predictions from text when using cloze procedure.

Shared Reading Plan

Title of Book	Setting	Characters	Problem	Solution	
Comprehension	Phonological and Phonemic Awareness (if applicable)	Phonics	Vocabulary	Fluency	Literacy Corners

Shared Reading Plan

Title of Book	Setting	Characters	Problem	Solution
The Farm Concert	On a farm	The farmer, cow, sheep, pig, dog, frog, and duck	The animals were all making loud animal noises at the same time (in concert with each other) and the farmer couldn't sleep.	The farmer yelled at the animals. Then the animals made softer noises so the farmer could sleep.

Comprehension	Phonological and Phonemic Awareness (if applicable)	Phonics	Vocabulary	Fluency
• *Inferring*: What did the author not tell us? • *Retelling*: What happened in the story? • *Connections*: Does this story remind you of . . . • *Questions*: Do you have any questions? Were your questions answered? • *Expression*: Acting out the story—drama	• Add the "er" sound to the end of farm. What's the new word? • Take away the /w/ sound in "went" and add the /s/ sound. What's the new word? • Add the /n/ sound to the end of moo. What is the new word? • What word rhymes with sheep? (sleep) • How are they the same (eep sound)	• Highlight the word "went." Students build "went" with magnetic letters or students write the word "went." Fluency practice: can, the	*Before Reading:* Concert: musical entertainment; harmony *After Reading:* T: We are having a Christmas musical later this month and we will all be singing in concert with each other. C: When we all read together, we are reading in concert with each other.	• Read text with fluency, intonation, and expression. • Revisited and reread text with fluency, intonation, and expression and invite and encourage participation.

Literacy Corners

- Reread text for enjoyment.
- Rebuild text beside pictures.
- Rebuild text and match pictures to text.
- Listen to tape of text.

APPENDIX SECTION II

Professional Development Activities

These activities are designed for literacy team meetings, whereby teachers engage in a reading workshop format that mirrors their work with students. It utilizes an apprenticeship philosophy of working together in social contexts to learn a new strategy or skill. For instance, if a teacher is learning to conduct book discussions with students, he or she should join a teacher book club and apply the process with other teachers. During literacy team meetings with colleagues, teachers can establish a workshop format that includes literature discussion groups, followed by debriefing conversations on the quality of the group's interaction. Similarly, if teachers expect students to use the rubrics in Section IV of this Appendix for assessing literature discussions, the first step would be to use the rubric with colleagues during book discussions. Or if a teacher is learning how to assess fluency, the literacy team meeting will provide a supportive context for acquiring this critical skill. During their participation in the team meeting, teachers should become aware of how language is used to communicate knowledge and foster deeper comprehension; they should also begin to notice the features of successful discourse—specifically, the responsibility of each member to listen, respond, and engage in constructive talk. Building this awareness is necessary for teachers' ability to provide similar experiences to students as they learn how to build discourse chains around common literacy events. All professional activities in this section are intended to provide meaningful and relevant practice that will parallel reading instruction in the classroom. Teachers are encouraged to read and revisit related chapters of this book as they engage in the professional activities.

Teacher Book Clubs

A teacher of reading must also be a motivated consumer of books. The best professional development for teachers is to participate in book discussions with others. Teacher book clubs should become a natural part of a school's literacy plan. Here are some things to consider for starting a teacher book club:

- Find a common time when teachers can meet together for 20–30 minutes to discuss books. Establish a schedule for meetings (at least once a month), arrange for refreshments, and generally provide a relaxing environment for talking about books.
- Establish guidelines for how the book club will function—for example, how to select books for discussion, how to prepare for the discussion group, and how to engage in constructive conversations. At the end of each book discussion, take a few moments to reflect on your own comprehending process. Use the rubrics in Section IV of this Appendix to assess how well the group participated in the book discussion.
- Apply this process to your work with students—specifically on how language is used to promote deeper comprehension. You may want to videotape a teacher book discussion and share this example with your students. Encourage your students to observe how discussion groups share similar features.

Teacher Reading Log

Over years of successful reading, teachers have acquired a mental toolbox of effective strategies. These strategies should be shared with students. One of the best ways to do this is by keeping a personal reading log. Here, teachers demonstrate the value of reading through literate actions, not just "instructional words." Your reading log can be a valuable teaching tool, serving as a model for scaffolding students toward similar goals. A teacher's reading log might include the following sections:

- Reflections on how you learned to read, including important strategies that you use each time you read.
- A cumulative listing of books you have read, including date, type of book, brief summary of 2–3 sentences, and a personal rating.
- Favorite words and phrases from books (be sure to include a note on the source and page number for each).
- Book reflections, including questions and comments.

Reading Survey

Take the following survey to rate your reading behavior. How do your perceptions and habits influence the way you teach reading in your own classroom?

- Do you have a habit of reading for pleasure?
- Do you read a variety of books, including different genres and authors?
- Do you regularly share books you are reading with your students?
- Are books a common topic of discussion among your friends and family?
- Do you frequently visit the library or bookstore for enjoyment?
- Do you frequently purchase books for friends and family?

Literacy team meetings should be based on a workshop approach and should include time to read books. Teachers can bring in several copies of favorite books and talk briefly about each.

Then teachers can select one or more books for independent reading. We see independent reading as a critical component of reading workshop in the classroom, so let's place the same value on time for teachers to engage in independent reading during team meetings. Create a plan of action to significantly increase the number of books that you read each year. Record the number of books read on the team meeting wall, including genres and recommendations. Use anchor charts and text maps to deepen your understanding of the books you read. Whatever we expect of our students, we teachers should expect the same for ourselves. Create a literate environment during literacy team meetings that echoes the literate environment of your classroom. Share this information with students.

Planning for Shared Reading

Reread the section of Chapter 3 on shared reading and discuss with the literacy team. Analyze the shared reading charts for how to integrate the reading process, including strategies for word solving, fluency, vocabulary, and comprehension. View the videotaped lessons on shared reading from the DVD that accompanies this book. Record observations of teacher-student interactions and analyze these according to a scale of help. Discuss the example of *The Farm Concert* from the Shared Reading Plan in Section I of this Appendix, and use the blank planning guide to guide your analysis of other shared reading texts.

Prompting Versus Teaching

- Reread and discuss the sections from Chapter 3 on questioning and prompting. Observe videotaped lessons of teacher-student interactions during reading groups. Record examples of the teacher's language and code these as questions or prompts. Discuss how the language is promoting (or interfering with) deeper comprehension.
- Audiotape your interactions with two different groups of readers—for example, an emergent and a transitional reading group. How do you adjust your language to reflect the learning needs of each group? Record a few examples and bring to your literacy team meeting for colleague discussion.

Strategic Processes for Comprehending

- Reread and discuss Chapters 4 and 5 on strategic behaviors. Analyze your own reading behaviors and discuss these with colleagues. Become more aware of how you comprehend when you read. What are the most important strategies you use to construct meaning? Reflect on this in your reading log.
- Discuss the importance of self-correcting behavior for developing deeper comprehension. Look at the videos from Tape 2 of *Results That Last* (Dorn and Soffos 2002) and examine the self-correcting behaviors of the different readers. Look for evidence of self-correcting behavior in general life, language, writing, and reading. Consider the implications for this critical strategy in teaching for deep comprehension.
- Listen to several examples of fluent reading and use the NAEP fluency scale to assess the four fluency levels. Some teachers have found it helpful to use audio- or videotaped recordings of children's reading at different points on the rating scale. As students read, teachers can use a running record to document reading behaviors while simultaneously coding fluent reading with slash marks that indicate hesitations or parsing of words

into language phrases. Team meetings that focus on the characteristics of fluent reading can provide a problem-solving context for assessing fluency, followed by a plan of action to promote fluency during readers' workshop.
- Select three or more of the most important strategic behaviors described in Chapters 4 and 5 and create a plan for teaching them to your students. Reflect on your results in your reading log. Share this information with your colleagues and discuss what went well and what you might change.

The Classroom Library

Reread Chapter 6 on the reading workshop. Discuss the need for volume reading and the importance of creating a literate environment that includes a classroom library as the centerpiece of the reading workshop. Rate your classroom library on a scale of 1 (impoverished), 2 (neutral, some evidence), and 3 (enriched).

- The classroom environment includes comfortable places for children to read and relax. The space is utilized to accommodate independent reading, peer reading, and literature discussion groups with the teacher.
- The classroom library is central to the reading workshop, including predictable texts and easy books for beginning readers and more complex texts for transitional and fluent readers.
- The classroom library contains a variety of books, including a range of genres, collections by favorite authors, nonfiction texts, magazines, and other interesting reading materials.
- The classroom library is organized and run by the teacher and students, including a class-generated system for categorizing books in logical ways.
- The classroom library includes creative ways to advertise books, including attractive book displays with covers visible, spotlighted books (for instance, new books or a special author), and a chart with student recommended books.
- The classroom library includes a special section for student- or class-published books.

APPENDIX SECTION III

Glossary of Genres

Book Lists by Genre and Grade Level

Genre Descriptions, Questions, and Text Maps

Graphic Organizers

Glossary of Genres

Autobiography: The story of a real person's life that is written by that person.

Biography: The story of a real person's life that is written by another person.

Fable: A story that contains a moral and usually has animals that speak and act like human beings.

Fairy tale: A kind of folktale that almost always involves some element of magic, with good triumphing over evil.

Fantasy: A story containing elements that are not based in the world as it exists, such as talking animals or magic.

Folktale: A story, often with a message, that was initially passed on by word of mouth.

Historical fiction: A fictional story with real and invented characters that takes place during a historical time.

Memoir: A type of nonfiction that centers around an event, object, or person that was significant to the author.

Mystery: A suspenseful story about a puzzling event that is not solved until the end of the story.

Nonfiction: All of the text is based on facts and not made up.

Poetry: A verse written to inspire thought.

Realistic fiction: A story using made-up characters that takes place in modern times.

Science fiction: A story that blends futuristic technology with scientific fact and fiction.

Tall tale: A story where the main character is larger than life and has a specific job; the problem is solved in an incredible or funny way, and exaggerated details describe things greater than they really are.

Book Lists by Genre and Grade Level

Fairy Tales/Folktales

Grades K–2
Adelita, Tomie dePaola (Putnam)
Bubba the Cowboy Prince, A Fractured Texas Tale, Helen Ketteman (Scholastic)
Dinorella, A Prehistoric Fairy Tale, Pamela Duncan Edwards and Henry Cole (Scholastic)
Dusty Locks and the Three Bears, Susan Lowell (Scholastic)
The Fourth Little Pig, Teresa Celsi (Steck-Vaughn)
The Frog Prince Continued, Jon Scieszka (Scholastic)
Little Red Riding Hood, A Newfangled Prairie Tale, Lisa Campbell Ernst (Scholastic)
The Three Little Jaavelinas, Susan Lowell (Scholastic)
The Three Little Wolves and the Big Bad Pig, Eugene Trivizas
The Three Pigs, David Wiesner (Scholastic)
The True Story of the Three Little Pigs, Jon Scieszka (Scholastic)
Who's Been Eating My Porridge? Nick Ward (Scholastic)

Grades 3–5
Dove Isabau, Jane Yolen (Harcourt Brace)
The Dragon and the Unicorn, Lynne Cherry (Harcourt Brace)
The Egyptian Cinderella, Shirley Clemo (HarperCollins)
The Golden Sandal, A Middle Eastern Cinderella Story, Rebecca Hickox (Holiday House)
The Irish Cinderella, Shirley Clemo (HarperCollins)
The Korean Cinderella, Shirley Clemo (HarperCollins)
Lon Po Po, a Red Riding Hood Story from China, Ed Young (Scholastic)
Rapunzel, Paul O. Zelinsky (Ruffin)
Rumpelstiltskin, Paul O. Zelinsky (Ruffin)
Sleeping Ugly, Jane Yolen (Coward McCann)
The Stinky Cheese Man and Other Fairly Stupid Tales, Jon Scieszka and Lane Smith

The Twelve Dancing Princesses, Marianna Mayer (Mulberry Books)

Tall Tales

Suitable for All Grades
The Bunyans, Audrey Wood (Scholastic)
John Henry, Julius Lester (Scholastic)
Johnny Appleseed, Steven Kelogg (Scholastic)
Mike Fink, Steven Kelogg (Scholastic)
New York's Bravest, Mary Pope Osborne (Knopf Books for Young Readers)
Paul Bunyan, Steven Kelogg (Scholastic)
Pecos Bill, Steven Kelogg (Scholastic)
Swamp Angel, Anne Isaacs (Scholastic)

Grades K–2
The Checker Playing Hound Dog: Tall Tales from a Southwestern Storyteller, Joe Hayes (Mariposa)
Feliciana Feydra Leroux, Tynia Thomassie and Cat Bowman Smith (Little, Brown)
I Was Born About 10,000 Years Ago: A Tall Tale, Steven Kelogg (William Morrow)
Master Man: A Tall Tale of Nigeria (West African Folktales), Aaron Shepard and David Wisniewski (HarperCollins)
A Million Fish More or Less, Patricia McKissack (Knopf)
Shaq and the Beanstalk and Other Very Tall Tales, Shaquille O'Neal and Shane Evans (Jump at the Sun)
Tailypo: A Newfangled Tall Tale, Angela Shelf Medearis (Sterling Brown)

Grades 3–5
Mountain Men: True Grit and Tall Tales, Andrew Glass (Doubleday Books for Young Readers)
A Small Tall Tale from the Far Far North, Peter Sis (Farrar, Straus, and Giroux)

The Tallest Leprechaun: A Tall Tale of Terrible Teasing, Emily Grace Koenig (Little Treasure Publications)
Three Strong Women: A Tall Tale from Japan, Claus Stamm (Viking Books)

Fables

Suitable for All Grades
Fables, Arnold Lobel (Harper Trophy)
Fabulous Fables: Using Fables with Children, Grades 2–4 (Good Year Books)
Greek Myths for Young Children, Marcia Williams (Candlewick)
The Maestro, Number 2: Preposterous Fables for Unusual Children, Judd Palmer (Bayeux Arts)
The Magic Fish, Freya Littledale (Scholastic)
Multicultural Fables and Fairy Tales (Grades 1–4), Tara McCarthy (Scholastic)
Three Aesop Fox Fables, Paul Galdone (Seabury)

Grades K–2
The Ant and the Grasshopper, Amy Poole (Holiday House)
Fables from Aesop, Val Biro (Wright Group)
Fredrick, Leo Lionni (Pantheon)
Math Fables, Greg Tang (Scholastic)
Seven Blind Mice, Ed Young (Philomel)
Squids Will Be Squids: Fresh Morals, Beastly Fables, Jon Scieszka and Lane Smith (Puffin Books)
Town Mouse, Country Mouse, Jan Brett (Putnam)

Grades 3–5
Amos and Boris, William Steig (Farrar)
The Children of Odin: The Books of Northern Myths, Padraic Colum (Alladin)
The Lion and the Mouse, Ed Young (Doubleday)
The Monkey and the Crocodile, Paul Galone (Seabury)
Old Granny Fox, Thorton W. Burgess (Dover Publications)
The Rainstick, a Fable, Sandra Chisholm Robinson (Falcon)

A Sip of Aesop, Jane Yolen and Karen Barbour (Blue Sky)

Fantasy

Grades K–2
Abel's Island, William Steig (Farrar)
All I See, Cynthia Rylant (Orchard Books)
A Bear Called Paddington, Michael Bond (Houghton Mifflin)
Bunnicula, Deborah and James Howe (Atheneum)
Charlotte's Web, E. B. White (Harper and Row)
The Chocolate Touch, Patrick Catling (Morrow)
Click Clack Moo: Cows That Type, Doreen Cronin (Simon and Schuster)
The Cuckoo Child, Dick King-Smith (Hyperion)
Jumanji, Chris Van Allsburg (Houghton Mifflin)
Koala Lou, Mem Fox (Harcourt Brace)
Magic School Bus (series), Joanna Cole (Scholastic)
Magic Tree House (series), Mary Pope Osborne (Random House)
The Mouse and the Motorcycle, Beverly Cleary (Morrow)
Pippi Longstocking, Astrid Lindgren (Viking)
Possum Magic, Mem Fox (Harcourt Brace)
Shrek, Wiliam Steig (Farrar)
Stuart Little, E. B. White (Harper and Row)
Time Warp Trio, Jon Scieszka (Viking)
Wemberly Worried, Kevin Henkes (Greenwillow)
The Wind in the Willows, Kenneth Grahame (Holiday House)
Winnie-the-Pooh, A. A. Milne (Dutton)

Grades 3–5
Alice's Adventures in Wonderland, Lewis Carroll (Macmillan)
The Borrowers, Mary Norton (Harcourt Brace)
Ella Enchanted, Gail Levine (HarperCollins)
The Garden of Abdul Gasazi, Chris Van Allsburg (Houghton Mifflin)
Harry Potter (series), J. K. Rowling (Scholastic)
James and the Giant Peach, Roald Dahl (Knopf)

The Lion, the Witch, and the Wardrobe, C. S. Lewis (Macmillan)
Mrs. Frisby and the Rats of NIMH, Robert O'Brien (Atheneum)
The Phantom Tollbooth, Norton Juster (Random House)
Poppy, Avi (Orchard)
Sector 7, David Wiesner (Clarion)
The Tale of Despereaux, Kate DiCamillo (Candlewick)
Tuck Everlasting, Natalie Babbit (HarperCollins)
Watership Down, Richard Adams (Macmillian)
A Wrinkle in Time, Madeleine L'Engle (Farrar)

Historical Fiction

Grades K–2
Dakota Dugout, Ann Tuner (Macmillan)
Little House in the Big Woods, Laura Ingalls Wilder (Harper)
Magic Tree House (series), Mary Pope Osborne (also fantasy) (Random House)
Mailing May, Michael Tunnell (Greenwillow)
My Brother's Keeper: Virginia's Diary (*My America* series), Mary Pope Osborne (Scholastic)
Night Journeys, Avi (Morrow)
Pink and Say, Patricia Polacco (Philomel)
Sadako and the Thousand Paper Cranes, Eleanor Coeer (Putnam)
The Salem Witch Trials : An Unsolved Mystery from History, Jane Yolen and Heidi Elisabet Yolen Stemple (Simon and Schuster)
Sarah, Plain and Tall, Patricia MacLachlan (Harper)
Shh! We're Writing the Constitution, Jean Fritz (Putnam)
Sleds on Boston Common, Louise Borden (McElderry)
Squanto's Journey, Joseph Bruchac (Harcourt)
Stone Fox, John Gardiner (Cronwell)
The Wall, Eve Bunting (Houghton Mifflin)

Grades 3–5
The Birchbark House, Louise Erdrich (Hyperion)
The Borning Room, Paul Fleischman (HarperCollins)
Bud, Not Buddy, Christopher Paul Curtis (Delacorte)
Bull Run, Paul Fleischman (HarperCollins)
Caddie Woodlawn, Carol Brink (Macmillan)
Charley Skedaddle, Patricia Beatty (Morrow)
Crispin: The Cross of Lead, Avi (Hyperion)
Dandelions, Eve Bunting (Harcourt Brace)
The Devil's Arithmetic, Jane Yolen (Penguin)
Encounter, Jane Yolen (Harcourt)
Esperanza Rising, Pam Munoz Ryan (Scholastic)
Hundred Dresses, Elenor Estes (Harcourt)
Jip: His Story, Katherine Paterson (Lodestar)
Johnny Tremain, Ester Forbes (Houghton Mifflin)
A Long Way from Chicago, Richard Peck (Dial)
The Midwife's Apprentice, Karen Cushman (Clarion)
Morning Girl, Michael Dorris (Hyperion)
Nettie's Trip South, Ann Turner (Macmillan)
Nightjohn, Gary Paulsen (Delacorte)
Nora Ryan's Song, Patricia Reilly Giff (Delacorte)
Number the Stars, Lois Lowry (Houghton Mifflin)
Our Only May Amelia, Jennifer Holm (HarperCollins)
Out of the Dust, Karen Hesse (Scholastic)
Roll of Thunder, Hear My Cry, Mildred Taylor (Dial)
Rose Blanche, Christophe Gallaz and Roberto Innocenti (Creative Education)
Shades of Gray, Carolyn Reeder (Macmillan)
A Single Shard, Linda Sue Park (Clarion)
The Slave Dancer, Paula Fox (Bradbury Press)
True Confessions of Charlotte Doyle, Avi (Orchard)
The Witch of Blackbird Pond, Elizabeth George Speare (Houghton Mifflin)
Year of Impossible Goodbyes, Sook Choi (Houghton Mifflin)

Realistic Fiction

Grades K–2
Alexander and the Terrible, Horrible, No Good, Very Bad Day, Judith Viorist (Antheneum)

Also Applesauce, Joanna Hurwitz (Morrow)
Amelia Bedelia, Peggy Parish (Harper and Row)
Attaboy, Sam! Lois Lowry (Houghton Mifflin)
The Best Christmas Pageant Ever, Barbara Robinson (Harper)
Cam Jenson (series), David Adler (Viking) (mystery)
Encyclopedia Brown, Boy Detective, Donald Sobol (Nelson)
Get Ready for Second Grade, Amber Brown, Paula Danziger (Putnam)
The Graduation of Jake Moon, Barbara Park (Antheneum)
Henry and Mudge: The First Book of Their Adventures, Cynthia Rylant (Bradbury)
Homesick, Jean Fritz (Putnam) (memoir)
Judy Moody, Megan McDonald (Candlewick)
Junie B. Jone, First Grader (at last!), Barbara Park (Farrar)
Locomotion, Jacqueline Woodsen (Grosset and Dunlap)
Marvin Redpost, Louis Sachar (Farrar)
Muggie Maggie, Beverly Cleary (Morrow)
Nana Upstairs and Nana Downstairs, Tomie dePaola (Viking)
Nate the Great, Marjorie Wiseman Sharmat (Putnam) (mystery)
Ramona the Pest, Beverly Cleary (Morrow)
Skinnybones, Barbara Park (Knopf)
The Stories Julian Tells, Ann Cameron (Knopf)
Thank You, Mr. Falker, Patricia Polacco (Philomel)
26 Fairmont Avenue, Tomie dePaola (Putnam) (memoir)

Grades 3–5

Anastasia Krupnik, Lois Lowry (Houghton Mifflin)
Are You There, God? It's Me, Margaret, Judy Blume (Bradbury)
Because of Winn-Dixie, Kate DiCamillo (Candlewick)
The Best Christmas Pageant Ever, Barbara Robinson (Harper)
Bridge to Terabithia, Katherine Paterson (Crowell)
Dear Mr. Henshaw, Beverly Cleary (Morrow)
The Egypt Game, Zilpha Snyder (Antheneum) (mystery)
Everything on a Waffle, Peggy Horvath (Farrar)
Frindle, Andrew Clements (Simon and Schuster)
From the Mixed-Up Files of Mrs. Basil E. Frankweiler, E. L. Konigsburg (Atheneum)
The Great Gilly Hopkins, Katherine Paterson (Crowell)
Hatchet, Gary Paulsen (Bradbury)
Holes, Louis Sachar (Farrar)
In the Year of the Boar and Jackie Robinson, Bette Bao Lord (Harper and Row)
Love, Ruby Lavender, Deborah Wiles (Harcourt Brace)
Love That Dog, Sharon Creech (Joanna Colter)
Maniac Magee, Jerry Spinelli (Little, Brown)
Nothing But the Truth, Avi (Orchard)
Ruby Hollar, Sharon Creech (HarperCollins)
Shiloh, Phyllis Naylor (Antheneum)
Tales of a Fourth Grade Nothing, Judy Blume (Dutton)
Toning the Sweep, Angela Johnson (Orchard)
The Trouble with Tuck, Theodore Taylor (Doubleday)
The View from Saturday, E. L. Konisburg (Antheneum)
Walk Two Moons, Sharon Creech (HarperCollins)
The Westing Game, Ellen Raskin (Dutton) (mystery)
Wringer, Jerry Spinelli (HarperCollins)
Yolanda's Genius, Carol Fenner (McElderry)

Biography

Alexander Graham Bell, Leonard Fisher (Atheneum)
The Amazing Life of Benjamin Franklin, James Giblin (Scholastic)
Amelia Earhart: Courage in the Sky, Mona Kerby (Viking)
Bigmama's, Donald Crews (Greenwillow) (autobiography)
Bill Peet: An Autobiography, Bill Peet (Houghton Mifflin)
Brave Harriet, Marissa Moss (Harcourt)

Appendix Section III Glossary of Genres; Book Lists; Genre Descriptions; Graphic Organizers

Brother Sun, Sister Moon: The Life and Stories of St. Francis, Margaret Mayo (Little, Brown)
The Dinosaurs of Waterhouse Hawkins, Barbara Kerley (Scholastic)
Don't You Know There's a War On? James Stevenson (Greenwillow) (autobiography)
Eleanor, Barbara Cooney (Viking)
Hank Aaron: Brave in Every Way, Peter Golenbock (Harcourt)
The Heroine of the Titanic: A Tale Both True and Otherwise of the Life of Molly Brown, Jan Blos (Morrow)
Johnny Appleseed, Steven Kellogg (Morrow)
Laura Ingalls Wilder: Young Pioneer, Beatrice Gormley (Aladdin)
The Librarian Who Measured the Earth, Katheryn Lasky (Little, Brown)
Lincoln: A Photobiography, Russell Freedman (Clarion)
Little Louis and the Jazz Band, Angela Meaderis (Lodestar)
Michelangelo, Diane Stanley (Harper)
Out of the Darkness: The Story of Louis Braille, Russell Freedman (Clarion)
Rocks in His Head, Carol Otis Hurst (Greenwillow)
Rosa Parks: My Story, Rosa Parks (Dial) (autobiography)
Shoeless Joe and Black Betsy, Phil Bildner (Simon and Schuster)
Shooting for the Moon: The Amazing Life and Times of Annie Oakley, Stephen Krensky (Farrar)
Snowflake Bentley, Jacqueline Briggs Martin (Houghton Mifflin)
So You Want to Be President? Judith St. George (Philomel)
The Story of Christopher Columbus, Admiral of the Ocean Sea, Mary Pope Osborne (Dell)
And Then What Happened, Paul Revere? Jean Fritz (Coward)
Through My Eyes, Ruby Bridges (Scholastic) (autobiography)
Traveling Man: The Journey of Ibn Battuta, James Rumford (Houghton Mifflin)
Ty Cobb: Bad Boy of Baseball, S. Dramer (Random House)
Who Was Ben Franklin? Dennis Brindell Fradin (Grosset and Dunlap)
You Forgot Your Skirt, Amelia Bloomer! Shana Corey (Scholastic)
You Want Women to Vote, Lizzie Stanton? Jean Fritz (Putnam)

Poetry

All the Small Poems and Fourteen More, Valerie Worth (Sunburst)
Antarctic Antics: A Book of Penguin Poems, Judy Sierra (Harcourt Brace)
Color Me a Rhyme, Jane Yolen (Wordsong and Boyds Mills Press)
Creatures of the Earth, Sea, and Sky, Georgia Heard (Wordsong)
Dogs Rule, Daniel Kirk (Hyperion Books)
The Dream Keeper and Other Poems, Langston Hughes (Scholastic)
The Golden Books Family Treasury of Poetry, selected by Louis Untermeyer (Golden Books)
Good Books, Good Times, selected by Lee Bennett Hopkins (Trumpet Club)
Hailstones and Halibut Bones, Mary O'Neill (Doubleday)
Honey, I Love, Eloise Greenfield (Harper Trophy)
Lizzards, Frogs, and Polliwogs, Douglas Florian (Scholastic)
Mrs. Cole on an Onion Roll and Other School Poems, Kalli Dakos (Scholastic)
Popcorn, James Stevenson (Scholastic)
Ride a Purple Pellican, Jack Prelutsky (Greenwillow)
The Great Frog Race and Other Poems, Kristine O'Connell George (Clarion)
The Random House Book of Poetry for Children, selected by Jack Prelutsky (Random House)
The Twentieth Century Children's Poetry Treasury, selected by Jack Prelutsky (Knopf)

Genre Descriptions, Questions, and Text Maps
Fiction

Background Information

The term fiction is used to describe works of the imagination. A large part of the appeal of fiction is its ability to evoke the entire spectrum of human emotion: to distract our minds, to give us hope in times of despair, to make us laugh, or to let us experience empathy without attachment. Fictional works—novels, pictures, stories, fairy tales, fables, films, comics—may be partly based on factual occurrences but always contain some imaginary content.

Questions for Fiction

The following questions can be used with any fiction book or story. Choose the questions that fit the level of your children and the level of the story read. The children are to give reasons for their answers to the yes/no questions.

Setting

1. Where did the book take place?
2. Why did it take place there?
3. Could it have taken place anywhere else?
4. Does the setting play a major role in the story?
5. How accurately are you able to see the place when the story occurs in your mind? Explain.
6. How does the character use the environment?
7. When does the story take place?
8. Did it happen before you were born?
9. Does the time play a major role in the story?
10. Does the story happen in an appropriate place and time?
11. Could it happen now?
12. Could this story really happen?
13. Could it happen to you?
14. Would you like it to happen to you? Why?
15. Is there sufficient description?
16. Is there a unity of time and place, or does the story change from time to time or place to place?

Characters

1. Who is the main character?
   a. Is he/she believable?
   b. Is the main character simple or complex?
2. What techniques did the author use to portray the character?
3. How is the main character consistent in the story?
4. Who were the other characters?
5. Which characters do you like best and why?
6. Would you or your family like to have the character for a friend?
7. Have you ever done the same thing as this character?
8. How would you have acted differently from the way any characters acted during the crucial points of the story?
9. Is there a character you read about who is like you? In what ways?
10. How is a character in the story made to seem good or bad, likable or unlikable, interesting or dull?
11. Are characters driven by forces within themselves that they cannot control?
12. Are characters driven by forces around them that they cannot control (society, the times they live in, situations, other characters, etc.)?
13. Are characters driven by events they cannot control?
14. Does the author justify actions of characters that you feel are wrong?

15. Do the characters always act in ways that you think are appropriate for them?
16. Can you make a list of the good and bad points of a main character?

Plot

1. What would you change about the beginning or ending of the story?
2. How well are events in the story tied together?
3. Do you feel the story moves rapidly enough?
4. Name at least two problems or conflicts in the story. What were the author's solutions? Categorize these under Man vs. Man, Man vs. Nature, Man vs. Society, or Man vs. Himself/Herself.
5. Do you feel caught up, excited, and involved in the action of the story?
6. Are the events in the story important?
7. Is the story believable?

Mood

1. Does the author communicate a feeling that goes with the story?
2. What words characterize the story?
3. How were your feelings changed as you read the story?
4. Is there an undercurrent or hidden mood in the story?
5. Is there a tension in the story that makes you want to finish it?
6. How real is the mood?
7. How could the author have enhanced the mood or made it more subtle?

Theme or Moral

1. Does the title state the theme?
2. What are you going to remember about this book?
3. What is the purpose of the story?
4. What is the subject of the book?
5. Does your book teach a moral? What is it?
6. Do you agree with the author's ideas?
7. Have you read another book with the same main ideas? What is the title?
8. Would you like everyone to know this main idea? Why?
9. What general truth does the author seem to be stating about human nature?
10. Are there morals or lessons in the story? What do you think of them?
11. What things does the reader have to know to understand the story?
12. What attitudes does the author assume that the reader has?
13. What devices does the author use to deliver the message?

Fiction

Title	Type of Literature	Setting	Main Character	Qualities of Main Character	Other Characters	Plot (one-sentence summary)	Type of Conflict	Mood	Theme or Moral

Genre Descriptions, Questions, and Text Maps
Biography

Background Information

Children tend to prefer history told as a living story. Children read biography as they read fiction—for the story or plot. Children demand a fast-moving narrative. In biographies, events and actions become even more exciting because they really happened. A biography must help the children know the person as a living human being.

Questions for Biography

1. What is the title?
2. Who is the main character?
3. What has the main character done to deserve having a book written about him or her?
4. Is the book about the childhood or adult life of the character?
5. What contributions have been made by the main character?
6. From where did the information about the main character originate? (Personal interview, interview with friends or family, historical records, etc.)
7. Was the book about the entire life of the character or only about a part of his or her life?
8. How did the setting (time and place) affect the main character's life?
9. Can you name three events or people that influenced the main character's life?

Biography

Title	Main Character	Contribution of Character	Childhood or Adult Life of Character Portrayed	Source of Information Used in Book	Setting

Genre Descriptions, Questions, and Text Maps
Fairy Tales

Background Information

The traditional folk or fairy tale had no identifiable author but was passed down by word of mouth from one generation to the next. While the names of Grimm and Jacobs have been associated with some of these tales, they did not write the stories but compiled the folktales of Germany and England. The modern fairy tale utilizes the form of the old tales, but has an identifiable author. Hans Christian Andersen is generally credited with being the first author of modern fairy tales, although even some of his stories are adaptations of old folktales. Two of Andersen's tales are said to be autobiographical—"The Ugly Duckling" and "The Steadfast Tin Soldier." Andersen was not afraid to show children cruelty, morbidity, sorrow, and even death. A few stories, such as "The Tender Thumbelina," end happily, but most of his tales contain a thread of tragedy.

In many instances, modern writers have written different versions of the old fairy tale form. The settings are medieval, in the days of kings and queens and beautiful princesses. The language reflects the manners of the period, and the usual "Once upon a time" beginning and "They lived happily ever after" ending are present, but the conflict has a modern twist. True to all fairy tales, virtue is rewarded and evil overcome.

Questions for Fairy Tales

1. What is the title?
2. What country does the fairy tale come from?
3. Who is the main character?
4. How is the main character described?
5. Other characters?
6. Setting?
7. What are the magic elements in the story?
8. What is the problem in the story?
9. How is the problem resolved?
10. What lesson can be learned from the story?

Fairy Tales

Title	Country Tale Came From	Main Character	Character Description	Other Characters	Setting	Magical Elements in Story	Problem in Story	How Problem Solved	Lessons to Be Learned from Story

Genre Descriptions, Questions, and Text Maps
Folktales

Background Information

Folktales are written or oral narratives that have been handed down in oral form through the years. Hans Christian Andersen's fairy tales are part of the heritage that might be described as folktales, but they originated in written, rather than oral, form.

The plot structure of the longer folktale is usually simple and direct. Repetition is a basic element in many folktales. Frequently, the number three is used—there are three pigs; the wolf gives three challenges to the pig in the brick house. Repetition of responses, chants, or poems is frequently part of the structure. In folktales, time and events pass quickly. The setting of the folktale is not specific, but is in a faraway land, a cottage in the woods, or a beautiful place. The reader of a folktale is fully aware that the folktale will usually have a happy ending, that the hero will be successful in his quest, the children will be saved, the prince will marry the princess. The introduction to a folktale usually presents the conflict, characters, and setting in a few sentences. In one sentence a storyteller can establish setting: "Once upon a time there was a fisherman who lived with his wife in a miserable house close by the sea, and every day he went fishing." The conclusion of the story follows the climax very quickly and includes few details. Characters in folktales are symbolic, usually completely good or evil. Dialogue makes a folktale more readable and interesting, although some are written without it.

The major criteria for the style of a written folktale are that it maintain the atmosphere of the country from which it originated and that it truly seems to be a tale told by a storyteller.

The basic purpose of the folktale is to tell an entertaining story, yet these stories do present themes.

Questions for Folktales

1. What is the title of the book?
2. What country did the story come from?
3. Who is the hero/heroine?
4. What kinds of qualities does the hero/heroine have?
5. Who are the other characters in the story?
6. What kinds of qualities do the other characters have?
7. What is the setting?
8. What was the quest or goal?
9. What difficulties or obstacles did the hero/heroine encounter?
10. What was the hero/heroine's accomplishment?
11. What price did the hero/heroine pay?
12. What lesson was learned or could be learned from the story?

Folktales

Title	Country Story Came From	Hero/Heroine	Character Qualities of Hero/Heroine	Other Characters	Qualities of Other Characters	Setting (When/Where)	Quest/Goal	Difficulties/Obstacles	Hero/Heroine's Accomplishments	Price Paid

Genre Descriptions, Questions, and Text Maps
Historical Fiction

Background Information

Historical fiction is a fictional story with a historical background. These books supplement the information obtained form factual books and biographies. Historical fiction for children seeks to reconstruct the life and thought of an age or period of time other than that of the present generation. The characters, setting, and events are drawn from the past or the author may invent plots, characters, and events, provided that basic historical facts are not altered.

Questions for Historical Fiction

1. What is the title?
2. Who is the main character?
3. What are the main character's qualities?
4. Who are the other characters?
5. What are the other characters' qualities?
6. What is the setting?
7. In what time does the story take place?
8. What events were directly related to the historical period in which the book took place and not at any other time?
9. What is the problem in the story?
10. How is the problem resolved?
11. What is the lesson/theme of the story?

Historical Fiction

Title	Main Character	Qualities of Main Character	Other Characters	Qualities of Other Characters	Setting/Time/Place	Problem	Solution

Genre Descriptions, Questions, and Text Maps
Modern Fantasy

Background Information

Books of modern fantasy encourage the creative powers of children. Children vary in their capacity for imaginative thinking. The literal-minded child finds it more difficult to pass from reality to fantasy. Other children relish the opportunity to enter the world of enchantment. Frequently, taste for fantasy may be developed by reading a fantasy aloud. Books of modern fantasy are usually longer than fairy tales and may take a variety of forms. All contain some imaginary elements that are contrary to reality as we know it today—for example, the stories may personify animals or toys, create new worlds, change the size of human beings, give humans unusual powers, or manipulate time patterns. Some fantasies utilize several of these features. Characteristic of most modern fantasies, like the fairy tales of old, is the presentation of a universal truth or a hidden meaning—that love overcomes hate, that fools may be wiser than the wise men, that the granting of wishes may not mean happiness. Well-written fantasy, like other fiction, has a well-constructed plot, convincing characterization, worthwhile theme, and appropriate style. However, additional considerations need to guide the evaluation of fantasy.

The primary concern in fantasy is whether the author made the story believable. Another point to be considered in a fantasy is that the plot should be original—it should display creativity.

Types of Fantasy:

Strange and curious worlds
Imaginary kingdoms
Animal
World of dolls and toys
Lilliputian worlds
Fabulous flights
Magical powers
Overcoming evil
Time magic

Questions for Modern Fantasy

1. What is the title of the book?
2. Who tells the story? (point of view)
3. What is the setting? (real world with unreal occurrences, or "low" fantasy; in another world, or "high" fantasy)
4. What does the author do to make the setting believable?
5. Who is the main character?
6. Can you describe the qualities of the main character?
7. How does the author make the main character believable?
8. Who are the other characters in the book?
9. What are their characteristics?
10. What is the problem in the book?
11. How is the problem resolved?
12. What is the lesson, or theme, of the book?

Modern Fantasy

Title	Who Tells Story (Point of View)	Setting	How Author Makes Setting Believable	Main Character	Qualities of Main Character	How Author Makes Main Character Believable	Other Characters	Problem	Solution	Lesson or Theme

Graphic Organizers

Cause/Effect

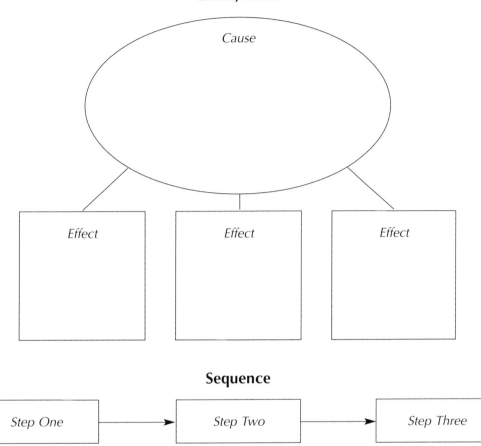

Sequence

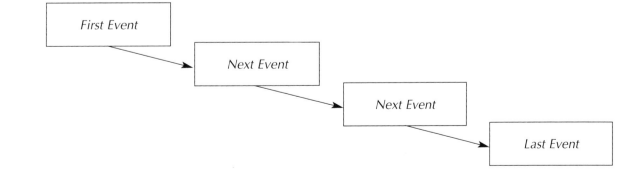

Graphic Organizers

Problem/Solution

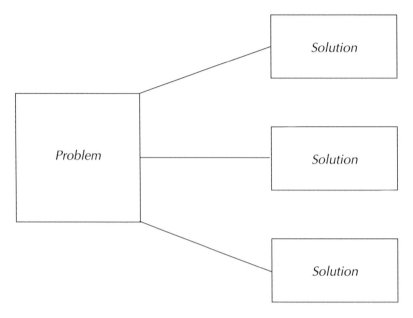

Descriptive

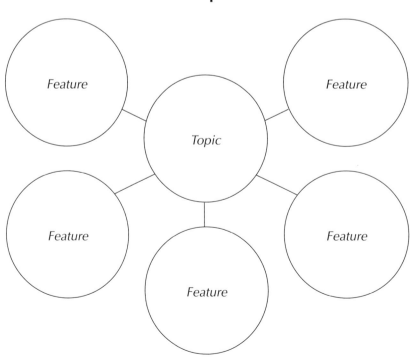

Appendix Section III Glossary of Genres; Book Lists; Genre Descriptions; Graphic Organizers 153

Graphic Organizers

Looking More Closely

What is the photo or picture about?

Describe the way it looks.

Draw a picture or paste your photo here.

Describe the way it sounds or tastes.

Describe the way it feels or makes you feel.

Graphic Organizers

Sequencing Chart

First _____

_____

_____

↓

Next _____

_____

_____

↓

Then _____

_____

_____

↓

Finally _____

_____

_____

Graphic Organizers

Problem/Solution

The Problem

Solution 1

Solution 2

The Best Solution

Graphic Organizers

Character's Traits

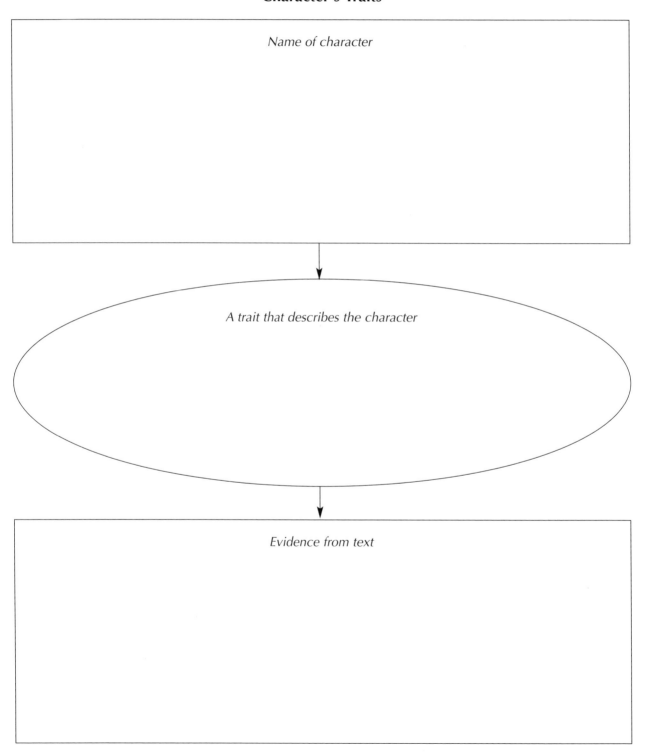

APPENDIX SECTION IV

Rubrics for Assessment

Rubric for Assessing Literature Discussion Groups

Name: _____ Date: _____

Goal: To enjoy, share ideas, and learn from each other through literature discussion groups.

4
- Prepares for group meeting (i.e., log section is marked and thinking is clearly visible).
- Comes to group meeting excited and ready to begin discussion.
- Actively participates in book discussion (i.e., shares thinking).
- Supports thinking using evidence from text.
- Stays on topic.
- Makes eye contact with person speaking.
- Listens carefully to others' thinking.
- Offers opinion and/or builds on ideas at appropriate times.
- Respects others' thinking and reacts using appropriate language.
- Asks questions when needed to clarify understanding.
- Achieves deeper comprehension through discussion.

3
- Prepares for group meeting (i.e., log section is marked and thinking is clearly visible).
- Comes to group meeting excited and ready to begin discussion.
- Actively participates in book discussion (i.e., shares thinking).
- Supports thinking using evidence from text; requires few reminders.
- Stays on topic.
- Makes eye contact with person speaking.
- Listens carefully to others' thinking; requires few reminders.
- Offers opinion and/or builds on others' ideas at appropriate times.
- Respects others' thinking and reacts using appropriate language.
- Asks questions when needed to clarify understanding.
- Achieves deeper comprehension through discussion.

2
- Prepares for group meeting (i.e., log section is marked and thinking is clearly visible; requires many reminders).
- Comes to group meeting excited and ready to begin discussion.
- Actively participates in book discussion (i.e., shares thinking).
- Supports thinking using evidence from text; requires many reminders.
- Stays on topic; requires many reminders.
- Makes eye contact with person speaking.
- Listens carefully to others' thinking; requires many reminders.
- Offers opinion and/or builds on others' ideas at appropriate times; requires many reminders.
- Respects others' thinking and reacts using appropriate language; requires many reminders.
- Asks questions when needed to clarify understanding; requires reminders.
- Achieves deeper comprehension through discussion.

1
- Prepares for group meeting (i.e., log section is marked and thinking is clearly visible; requires full support).
- Comes to group meeting excited and ready to begin discussion.
- Actively participates in book discussion (i.e., shares thinking).
- Supports thinking using evidence from text; requires full support.
- Stays on topic; requires full support.
- Makes eye contact with person speaking; requires full support.
- Listens carefully to others' thinking; requires full support.
- Offers opinion and/or builds on others' ideas at appropriate time; requires full support.
- Respects others' thinking and reacts using appropriate language; requires full support.
- Asks questions when needed to clarify understanding; requires full support.
- Achieves deeper comprehension through discussion.

What Are "Thoughtful" Log Entries?

- **Respond personally to the text**
    - How do you feel about the text and why?
    - How has the text changed your life in some way?
    - What is your favorite or least favorite part of the book and why?

- **Respond to the theme and/or author's purpose**
    - What is the author trying to teach you?
    - What is the author's purpose or message in the text?
    - Why do you think the author wrote this text?

- **Offer opinion of text**
    - Do you like or dislike the text and why?
    - Who is your favorite or least favorite character and why?
    - Will you read this book again? Why or why not?
    - Will you recommend this book to a friend?

- **Ask questions**
    - What does the word/phrase —— mean?
    - Why did the character act this way?
    - What did the author mean when . . . ?
    - What is the author trying to teach you?

- **Make predictions/inferences**
    - What do you think might happen and why?
    - I think —— because . . .

- **Respond to the writing style or author's language**
    - How does the author use language to create sensory images?
    - How does the author's language deepen your understanding?

- **Respond to the traits and/or actions of the character(s)**
    - Do you like, dislike, or admire the character(s) and why?
    - Would you act/react differently and why?

- **Share connections**
    - Does any part of the book remind you of the world and what is occurring now or has happened in the past?
    - How have your own experiences deepened your understanding?
    - How is this text (characters or events) similar to another book (characters or events)?
    - Do you connect in any way with a character from the text?

- **Critique the text**
    - Did the author do a good job organizing the text? crafting the text?
    - What are the resources the author used to provide you with accurate and current information?
    - Did the author use text features to help you understand the information?
    - Did the author follow the text structures for the genre?

Rubric for Assessing Log Entries

Name: _____ Date: _____

Goal: Log is organized and contains thoughtful entries (i.e., thinking while reading is reflected upon). After reading, thinking is made visible for sharing and additional learning.

4	• Log is organized and contains evidence of volume reading (self-selected and assigned reading texts)—i.e., texts, genres, and dates are recorded in front of log. • Reflections are clearly labeled and easy to locate. • Log contains thoughtful entries, reflecting some of the following: makes personal responses to text; identifies and responds to theme(s) and/or author's purpose; offers opinion of text; notes connections; wonders or questions; seeks answers; shares predictions; responds to author's language; creates sensory images; notes inferences; writes letters; compares and contrasts information; reacts and responds to the character(s); responds to text at the synthesis level; critiques text. • Log entries are supported by evidence from the text.
3	• Log is organized and contains evidence of volume reading (self-selected and assigned reading texts)—i.e., texts, genres, and dates are recorded in front of log. • Reflections for group sharing are clearly labeled and easy to locate. • Log contains thoughtful entries, reflecting some of the following: makes personal responses to text; identifies and responds to theme(s) and/or author's purpose; offers opinion of text; notes connections; wonders or questions; seeks answers; shares predictions; responds to author's language; creates sensory images; notes inferences; writes letters; compares and contrasts information; reacts and responds to the character(s); responds to text at the synthesis level; critiques text. • Log entries are supported with evidence from text most of the time.
2	• Log is organized and contains some evidence of volume reading (self-selected and assigned reading texts)—i.e., texts, genres, and dates are recorded in front of log. • Reflections for group sharing are unorganized and are difficult to locate. • Log entries reflect surface level thinking, reflecting some of the following: makes personal responses to text; identifies and responds to theme(s) and/or author's purpose; offers opinion of text; notes connections; wonders or questions; seeks answers; shares predictions; responds to author's language; creates sensory images; notes inferences; writes letters; compares and contrasts information; reacts and responds to the character(s); responds to text at the synthesis level; critiques text. • Log entries are not supported with evidence from text.
1	• Log is unorganized and contains no evidence of volume reading (self-selected and assigned reading texts)—i.e., texts, genres, and dates are not recorded in front of log. • Reflections for group sharing are unorganized and are difficult to locate. • Log entries reflect random thinking and do not reflect any of the following: makes personal responses to text; identifies and responds to theme(s) and/or author's purpose; offers opinion of text; notes connections; wonders or questions; seeks answers; shares predictions; responds to author's language; creates sensory images; notes inferences; writes letters; compares and contrasts information; reacts and responds to the character(s); responds to text at the synthesis level; critiques text. • Log entries are not supported with evidence from text.

Appendix Section IV Rubrics for Assessment

Rubric for Assessing Independent Reading Time

Name: _____ Date: _____

Goal: Use reading workshop time wisely, resulting in many opportunities for volume reading.

4	<ul><li>Chooses suitable texts for self-selected reading.</li><li>Locates an area for reading and begins reading immediately.</li><li>Uses reading workshop time wisely, resulting in opportunities for volume reading.</li><li>Completes group assignment before self-selecting another reading option.</li><li>Respects other readers by reading or discussing books quietly.</li></ul>
3	<ul><li>Chooses suitable texts for self-selected reading.</li><li>Locates an area for reading and begins reading immediately; requires few reminders.</li><li>Uses reading workshop time wisely; requires few reminders, resulting in many opportunities for reading.</li><li>Completes group assignment before self-selecting another reading option most of the time; requires few reminders.</li><li>Respects others by reading or discussing books quietly.</li></ul>
2	<ul><li>Chooses suitable texts for self-selected reading; requires many reminders.</li><li>Locates an area for reading with difficulty (moves from spot to spot); requires many reminders before beginning to read.</li><li>Uses very little of the reading workshop time wisely; requires many reminders, resulting in few reading opportunities.</li><li>Completes group assignment before self-selecting another reading option; requires many reminders.</li><li>Respects others by reading or discussing books quietly; requires many reminders.</li></ul>
1	<ul><li>Chooses suitable texts for self-selected reading; requires full support.</li><li>Locates an area for reading with difficulty (moves from spot to spot); requires full support before beginning to read.</li><li>Uses very little reading workshop time wisely; requires full support resulting in little or no reading opportunities.</li><li>Completes group assignments before self-selecting another reading option; requires full support.</li><li>Respects others by reading or discussing books quietly; requires full support.</li></ul>

Correlation of DVD Chapters and Segments to Book Chapters

DVD Chapter/Segment	DVD Segment Title	Title of Text	Prompts to Guide Viewing	Related Book Chapter Readings
Chapter 1 Shared Reading Segment 1	Before Reading: Introducing Text During Reading: Interacting with Text After Reading: Identifying Theme	*The Little Red Hen*	How does Vicki engage the students in building meaning for the story? Describe how Vicki promotes fluency, expression, and comprehension during and after the first reading.	Chap. 2: Fluency Chap. 3: Shared reading Chap. 4: Comprehension strategies Appendix Section I: Shared reading aids
	Explicit Teaching: Cloze Procedure	*The Little Red Hen*	How does the cloze procedure help students learn an important strategy about problem solving?	Chap. 3: Shared reading Chap. 4: Comprehension strategies Appendix Section I: Shared reading aids
Shared Reading Segment 2	Before Reading: Introducing Text During Reading: Interacting with Text After Reading: Explicit Teaching; Recording Favorite Words	*Who's in the Shed?*	How does Vicki engage the students in building meaning for the story? Describe how Vicki promotes fluency, expression, and comprehension during and after the first reading. What strategic behavior is being demonstrated? How does Vicki prompt the students to apply strategic processes to their independent work?	Chap. 3: Shared reading Chap. 4: Comprehension strategies Appendix Section I: Shared reading aids Chap. 3: Shared reading Chap. 4: Comprehension strategies Chap. 5: Language strategies Appendix Section I: Shared reading aids
Shared Reading Segment 3	Explicit Teaching: Exploring the Use of Labels	*Caterpillar Diary*	What strategic behaviors are being demonstrated?	Chap. 3: Shared reading Chap. 4: Comprehension strategies

Appendix Section V Correlation of DVD Chapters and Segments to Book Chapters

DVD Chapter/Segment	DVD Segment Title	Title of Text	Prompts to Guide Viewing	Related Book Chapter Readings
			How does Vicki prompt the students to apply strategic processes to their independent work?	Appendix Section I: Shared reading aids
Shared Reading Segment 4	Share Time/Reflection		Describe the social context of share time. How does this context provide Vicki with an opportunity to assess the students' learning? How does share time provide the students with an opportunity to reflect on their reading habits?	Chap. 4: Writing in response logs Chap. 6: Reading workshop Appendix Section IV: Rubric for assessing independent reading
Chapter 2 Author Study Segment 1	Interactive Read-Aloud; Listening for Powerful Language	*Jin Woo*	How does Vicki use an interactive read aloud to demonstrate language strategies? What strategic behavior is being demonstrated? How does Vicki prompt the students to apply strategic processes to their independent work?	Chap. 3: Reading aloud to students Chap. 5: Language strategies
Author Study Segment 2	Share Time		Describe the social context of share time. How does this context provide Vicki with an opportunity to assess the students' learning?	Chap. 6: Reading workshop Appendix Section IV: Rubric for assessing log entries; thoughtful log entries

DVD Chapter/ Segment	DVD Segment Title	Title of Text	Prompts to Guide Viewing	Related Book Chapter Readings
Author Study Segment 3	Mini-Lesson	*Secret Home* *Fly Away Home* *The Wall* *Jin Woo* *The Memory String* *A Picnic in October*	How does Vicki use a mini-lesson to build connections between reading and writing? What strategic behavior is being demonstrated?	Chap. 2: Text structure Chap. 4: Comprehension strategies Chap. 6: Mini-lesson
Author Study Segment 4	Small-Group Mini-Lesson: Surveying and Previewing Text		What strategic behavior is being demonstrated?	Chap. 4: Comprehension strategies Chap. 6: Mini-lesson
Author Study Segment 5	One-to-One Conference		Describe the teacher/child interaction during the one-to-one conference. What strategic behavior is being demonstrated?	Chap. 4: Comprehension strategies Chap. 5: Language strategies Chap. 6: Reading conference
Chapter 3 Book Discussion Segment 1	Teacher Book Discussion	*Black-Eyed Suzie*	Describe how teachers used language to interact with one another. How do the teachers use a flexible range of comprehending strategies to construct deeper meanings?	Chap. 1: Understanding comprehension Chap. 2: Reading for deep comprehension Chap. 4: Comprehension strategies Chap. 7: Literature discussion groups
Book Discussion Segment 2	Teacher Book Discussion	*Beachmont Letters*	Describe how teachers used language to interact with one another. How do the teachers use a flexible range of comprehending strategies to construct deeper meanings?	Chap. 1: Understanding comprehension Chap. 2: Reading for deep comprehension Chap. 4: Comprehension strategies Chap. 7: Literature discussion groups

Appendix Section V Correlation of DVD Chapters and Segments to Book Chapters

DVD Chapter/ Segment	DVD Segment Title	Title of Text	Prompts to Guide Viewing	Related Book Chapter Readings
Chapter 4 Mini-Lesson Segment 1	Mini-Lesson Character Analysis	*An Angel for Solomon Singer*	How does Jill promote deeper comprehension through character analysis?	Chap. 2: Character relationships Chap. 4: Comprehension strategies Chap. 6: Mini-lesson
Chapter 5 Literature Discussion Group Segment 1	Reviewing Conversational Moves	*The Summer My Father Was Ten*	Discuss how conversational moves lead to sustained discourse among the group.	Chap. 4: Comprehension strategies Chap. 7: Literature discussion groups Appendix Section IV: Rubric for assessing literature discussion groups
	Literature Discussion Group		How does Jill provide a scale of help for assisting the students to think at deeper levels? What is her role in the literature discussion group?	
	Reflecting on Group Discussion		Discuss how the students reflect on their own conversational moves.	
Literature Discussion Group Segment 2	Literature Discussion Group	*Honeysuckle House*	How does Priscilla provide a scale of help for assisting the students to think at deeper levels? What is her role in the literature discussion groups? Discuss the difference in teacher support between the two groups.	Chap. 4: Comprehension strategies Chap. 7: Literature discussion groups Appendix Section IV: Rubric for assessing literature discussion groups

References

Professional References

Baker, Linda, and Ann L. Brown. 2002. Metacognitive skills and reading. In P. David Pearson, ed., *Handbook of Reading Research*, pp. 353–394. Mahwah, NJ: Lawrence Erlbaum.

Beck, Isabel L., Margaret G. McKewon, Rebecca L. Hamilton, and Linda Kucan. 1997. *Questioning the Author: An Approach for Enhancing Student Engagement with Text.* Newark, DE: International Reading Association.

Block, Cathy Collins, and Michael Pressley. 2002. *Comprehension Instruction: Research-Based Best Practices.* New York: Guilford Press.

Britton, Bruce K., and Shawn M. Glynn, eds. 1987. *Executive Control Processes in Reading.* Hillsdale, NJ: Lawrence Erlbaum.

Britton, James. 1970. *Language and Learning: The Importance of Speech.* Portsmouth, NH: Heinemann.

Calkins, Lucy. 2001. *The Art of Teaching Reading.* New York: Addison-Wesley Educational Publishers.

Chambers, Arian. 1996. *Tell Me.* Portland, ME: Stenhouse.

Clay, Marie. 1991. *Becoming Literate: The Construction of Inner Control.* Portsmouth, NH: Heinemann.

———. 1998. *By Different Paths to Common Outcomes.* Portland, ME: Stenhouse.

———. 2001. *Change over Time in Children's Literacy Development.* Portsmouth, NH: Heinemann.

Dorn, Linda, Cathy French, and Tammy Jones. 1998. *Apprenticeship in Literacy: Transitions Across Reading and Writing.* Portland, ME: Stenhouse.

Dorn, Linda, and Carla Soffos. 2001a. *Scaffolding Young Writers: A Writers' Workshop Approach.* Portland, ME: Stenhouse.

———. 2001b. *Shaping Literate Minds: Developing Self-Regulated Learners.* Portland, ME: Stenhouse.

———. 2002. *Results That Last: A Model for School Change.* Video Staff Development Series. Portland, ME: Stenhouse.

———. 2003. *Developing Independent Learners: A Reading/Writing Workshop Approach.* Video Staff Development Series. Portland, ME: Stenhouse.

Duke, Neil K., and P. David Pearson. 2002. Effective practices for developing reading comprehension. In Allan Farstrup and S. Jay Samuels, eds., *What Research Has to Say About Reading Instruction,* 3rd ed., pp. 205–242. Newark, DE: International Reading Association.

Durkin, Dolores. 1966. *Children Who Read Early.* New York: Teachers College Press.

Farstrup, Allan, and S. Jay Samuels, eds. 2002. *What Research Has to Say About Reading Instruction.* 3rd ed. Newark, DE: International Reading Association.

Fitzgerald, J. 1984. The relationship between reading ability and expectations for story structures. *Discourse Processes* 7: 21–41.

Foertsch, M. A. 1992. *Reading in and out of School: Achievement of American students in Grades 4, 8, and 12 in 1989–90.* Washington, DC: US Government Printing Office, National Center for Educational Statistics.

Fountas, Irene, and Gay Su Pinnell. 2001. *Guided Reading and Writers, Grades 3–6: Teaching Comprehension, Genre, and Content Literacy.* Portsmouth, NH: Heinemann.

Gambrell, L. B., and P. S. Koskinen. 2002. Imagery: A strategy for enhancing comprehension. In Cathy Collins Block and Michael Pressley, eds., *Comprehension Instruction: Research-Based Best Practices,* pp. 305–318. New York: Guilford Press.

Glaessar, Arthur, Karl Haberlandt, and David Koizumi. 1987. How is reading time influenced by knowledge-based inferences and world knowledge? In Bruce Britton and Shawn M. Glynn, eds., *Executive Control Processes in Reading,* pp. 217–252. Hillsdale, NJ: Lawrence Erlbaum.

Graesser, A. C., and L. F. Clark. 1985. *Structures and Procedures of Implicit Knowledge.* Norwood, NJ: Ablex.

Graves, Michael. 1985. *A Word Is a Word . . . or Is It?* Ontario, Canada: Scholastic.

Hillenbrand, Laura. 2001. *Seabiscuit: An American Legend.* New York: Ballantine Books.

Holdaway, Don. 1979. *Foundations of Literacy.* Portsmouth, NH: Heinemann.

Houston, Gloria. 2003. *How Writing Works: Imposing Organizational Structures Within the Writing Process.* Boston: Pearson Education.

Hoyt, Linda. 2005. *Spotlight on Comprehension: Building a Literacy of Thoughtfulness.* Portsmouth, NH: Heinemann.

Kaufmann, G. 1979. *Visual Imagery and Its Relation to Problem-Solving.* New York: Columbia University Press.

King, Stephen. 2000. *On Writing: A Memoir of the Craft.* New York: Scribner.

Laminack, Lester. 2004. Making meaning from memories: Writing and reading memoir in the elementary classroom. Keynote presentation, Reading Recovery and Comprehensive Literacy Conference, October 12, 2004, Little Rock, AR.

Lattimere, Heather. 2003. *Thinking Through Genre: Units of Study in Reading and Writing Workshops, 4–12.* Portland, ME: Stenhouse.

Levine, Mel. 2002. *A Mind at a Time.* New York: Simon and Schuster.

Lindfors, Judith. 1999. *Children's Inquiry: Using Language to Make Sense of the World.* New York: National Council of Teachers of English.

Lyons, Carol. 2003. *Teaching Struggling Readers: How to Use Brain-Based Research to Maximize Learning.* Portsmouth, NH: Heinemann.

McBride-Chang, C., F. Manis, M. Seidenberg, R. Custodio, and L. Doi. 1993. Print Exposure as a Predictor of Word Reading and Reading Comprehension in Disabled and

Nondisabled Readers. *Journal of Educational Psychology:* 230–238.

McGee, L. M. 1982. Awareness of text structure: Effects on children's recall of expository text. *Reading Research Quarterly* 17: 581–592.

Meek, Margaret. 1991. *On Being Literate.* Portsmouth, NH: Heinemann.

Mercer, Neil. 1995. *The Guided Construction of Knowledge: Talk Amongst Teachers and Learners.* Philadelphia: Multilingual Matters.

Moline, Steve. 1995. *I See What You Mean: Children at Work with Visual Information.* Portland, ME: Stenhouse.

Morrison, Toni. 1997. *Beloved.* New York: Penguin.

———. 2000. *The Bluest Eye.* New York: Penguin.

Parsons, L. 2001. *Response Journals Revisited.* Portland, ME: Stenhouse.

Patterson, James. 2001. *Suzanne's Diary for Nicholas.* New York: Warner.

Pearson, D. P., ed. 2002. *Handbook of Reading Research.* Mahwah, NJ: Lawrence Erlbaum.

Pearson, P. David, and Nell K. Duke. 2002. Comprehension instruction in the primary grades. In Cathy Collins Block and Michael Pressley, eds., *Comprehension Instruction: Research-Based Best Practices,* pp. 247–258. New York: Guilford Press.

Pearson, P. David, and M. C. Gallagher. 1983. The instruction of reading comprehension. *Contemporary Education Psychology* 8: 317–344.

Pearson, P. David, and Dale D. Johnson. 1972. *Teaching Reading Comprehension.* New York: Holt, Rinehart, and Winston.

Pinnell, Gay Su. 2001. What does it mean to comprehend a text? In Gay Su Pinnell and Patricia L. Scharer, eds., *Teaching for Comprehension in Reading: Grades K–2.* New York: Scholastic.

Pinnell, Gay Su, and Patricia L. Scharer. 2003. *Teaching for Comprehension in Reading: Grades K–2.* New York: Scholastic.

Rasinski, T. 2003. *The Fluent Reader: Oral Reading Strategies for Building Word Recognition, Fluency, and Comprehension.* New York: Scholastic.

Ratey, John J. 2001. *A User's Guide to the Brain: Perception, Attention, and the Four Theaters of the Brain.* New York: Allyn and Bacon.

Rogoff, Barbara. 1990. *Apprenticeship in Thinking: Cognitive Development in Social Contexts.* New York: Oxford University Press.

Routman, Regie. 2003. *Reading Essentials: The Specifics You Need to Teach Reading Well.* Portsmouth, NH: Heinemann.

Ruddell, Robert B., Martha R. Ruddell, and Harry Singer, eds. 1994. *Theoretical Models and Processes of Reading.* 4th ed. Newark, DE: International Reading Association.

Samuels, S. Jay, and Allan Farstrup, eds. 1992. *What Research Has to Say About Reading Instruction.* 2nd ed. Newark, DE: International Reading Association.

Singer, Harry. 1994. The substrata-factor theory of reading. In Robert B. Ruddell, Martha R. Ruddell, and Harry Singer, eds., *Theoretical Models and Processes of Reading,* 4th ed., pp. 895–927. Newark, DE: International Reading Association.

Smith, Frank. 1976. *Comprehension and Learning: A Conceptual Framework for Teachers.* New York: Richard C. Owen.

———. 1994. *Understanding Reading: A Psycholinguistic Analysis of Reading and Learning to Read.* 5th ed. Hillsdale, NJ: Lawrence Erlbaum.

Stead, Tony. 2006a. *Guided Reading with Nonfiction.* Video series. Portland, ME: Stenhouse.

———. 2006b. *The Tony Stead Nonfiction Independent Reading Collection.* New York: Rosen Publishing Group.

Steinbeck. John. 1939. *The Grapes of Wrath.* New York: Viking Penguin.

Taylor, Barbara. 1992. Text structure, comprehension, and recall. In S. Jay Samuels and Allan Farstrup, eds., *What Research Has to Say About Reading Instruction,* 2nd ed., pp. 220–235.

Newark, DE: International Reading Association.
Truss, Lynne. 2003. *Eats, Shoots, and Leaves.* New York: Gotham Books.
Vygotsky, Lev. 1978. *Mind in Society: The Development of Higher Psychological Processes.* Cambridge, MA: Harvard University Press.
———. 1986. *Thought and Language.* Cambridge, MA: MIT Press.
Wagner, Richard, and Robert Sternberg. 1987. Executive control in reading comprehension. In Bruce K. Britton and Shawn M. Glynn, eds., *Executive Control Processes in Reading.* Hillsdale, NJ: Lawrence Erlbaum.
Wells, G., and Gen Ling Chang-Wells. 1992. *Constructing Knowledge Together: Classrooms as Centers of Inquiry and Literacy.* Portsmouth, NH: Heinemann.
Wood, David. 1998. *How Children Think and Learn.* 2nd ed. Oxford, UK: Blackwell.

Children's Book References

Armstrong, William H. 1969. *Sounder.* New York: Harper Trophy.
Brisson, Pat. 1999. *The Summer My Father Was Ten.* Honesdale, PA: Boyds Mills Press.
Byars, Betsy. 1977. *The Pinballs.* New York: Harper Trophy.
Cheng, Andrea. 2004. *Honeysuckle House.* Honesdale, PA: Front Street.
Coerr, Eleanor. 1977. *Sadak and the Thousand Paper Cranes.* New York: Bantam Doubleday Dell.
Cole, Robert. 1995. *The Story of Ruby Bridges.* New York: Scholastic.
Curtis, Christopher Paul. 1995. *The Watsons Go to Birmingham, 1963.* New York: Bantam Doubleday.
———. 1999. *Bud, not Buddy.* New York: Scholastic.
DiCamillo, Kate. 2000. *Because of Winn-Dixie.* Cambridge, MA: Candlewick Press.
Drew, David. 1987. *Caterpillar Diary.* Crystal Lake, IL: Rigby.
Fraustino, Lisa Rowe. 2001. *The Hickory Chair.* New York: Scholastic Press.
Gardiner, John Reynolds. 1980. *Stone Fox.* New York: Crowell.
Giff, Patricia. R. 2002. *Pictures of Hollis Wood.* New York: Wendy Lamb Books.
Gray, Libba Moore. 1999. *My Mama Had a Dancing Heart.* New York: Orchard Farm.
Houston, Gloria. 2002. *My Great Aunt Arizona.* New York: HarperCollins.
Hesse, Karen. 1994. *Sable.* New York: Henry Holt and Co.
———. 1997a. *Out of the Dust.* New York: Scholastic.
———. 1997b. *A Time for Angels.* New York: Hyperion.
MacLachlan, Patricia. 1995. *What You Know First.* New York: Joanna Cotler Books/Harper Trophy.
Martin, Rafe. 1992. *The Rough Faced Girl.* New York: Scholastic.
McGill, Alice. 1999. *Molly Bannaky.* Boston: Houghton Mifflin.
McKissack, P. 1986. *Flossie and the Fox.* New York: Dial Books for Young Readers.
———. *Mirandy and Brother Wind.* New York: Alfread A. Knopf.
———. 1989. *Nettie Jo's Friends.* New York: Alfred A. Knopf.
Parkes, Brenda. 1997a. *The Little Red Hen.* Crystal Lake, IL: Rigby.
———. 1997b. *Who's in the Shed?* Crystal Lake, IL: Rigby.
Patterson, Katherine. 1977. *Bridge to Terabithia.* New York: HarperCollins.
Peck, Richard. 2000. *A Year Down Yonder.* New York: Penguin Putnam.
Polacco, Patricia. 1990. *Thundercake.* New York: Putnam and Grosset Group.
———. 1998. *Thank You, Mr. Falker.* New York: Penguin Putnam.

References

Randall, Beverly. 1994. *Tiger, Tiger.* Crystal Lake, IL: Rigby.

Riggo, Anita. 1997. *Secret Signs: Along the Underground Railroad.* Honesdale, PA: Boyds Mills Press.

Root, Phyllis. 1998. *Aunt Nancy and Cousin Lazybones.* Cambridge, MA: Candlewick Press.

Rylant, Cynthia. 1996. *An Angel for Solomon Singer.* New York: Scholastic.

Shaw, Susan. 2002. *Black-Eyed Suzie.* Honesdale, PA: Boyds Mills Press.

Smith, Doris B. 1973. *A Taste of Blackberries.* New York: Scholastic.

Springer, Nancy. 1994. *Music of Their Hooves.* Honesdale, PA: Boyds Mills Press.

Twomey, Cathleen. 2003. *Beachmont Letters.* Honesdale, PA: Boyds Mills Press.

White, E. B. 1952. *Charlotte's Web.* New York: Scholastic.

Yolen, Jane. 2001. *Welcome to the River of Grass.* New York: G. P. Putnam's Sons.

Index

Abernathy, Rosa, 29
adjectives, 52, 54–55
adjustable language support, 32–35
adverbs, 56
Altland, Vicki, xv, xvi, 45, 62, 72, 75, 76, 89, 164
Amelia Bedelia books (Parish), 60
analytical readers, 44
anchor chart examples
   "Guidelines for Engaging in Literature Discussion Group," 84
   "Guidelines for Literature Group Discussions," 69
   "Guidelines for Self-Selecting Books," 77
   "Preparing for Book Talks," 73
   "Preparing for Literature Discussion Groups," 84
   "Presenting Book Talks," 73
   "Strategies Used by Good Readers," 69
anchor charts, 62, 68–70, 73
   defined, 68–69
   for literature discussion groups, 84
   planning, 70
   reviewing, 96
   for reviewing comprehension strategies, 96
   student-created, 70
Anderson, Hans Christian, 143, 145
Angel for Solomon Singer, An, 167
apostrophes, 57
Apprenticeship in Literacy (Dorn, French, and Jones), xv, 3
apprenticeship learning, 81, 92. *See also* models; scaffolding

   cognitive, 81
   professional development activities, 127–30
Armstrong, William H., 58
assessment
   of deep comprehension, 15
   of independent reading time, 161
   in literature discussion groups, 85
   of log entries, 159–60
   in reading workshop, 67
   rubrics, 158–61
-ation suffix, 46
Aunt Nancy and Cousin Lazybones (Root), 60
authors
   creative use of adjectives by, 52, 54–55
   discussing message of, 88
   language studies based on, 62
   questioning, 43, 85
   style of, 90
author studies
   conducting, 91–92
   DVD chapter/segments, 165–66
   example, 93
   value of, 92–93
autobiography, 132

background experience
   deep-level comprehension and, 15
   problem-solving and, 8
background knowledge
   comprehension and, 17, 29
   inferential thinking and, 19
   visualization strategies and, 9
Baker, Linda, 6

Beachmont Letters, 166
Because of Winn-Dixie (DiCamillo), 21, 58, 89, 90
Beck, Isabel L., 44, 80–81
beginning novels, 60
beginning readers. *See also* emergent readers
   author studies for, 91–92
behaviors. *See also* strategic behaviors
   defined, 41
   indicating problem-solving strategies, 38
   indicating reading strategies, 41
   strategies *vs.*, 41
Behrend, Janet, xvi
Beloved (Morrison), xi, 51–52
Big Books, 45
biography
   book lists, 136–37
   defined, 132, 141
   form, 142
   questions for, 141
Black-Eyed Suzie, 166
Block, Cathy Collins, 6
Bluest Eye, The (Morrison), 52–53
book choice. *See also* texts
   for literature discussion groups, 83–84
   rhythmic learning and, 32
   self-selection, 72–73, 77
book clubs, for teachers, 128
book discussions. *See also* literature discussion groups; texts
   after shared reading, 31
   character analysis in, 23
   comprehension and, 17–18

book discussions (continued)
  DVD chapter/segments, 166
  inquiry-driven, 80–81
  meaning-making chains and, 80
  mini-lessons for, 83, 106
  models for, 82–83
  question-driven, 80–81
  in reading workshop, 71
  scaffolding and, 80
  as strategic behavior, 48
  by teachers, 21, 127
  teacher's role in, 80–81
  value of, 13–14
  videotapes of, 83
book lists, 133–39
book orientations, 31, 43
books. *See* texts
book talks, 73, 75–76
Bridge to Terabithia (Patterson), 56
Britton, James, 79–80
Brown, Ann L., 6
Brown, Marc, 90
Bud, not Buddy (Curtis), 60
buddy reading, 71, 73
Buddy Reading icon, 73
bullets, 45
Byars, Betsy, 60

captions, 45
Carle, Eric, 93
Caterpillar Diary, 164
cause/effect
  graphic organizer, 151
  in nonfiction texts, 44
challenging work, rhythmic pattern
    and, 29–30
*Change Over Time in Children's Literacy
    Development* (Clay), xvii, 38
Chang-Wells, Gen Ling, 29
chapter books, 60
chapters, organization and, 59
character relationships, 19–23
  deep comprehension and, 19
  prompts about, 22–23
characters
  analysis of, 22–23
  in fiction, 138–39
  influences on other characters, 21
  recurring, 42
  strong, 22
character's traits graphic organizer, 156
Charlotte's Web (White), 56, 60
chart paper, 124
Cherry, Mavis, xvii
Choate, Connie, xvi
chronology, in nonfiction texts, 44
Clark, L. F., 15
classroom libraries, 74–77
  creating, 75–76
  defined, 76
  investigating figurative language in,
      62

  as literate environments, 130
  organizing, 74–75
  previewing or surveying texts in, 43
  self-selecting books from, 72
  teacher rating of, 130
classroom management, 70
Clay, Marie, xvii, 7, 11, 37–38, 41, 42
Cleary, Beverly, 60, 65
close-ups, 45
closing sentences, 59
cloze activities, 56
co-construction of knowledge, 80
Coffman, Debbie, xv, xvi
cognition, perception and, 6
cognitive apprenticeship, 81
cognitive strategies, 8
Cole, Robert, 85
collaborative language, 48
commas, 57
comparison/contrast, in nonfiction
    texts, 44, 45
complex sentences, 57–58
composing. *See also* writing
  comprehension and, 24–25
comprehending process, 7
comprehension. *See also* deep compre-
    hension
  assessing, 85
  assumptions about, 12
  challenges in teaching for, 7
  character relationships and, 19
  as a cognitive process, 1–2
  complexity of, xi–xii
  composing and, 24–25
  comprehending *vs.*, 7
  as a constructive process, 1–2
  defined, xi–xii, 18
  factors affecting, 6–7
  importance of, xi
  inferential thinking and, 19
  language and, 52–54
  levels of, 14–15
  meaning-making and, 37–38
  mini-lessons on skills, 98
  models as barriers to, 2
  as orchestration process, 11–12
  as outcome, 7
  personal, 15
  as process, 1–2, 7, 12
  questioning and, 36
  self-reflection and, 16–18
  strategies and, 2
  surface level, 14–15
  teachers' theories of, 15
  text conventions for, 23–24
  visualization strategies for, 8–11
comprehension strategies, 38–41. *See
    also* strategies
  behaviors *vs.*, 41
  for fluency, 39–40
  mini-lessons on, 98
  modeling in mini-lessons, 96

  processes, 129–30
  self-correcting, 40–41
  shared reading and, 32
comprehension task cards, for charac-
    ter analysis, 23
conclusions, transitional words and
    phrases, 63
concrete words, 55
conferences
  for literature discussion groups,
      84–85
  in reading workshop, 67
Conner, Patsy, xvi
content workshop, 67, 68
context
  inferring meaning from, 46
  mini-lesson on, 104–5
contingent scaffolding, 33–35, 82
conventions. *See* text conventions;
    writing conventions
conversation, 79–80. *See also* book dis-
    cussions; literature discussion
    groups
Crash (Spinelli), 60
critical skills mini-lessons, 98–99
curriculum libraries, 76–77
Curtis, Christopher Paul, 56, 60, 61
cutaways, 45

dashes, 57
Dear Mr. Henshaw (Cleary), 65
deep comprehension, 13–25. *See also*
    comprehension
  assessment of, 15
  book selection and, 77
  character relationships and, 19–23
  complex sentences and, 58
  comprehension levels, 14–15
  conditions for, 17–18
  defined, 1–2
  as goal of reading, 12
  inferential thinking and, 18–19
  knowledge types and, 15–16
  language and, 82
  questioning and, 43
  self-reflection and, 17–18
  strategies for, 38–41, 49
  text structure and, 23–25
descriptive graphic organizer, 152
descriptive structure, in nonfiction
    texts, 44
dialogue
  describing, 60
  extending meaning with, 60–61
dialogue carrier, 60
DiCamillo, Katie, 21, 58, 89
differentiated instruction
  reading environment and, 66
  in reading workshop, 77
  theory of, 82
directions, transitional words and
    phrases, 63

Index

Dorn, Linda, xi–xiii, xv, 3, 28, 30, 32, 35, 42, 67, 81, 82, 83, 95, 96, 129
dry-erase marker boards, 31, 34, 124
Duke, Nell K., 7, 32
Durkin, Dolores, 29
DVD chapters, correlating to book chapters, 163–67

early readers
　author studies for, 92
　classroom libraries and, 75
　fiction reading, 113–15
　framing cards and highlighter tape for, 122
　language support for, 33–35
　nonfiction reading, 118–19
　sentence strips, pocket charts and word cards for, 123
　sticky notes and flags for, 121
　visual searching strategies for, 33–34
　wipe-off board and chart paper for, 124
East, Pam, xv
easy readers, 60
easy work, rhythmic pattern for, 29–30
Eats, Shoots, and Leaves (Truss), 57
emergent readers
　author studies for, 91–92
　classroom libraries and, 75
　comprehension strategies used by, 22
　fiction reading, 110–12
　framing cards and highlighter tape for, 122
　language support for, 35
　nonfiction reading, 116–17
　rereading by, 42
　sentence strips, pocket charts and word cards for, 123
　sticky notes and flags for, 121
　wipe-off board and chart paper for, 124
emotions, 6
emphasis, 63
examples, 63
exclamation points, 57
expository texts, 19
expressiveness, in student reading, 40

fables
　book lists, 134
　defined, 132
fairy tales
　book lists, 133
　defined, 132, 143
　features of, 44
　form, 144
　questions for, 143
　structure of, 18
　writing process, 25
familiar texts, for shared reading, 30–31

fantasy. *See also* modern fantasy
　book lists, 134–35
　defined, 132
Farm Concert, The, 126, 129
Farstrup, Alan, 6
fiction. *See also* specific genres
　beginning novels, 60
　characters, 138–39
　defined, 138
　early readers and, 113–15
　emergent readers and, 110–12
　form, 140
　inferential thinking and, 18–19
　mood, 139
　plot, 139
　questions for, 138
　theme or moral, 139
　transitional readers and, 113–15
figurative language, 61–62
Fitzgerald, J., 23
flexibility, fluency and, 39, 40
Flossie and the Fox (McKissack), 83
fluency
　comprehension and, 39
　elements of, 39, 40
　memory capacity and, 39
　NAEP scale, 39–40, 129
　prompting for, 39
　self-correcting and, 41
fluent readers
　author studies for, 92
　inferential thinking by, 19
　strategic behaviors of, 42
　strategy use by, 22, 98
Fly Away Home, 166
focus groups, 89–90
Foertsch, M. A., 74
folktales
　book lists, 133
　defined, 132, 145
　form, 146
　questions for, 145
Foundations of Literacy (Holdaway), 29
Fox, Mem, 24, 60
framing cards, 122
Fraustino, Lisa Rowe, 57, 60
French, Cathy, xv, 3, 28, 30, 67, 82
Frog and Toad books (Lobel), 60

Gallagher, M. C., 97
Gambrell, L. B., 9
Gardiner, John Reynolds, 21
generic knowledge, 15–16
genres. *See also* texts
　autobiography, 132
　biography, 132, 136–37, 141–42
　book lists by, 133–37
　descriptions, questions and text maps, 138–50
　fables, 132, 134
　fairy tales, 18, 25, 44, 132, 133, 143–44
　fantasy, 132, 134–35

　fiction, 110–15, 138–40
　folk tales, 132, 133, 145–46
　glossary of terms, 132
　historical fiction, 132, 135, 147–48
　mini-lesson on, 102–3
　modern fantasy, 149–50
　picture books, 59, 60
　poetry, 10–11, 132, 137
　for reading aloud, 29
　realistic fiction, 24, 132, 135–36
　tall tales, 24, 132, 133–34
　text conventions for, 24
　using knowledge of, 44
genre studies
　conducting, 90–91
　value of, 92–93
Gerke, Susan, xvi
Gibbs International Magnet School, xv
Giff, Patricia R., 53, 60, 61
Glaessar, Arthur, 18–19
glossary, 45
gradual-release-of-responsibility model, 32, 97
Graesser, A. C., 15
Grapes of Wrath, The (Steinbeck), xi, 5–6, 7, 11–12, 79
graphic organizers, 151–56
　cause/effect, 151
　character's traits, 156
　descriptive, 152
　looking more closely, 153
　problem/solution, 152, 153
　sequence, 151
　sequencing chart, 154
Graves, Michael, 63
Gray, Libba Moore, 55
Grouchy Ladybug, The (Carle), 93
guided participation, 81
guided practice
　in mini-lessons, 96–97
　value of, 95
guided reading
　early readers of fiction and, 113–15
　early readers of nonfiction and, 118–19
　emergent readers of fiction and, 110–12
　emergent readers of nonfiction and, 116–17
　shared reading and, 30
　transitional readers of fiction and, 113–15
　transitional readers of nonfiction and, 118–19
guided reading library, 77
"Guidelines for Conducting Good Book Discussions" chart, 83
"Guidelines for Engaging in Literature Discussion Group" anchor chart, 84
"Guidelines for Literature Group Discussions" anchor chart, 69

"Guidelines for Self-Selecting Books" anchor chart, 77

Haberlandt, Karl, 18–19
Hamilton, Rebecca L., 44, 80–81
Harrison, Laurie, xvi
headings, 45
Henry Huggins books (Cleary), 60
Hesse, Karen, 9, 53, 56
Hickory Chair, The (Fraustino), 57, 60
higher-level thinking, self-correcting strategies and, 40
high language support, 32–35
highlighter tape, 122
highlighting texts, 46
Hillenbrand, Laura, xi, 14
historical fiction
　book lists, 135
　defined, 132, 147
　form, 148
　questions for, 147
Hobbs, Felicia, xv, xvii
Holdaway, Don, xviii, 29, 38
Honeysuckle House, 167
Houston, Gloria, 24, 60
How Writing Works (Houston), 24
Hoyt, Linda, xvi, 10
hyphens, 57

illustrations
　extending meaning with, 45
　in nonfiction texts, 45
imagery, 61–62. *See also* visualization strategies
in-and-out support, 30
independent practice
　in mini-lessons, 97–98
　in reading workshop, 67
independent reading
　in reading workshop, 71
　rubric for assessing, 161
　by teachers, 129
index, 45
index cards, 123
inferential thinking, 18–19
　mini-lessons on, 98
　reader's questions, 20
inquiry attitude, 43. *See also* questioning
inquiry-based language, 48
inquiry-driven discussion, 80–81
interactive language experiences, in shared reading, 30
I See What You Mean (Moline), 45

James, Karen, xvi
Jefferson, Thomas, 74
Jin Woo, 165, 166
Johnson, Jill, xv
Jones, Tammy, xv, 3, 28, 30, 67, 82
Junie B. Jones books (Park), 60

Kaufmann, G., 9
Keith, Rebecca, xvi, 75

Keogh, Ruth, xvi
Kids of Polk Street, The (Giff), 60
King, Stephen, 22
knowledge
　co-construction and, 80
　types of, 15–16
Koizumi, David, 18–19
Koskinen, P. S., 9
Kucan, Linda, 44, 80–81

labels, 45
Laminack, Lester, 29
language, 27–36
　awareness of, 63
　becoming literate through, 28–29, 106–7
　comprehension and, 52–54
　forms and functions of, 64
　as instructional tool, 81–82
　learning in meaningful contexts, 53–54
　before literacy, 27–28
　literate, 80–81, 92
　reader/writer contract, 53
　rhythmic patterns in learning, 29–30
　scale of help for, 32–35
　self-reflection and, 52
　shared reading, 30–32
　skillful use of, 51–52
　teacher's, 35
Language and Learning: The Importance of Speech (Britton), 79–80
language-based strategies, 54–63
　complex sentences, 57–58
　dialogue, 60–61
　figurative language, 61–62
　manipulating parts of speech, 54–55
　mini-lessons on, 98
　organization, 58–60
　pronouns as nouns, 56–57
　transitional words and phrases, 63
　vocabulary, 62–63
　word choice, 55–56
language studies
　author-based, 62
　deep comprehension and, 54
　in reading workshop, 54, 71
　value of, 63–64
language support
　adjustable, 32–35
　high, 32–35
　low, 32–35
　moderate, 32–35
Lattimer, Heather, 23
leading from behind, 81
learning. *See also* apprenticeship learning; literacy learning
　organic, 29
　principles of, xii
　rhythmic nature of, 29–30, 32, 38, 66
　self-correction and, 40
　thought processes for, 7
Leibig, Priscella, xv

Levine, Mel, xviii, 7, 46–47, 80
libraries. *See also* classroom libraries
　types of, 76–77
Library of Congress, 74
Lindfors, Judith, 48
lists, 45
literacy learning. *See also* learning
　in-and-out support for, 30
　in meaningful contexts, 53–54
　process of, 28–29
　rhythmic patterns for, 29–30
　scale of help, 32–35
　shared reading and, 30–32
　through language, 27–36
　through reading aloud, 28
literacy team meetings
　book discussions during, 21
　professional development activities for, 127–30
literal skills mini-lessons, 98
literary extensions, 32
literate environment, 66, 130
literate language, 80–81, 92. *See also* language
literature discussion groups, 48, 79–93. *See also* book discussions
　anchor charts for, 84
　apprenticeship learning and, 81, 92
　author studies, 91–92
　book selection for, 83–84
　components of, 83–90
　conversation and, 79–80
　defined, 81
　DVD chapters/segments, 167
　extensions, 90
　genre studies, 90–91
　group discussion in, 85–88
　models for, 82–83
　participant-spectator theory and, 79–80
　peer discussion in, 88–89
　preparing for, 84
　prompts for, 84–85
　rubrics for assessing, 158
　scaffolding in, 87
　silent reading for, 84
　student-teacher interactions in, 80
　teacher conferences and, 84–85
　teacher practice with, 127
　teacher's roles in, 85–88
　value of, 92
Little Red Hen, The, 164
Lobel, Arnold, 60
Logan, Regina, xvi, 89
log entries rubric, 159–60
looking more closely graphic organizer, 153
low language support, 32–35
Lyons, Carol A., xi–xiii, xvi, xviii, 6

MacLachlan, Patricia, 6
maps, 45

Index   **179**

marking texts, 46
  mini-lesson, 103–4
Martin, Rafe, 18
math workshop, 67, 68
McBride-Chang, C., 74
McGee, L. M., 23
McGill, Alice, 60
McKeown, Margaret G., 44, 80–81
McKissack, Patricia, 60, 61
meaning
  comprehension and, 17
  inferring from context, 46
  monitoring, 38
  self-correcting strategies, 38
  word parts and, 46
meaning construction
  cognitive strategies for, 12
  comprehension and, 37–38
  self-correction and, 40–41
meaning-making chains, 80
Meek, Margaret, 37
memoirs, 132
memory capacity
  book discussions and, 80
  fluency and, 39
  reading aloud and, 28–29
  remembering process, 7
  rereading and, 42
Memory String, The, 166
Mercer, Neil, 80
metaphor, 61
Miller, Melanie, xv
Mind at a Time, A (Levine), 80
mini-lessons, 95–107
  anchor chart review of comprehension strategies, 96
  on asking questions, 100–101
  for book discussions, 83
  on character analysis, 23
  on context and parts of words, 104–5
  defined, 66–67
  on discussing ideas and impressions, 106
  DVD chapters/segments, 167
  framework for, 96–98
  gradual-release-of-responsibility model and, 97
  guided practice in, 96–97
  independent practice in, 97–98
  length of, 96
  on marking texts and recording notes, 103–4
  modeling comprehension strategies in, 96
  on previewing or surveying, 100
  purpose of, 96
  on reading aloud, 101–2
  on reading logs, 105–6
  in reading workshop, 71
  on rereading, 99–100
  scripted, 96
  sharing in, 98

  on strategies, 98–99
  on text aids, 103
  on text structure, genre, and writing conventions, 102–3
  types of, 98–99
Mirandy and Brother Wind (McKissack), 61
Misery (King), 22
models. *See also* apprenticeship learning; scaffolding
  as barriers to learning, 2, 95–96
  for book discussions, 82–83
  guided practice in using, 2
  in mini-lessons, 96
moderate language support, 32–35
modern fantasy. *See also* fantasy
  defined, 149
  form, 150
  questions for, 149
Moley, Pauline, xvi
Moline, Steve, 45
Molly Bannaky (McGill), 60
monitoring meaning, 38
mood, in fiction, 139
moral, in fiction, 139
more knowledgeable other, theory of, 81–82
Morrison, Toni, xi, 51–53
motivation, rhythmic learning pattern and, 29–30
Music of Their Hooves (Springer), 10–11
My Great Aunt Arizona (Houston), 60
My Mama Had a Dancing Heart (Gray), 55
mystery genre, 91, 132

narrative texts, inferential thinking and, 18–19
Nate the Great books (Sharmat), 60
National Assessment of Educational Progress fluency scale, 39–40, 129
Nettie Jo's Friends (McKissack), 60, 61
nonfiction
  defined, 132
  early readers and, 118–19
  emergent readers and, 116–17
  features of, 32
  note-taking from, 46
  text features, 45
  text structures in, 44
  transitional readers and, 118–19
note taking, on/about texts, 46, 103–4
nouns, pronouns and, 56
novels, beginning, 60

On Being Literate (Meek), 37
one-to-one conferences, 67
onomatopoeia, 61
On Writing (King), 22
organic learning, 29
organization mini-lessons, 98
Organizing for Literacy (Treat), 3

outcome point of view, 7, 8
Out of the Dust (Hesse), 9
Owl Moon (Yolen), 60

pacing, fluency and, 39
paired reading, 71
paragraphs, 59
Parish, Peggy, 60
Park, Barbara, 60
participant-observers, teachers as, 86, 88
participant-spectator theory, 79–80
parts of speech
  manipulating, to express meaning, 54–55
  sentence transformations and, 58
Patterson, James, xi, 13, 14
Patterson, Katherine, 56
Pearson, P. David, xvi, xviii, 6, 7, 32, 97
Peck, Richard, 20
peer discussion, 88–89
peer projects, 67
perceptions, 6
personal connections, 1, 6, 14. *See also* text-to-life connections
photographs, 45
Picnic in October, A, 166
picture books, 59, 60
Pictures of Hollis Wood (Giff), 53, 61
Pinballs, The (Byars), 60
Pinnell, Gay Su, 10, 11
plot, 139
pocket charts, 123
"Poem of ATIONS, A," 46
poetry
  book lists, 137
  defined, 132
  visualization strategies for, 10–11
Polacco, Patricia, 60, 62
poor readers, strategy use by, 98
"Preparing for Book Talks" anchor chart, 73
"Preparing for Literature Discussion Groups" anchor chart, 84
"Presenting Book Talks" anchor chart, 73
Pressley, Michael, 6
previewing texts
  mini-lesson on, 100
  as strategic behavior, 42–43
print, types of, 45
print concepts, shared reading and, 32
problem/solution graphic organizer, 152, 155
problem/solution structure, 44
problem-solving
  adjustable language support and, 32–35
  background experience and, 8
  outcome and process in, 8
  processing cycle, 39
  process of, 7–9
  rhythmic learning patterns and, 38

problem-solving strategies
  cognitive, 8
  for general thinking, 7–8
  learning, 38
  self-monitoring, 8
  shared reading and, 32
  student behaviors indicating, 38
  visual imagery and, 8–9
procedures mini-lessons, 98
process approach, 7, 8, 25
professional development activities, 127–30
  classroom libraries, 130
  planning for shared reading, 129
  prompting *vs.* teaching, 129
  reading surveys, 128–29
  strategic process for comprehending, 129–30
  teacher book clubs, 128
  teacher reading logs, 128
  value of, xii
professional library, 77
proficient readers. *See* fluent readers
prompting
  on character relationships, 22–23
  defined, 36
  for fluency, 39
  for literature discussion groups, 84–85
  questioning *vs.*, 36, 81, 129
  for reading response logs, 47
  for rereading, 42
  for self-reflection, 18
  teaching *vs.*, 129
  for text-to-life connections, 18
pronouns, nouns and, 56
punctuation
  authors' use of, 53
  clarifying meaning with, 57
  regulating fluency with, 57

question-driven discussion, 80–81
questioning
  authors, 43, 85
  for biography, 141
  defined, 36
  examples, 44
  for fairy tales, 143
  for fiction, 138–39
  for folk tales, 145
  for historical fiction, 147
  mini-lesson on, 100–101
  for modern fantasy, 149
  promoting comprehension with, 36
  prompting *vs.*, 36, 81, 129
  self-, 52
  as strategic behavior, 43–44
Questioning the Author (Beck, McKeown, Hamilton, and Kucan), 80–81
question marks, 57
quotation marks, 57

Ramona books (Cleary), 60
Randall, Beverly, 19
Rasinski, T., 39, 74
Ratey, John J., 6
reaction, self-reflection vs., 18
reader/writer contract, 53
reading aloud
  building memory capacity through, 28–29
  to clarify thinking, 44, 101–2
  genres for, 29
  mini-lesson on, 101–2
  in reading workshop, 71
  as strategic behavior, 44
  student fluency, 39–40
  text types for, 29
  value of, 28–29
reading environment, 66, 130
reading habits
  defined, 77
  developing, 65–66
  volume reading and, 74
reading logs
  categories in, 47–48
  for literature discussion groups, 84, 85, 88
  mini-lesson on, 105–6
  rubrics for assessing entries, 160
  self-reflection in, 17
  for teachers, 48, 128
  "thoughtful" log entries, 159
  writing in, 18, 46–48
reading surveys, 128–29
reading volume, 71, 74
reading workshop, 65–77. *See also* workshop approach
  anchor charts, 68–70
  assessment in, 67
  book talks, 73
  buddy reading, 73
  classroom library and, 74–77
  conferences, 67
  differential instruction in, 77
  environment, 66
  independent practice, 67
  mini-lessons, 66–67, 96
  organizing, 70–72
  peer projects, 67
  Phase 1, 67, 68
  Phase 2, 67, 68
  professional development activities, 127
  reading volume, 74
  schedules, 70–72
  self-selecting books, 72–73, 77
  share time, 67
  small-group instruction, 67
  workshop framework, 66–68
Reading Workshop Option Board, 71, 72, 73
realistic fiction
  book lists, 135–36
  defined, 132
  text conventions for, 24
recall, surface-level comprehension and, 15
recorded reading, 71
recurring characters, rereading for information on, 42
reflection, xiii. *See also* self-reflection
reflective knowledge, 15–16
relationships between characters, 19–23
remembering, 7. *See also* memory capacity
rereading
  behavior changes over time, 42
  for enjoyment, 51–52
  mini-lesson on, 99
  as strategic behavior, 42
research studies, 25
restatements, 63
Results That Last: A Model for School Change (Dorn and Soffos), xvii, 129
retelling, surface-level comprehension and, 15
rhythm, fluency and, 39, 40
rhythmic learning patterns
  differentiated instruction and, 66
  problem-solving and, 38
  scale of help and, 32
  value of, 29–30, 38
Ribsy (Cleary), 60
Rice, Anne, 42
Richardson, Teresa, xv, xvii
Riggo, Anita, 83
Rogoff, Barbara, xviii, 8, 80, 81
Root, Phyllis, 60
root words, 46
Rough Faced Girl, The (Martin), 18
Routman, Regie, 11
rubrics, 158–61
  for independent reading time, 161
  for literature discussion groups, 158
  for log entries, 159, 160
  teacher practice with, 127
Ruddell, Martha R., 6
Ruddell, Robert B., 6
running records
  contingent scaffolding and, 33
  documenting behaviors with, 129–30
run-on sentences, 53

Sable (Hesse), 56
Sallie Cone Elementary School, xv
Samuels, S. Jay, 6
scaffolding. *See also* apprenticeship learning; models
  anchor charts for, 68–70
  book discussions and, 80
  character analysis and, 23
  contingent, 33–35, 82
  in literature discussion groups, 87
  for reading response logs, 47

Index

in reading workshop, 72
shared reading and, 32
scale of help, 32–35, 82
   high support, 32
   low support, 32
   moderate support, 32
   teacher decision making about, 82
Scharer, Patricia L., 10
Schubert, Barbara, xvi, xvii
science fiction, 132
Scott, Karen, xvi, xvii
scripted programs, 95–96
Seabiscuit: An American Legend (Hillenbrand), xi, 14, 19
Secret Home, 166
Secret Signs (Riggo), 83
self-correcting strategies, 38, 40–41, 129
self-monitoring strategies, 8
self-questioning, 52. *See also* questioning
self-reflection
   author's use of language and, 52
   comprehension and, 16–18
   deep comprehension and, 17–18
   low-level reaction *vs.*, 18
   prompting for, 18
   by teachers, 17, 18
   teaching, 16–18
   value of, 18
   writing in reading logs, 18
self-regulation strategies, 38–41
   fluency, 39–40
   self-correction, 40–41
self-selection of texts, 72–73, 77
semicolons, 57
sentences
   closing, 59
   combining, 57–58
   complex, 57–58
   fragments, 52
   organization and, 59
   run-on, 53
   topic, 59
   transformations, 58
   variety in, 57–58
sentence strips, 123
sequence, in nonfiction texts, 44
sequence graphic organizer, 151
sequencing chart graphic organizer, 154
Sewall, Angela, xvi
shared reading, 30–32
   book orientations for, 31
   charts, 129
   DVD chapter/segments, 164–65
   for early readers of fiction, 113–15
   for early readers of nonfiction, 118–19
   for emergent readers of fiction, 110–12
   for emergent readers of nonfiction, 116–17
   familiar texts for, 30–31

follow-up discussions, 31
framework for, 30–32
guided reading and, 30
literary extensions, 32
planning for, 129
steps in, 30
strategies for, 31
teacher's role in, 31
teaching points, 31–32
for transitional readers of fiction, 113–15
for transitional readers of nonfiction, 118–19
using text aids in, 45
value of, 30
Shared Reading Plan (form), 125–26
share time, 67
sharing, in mini-lessons, 98
showing, rather than telling, 22
sight words, 63
silent reading, for literature discussion groups, 84
simile, 61
Singer, Harry, xvii, 6
Skinner, Donnie, xvi, xvii, 10–11, 12, 81, 83, 96, 97
small-group conferences, 67
small-group instruction, 67
Smith, Doris Buchannan, 56
Smith, Frank, 7, 43, 53, 59
social contexts
   literacy learning in, 48
   for talking, 80
Soffos, Carla, xi–xiii, 3, 18, 32, 35, 42, 72, 81, 83, 85, 95, 96, 129
Sounder (Armstrong), 58
spectators, participants and, 80
speed, fluency and, 39, 40
Spinelli, Jerry, 60
spoken language
   rhythmic pattern of, 58
   written language and, 63
Spotlight on Comprehension: Building a Literacy of Thoughtfulness (Hoyt), xvi
Springer, Nancy, 10–11
"Steadfast Tin Soldier, The " (Anderson), 143
Steinbeck, John, xi, 5–6
sticky notes and flags, 31, 121
Stone Fox (Gardiner), 21, 22
story elements, 32
story maps, 84, 89–90
Story of Ruby Bridges, The (Cole), 85–88
story structure, 44
strategic behaviors, 41–48
   asking questions, 43–44
   context and word parts, 46
   defined, 41, 49
   discussing ideas with others, 48
   of good readers, 42
   marking texts, 46

mini-lessons on, 96, 98
note-taking, 46
previewing or surveying a text, 42–43, 100
professional development activities, 129–30
reading aloud, 44
rereading, 42
text structures and conventions, 44
visual aids, 45
writing in reading logs, 46–48
strategic knowledge, 15–16
strategies. *See also* comprehension strategies
   behaviors *vs.*, 41
   defined, 41, 49
   language-based, 54–63
   mini-lessons on, 98–99
   process approach and, 25
   as reason for reading, 2, 98
   for regulating comprehension, 38–41
   shared reading and, 31, 32
   similarities in, 25
   student behaviors indicating, 41
"Strategies Used by Good Readers" anchor chart, 69
student-teacher interaction, 80
subvocalizing, 44
suffixes, 46
Summer My Father Was Ten, The, 167
surface-level comprehension, 14–15
surveying texts
   mini-lesson on, 100
   as strategic behavior, 42–43
Suzanne's Diary for Nicholas (Patterson), xi, 13
syntax, student reading and, 40

table of contents, 45
tall tales
   book lists, 133–34
   defined, 132
   text conventions for, 24
Taste for Blackberries, A (Smith), 56
Taylor, Barbara, 23
teacher book clubs, 128
teachers
   adjustable language support by, 32–35
   book discussions for, 21
   book discussions modeled by, 82–83
   interaction with students, 80
   language of, 32, 35
   as learners, xii
   as more knowledgeable other, 81–82
   as participant-observers, 86, 88
   professional development, xii, 127–30
   reading logs, 48
   role in literature discussion groups, 85–88
   role in shared reading, 31
   scale of help and, 82

teachers (continued)
    self-reflections of, 17
    tools for, 120–24
teaching points, for shared reading, 31–32
teaching principles, xii
Teaching Reading Comprehension (Pearson), xvi
Teaching Struggling Readers: How to Use Brain-Based Research to Maximize Learning (Lyons), xvi
"Tender Thumbelina, The" (Anderson), 143
text aids, 120–24
    extending meaning with, 45
    mini-lesson on, 103
    for shared reading, 31
text conventions. *See also* writing conventions
    defined, 23
    for different genres, 24
    understanding, 58
text features, 90
text knowledge, 15–16
text mapping, 89–90. *See also* story maps
texts. *See also* genres
    beginning novels, 60
    book choice, 32, 72–73, 77, 83–84
    book lists by genre and grade level, 133–39
    chapter books, 60
    classification of, 74–75
    easy readers, 60
    familiar, 30–31
    genre lists, 133–37
    marking, 46, 103–4
    orientation to, 31
    picture books, 59–60
    previewing or surveying, 42–43, 100
    for reading aloud, 29
    self-selection of, 72–73, 77
    for shared reading, 30–31
    surveying, 42–43, 100
text structure
    mini-lesson on, 102
    in nonfiction texts, 44
    shared reading and, 32
    understanding, 23–25
text-to-life connections. *See also* personal connections
    comprehension and, 6
    prompting for, 18
    self-reflection and, 17
text tools. *See* text aids
Thank You, Mr. Falker (Polacco), 60–61
"Thank You, Stormy" (Springer), 10–11
theme, in fiction, 139
thinking
    activating, 81
    aloud, 44

general problem-solving strategies for, 7–8
    higher-level, 40
    inferential, 18–19, 20, 98
    organizing, by writing, 47
Thought and Language (Vygotsky), 55
Thunder Cake (Polacco), 60
Tiger, Tiger (Randall), 19, 20, 22
time, comprehension and, 17
Time for Angels, A (Hesse), 53
time order, in nonfiction texts, 44
tools, 120–24. *See also* text aids
topic sentences, 59
transitional readers
    author studies for, 92
    classroom libraries and, 75
    fiction reading, 113–15
    framing cards and highlighter tape for, 122
    nonfiction reading, 118–19
    sentence strips, pocket charts and word cards for, 123
    sticky notes and flags for, 121
    wipe-off board and chart paper for, 124
transitional words and phrases, 63
"traveling book club," 83
Treat, Teresa, 3
Truss, Lynne, 57

"Ugly Duckling, The" (Anderson), 143
underlining texts, 46
Underwood, Krista, xvi
unknown words
    analyzing, 46
    visual searching strategies for, 33–35

verbs
    creative use of, 55
    strong, 56
    for visual imagery, 9
Very Busy Spider, The (Carle), 93
Very Hungry Caterpillar (Carle), 93
Very Quiet Cricket, The (Carle), 93
visual aids, 45
visualization strategies
    background knowledge and, 9
    for increasing understanding, 8–9
    teaching, 10–11
    in text reading, 9
visual searching strategies, for unknown words, 33–34
vivid language, 9
vocabulary
    shared reading and, 32
    unknown words, 33–35, 46
    word relationships and patterns, 62–63
volume reading, 71, 74
Vygotsky, Lev, xviii, 8, 28, 52, 81–82

Wall, The, 166
Wallace, Vicki, xvi
Watsons Go to Birmingham, The (Curtis), 61
Wells, G., 29
What You Know First (MacLachlan), 6, 11–12
White, E. B., 56, 60
Who's in the Shell?, 164
wikki sticks, 31
Wilfred Gordon McDonald Partridge (Fox), 60
wipe-off boards, 31, 34, 124
Wood, David, xviii, 8, 32, 82
word cards (index cards), 123
word parts
    inferring meaning from, 46
    mini-lesson on, 104–5
words
    concrete, 55
    grouping/phrasing, 40
    invented, 55
    new, 63
    new concepts, 63
    new meanings for, 63
    organization and, 59
    precise, 55–56
    sight, 63
    transitional, 63
    unknown, 33–35, 46
    vocabulary, 32, 46, 62–63
word walls, 47
workshop approach. *See also* reading workshop; writing workshop
    reading workshop elements, 66–67
    teacher participation, xii
    typical schedules, 68–69
    workshop types, 67–68
writing
    comprehension and, 24–25
    fairy tales, 25
    literacy learning from, 53–54
    organizing thinking with, 47
    by readers, 53–54
    in reading response logs, 46–48, 105–6
    research studies, 25
writing conventions. *See also* text conventions
    authors and, 52–53
    mini-lesson on, 102–3
    using knowledge of, 44
writing workshop, 45, 67, 68

Year Down Yonder, A (Peck), 20
Yolen, Jane, 60